Media Across Borders

What happened when *Sesame Street* and *Big Brother* were adapted for African audiences? Or when video games *Final Fantasy* and *Assassins' Creed* were localized for the Spanish market? Or when Sherlock Holmes was transformed into a talking dog for the Japanese animation *Sherlock Hound*?

Bringing together leading international scholars working on localization in television, film and video games, *Media Across Borders* is a pioneering study of the myriad ways in which media content is adapted for different markets and across cultural borders. Contributors examine significant localization trends and practices such as: audiovisual translation and transcreation, dubbing and subtitling, international franchising, film remakes, TV format adaptation and video game localization.

Drawing together insights from across the audiovisual sector, this volume provides a number of innovative models for interrogating the international flow of media. By paying specific attention to the diverse ways in which cultural products are adapted across markets, this collection offers important new perspectives and theoretical frameworks for studying localization processes in the audiovisual sector.

For further resources, please see the Media Across Borders group website (www.mediaacrossborders.com), which hosts a 'localization' bibliography; links to relevant companies, institutions and publications, as well as conference papers and workshop summaries.

Andrea Esser is Principal Lecturer in Media and Communications at the University of Roehampton, UK.

Iain Robert Smith is Senior Lecturer in Film at the University of Roehampton, UK.

Miguel Á. Bernal-Merino is Senior Lecturer in Game and Media Localisation at the University of Roehampton, UK.

Routledge Advances in Internationalizing Media Studies

Edited by Daya Thussu, University of Westminster

1 Media Consumption and
Everyday Life in Asia
Edited by Youna Kim

2 Internationalizing
Internet Studies
Beyond Anglophone Paradigms
*Edited by Gerard Goggin and
Mark McLelland*

3 Iranian Media
The Paradox of Modernity
Gholam Khiabany

4 Media Globalization and the
Discovery Channel Networks
Ole J. Mjos

5 Audience Studies
A Japanese Perspective
Toshie Takahashi

6 Global Media Ecologies
Networked Production in Film
and Television
Doris Baltruschat

7 Music, Social Media and
Global Mobility
MySpace, Facebook, YouTube
Ole J. Mjøs

8 Media Power and
Democratization in Brazil
TV Globo and the Dilemmas of
Political Accountability
Mauro P. Porto

9 Popular Television in Eastern
Europe During and Since
Socialism
*Edited by Timothy Havens,
Anikó Imre, and Katalin Lustyik*

10 The Global News Challenge
Marketing Strategies of
International Broadcasting
Organizations in Developing
Countries
Anne Geniets

11 Al Jazeera and the Global
Media Landscape
The South is Talking Back
Tine Ustad Figenschou

12 Online Journalism in Africa
Trends, Practices and
Emerging Cultures
*Edited by Hayes Mawindi
Mabweazara, Okoth Fred
Mudhai and Jason Whittaker*

13 Modernization, Nation-
Building, and Television History
*Edited by Stewart Anderson
and Melissa Chakars*

14 Asian Perspectives on
Digital Culture
Emerging Phenomena,
Enduring Concepts
*Edited by Sun Sun Lim and
Cheryll Ruth R. Soriano*

15 Digital Politics and Culture in
Contemporary India
The Making of an Info-Nation
Biswarup Sen

16 Media Across Borders
Localizing TV, Film, and
Video Games
*Edited by Andrea Esser, Miguel
Á. Bernal-Merino, and Iain
Robert Smith*

Media Across Borders
Localizing TV, Film, and Video Games

Edited by
Andrea Esser,
Miguel Á. Bernal-Merino, and
Iain Robert Smith

Routledge
Taylor & Francis Group

NEW YORK AND LONDON

First published 2016
by Routledge
711 Third Avenue, New York, NY 10017

and by Routledge
2 Park Square, Milton Park, Abingdon, Oxon OX14 4RN

Routledge is an imprint of the Taylor & Francis Group, an informa business

Library of Congress Cataloging-in-Publication Data

Names: Esser, Andrea, 1968– editor. | Bernal-Merino, Miguel Á. editor. |
Smith, Iain Robert, editor.
Title: Media across borders: localizing tv, film and video games / edited by
Andrea Esser, Miguel Á. Bernal-Merino and Iain Robert Smith.
Description: New York: Routledge, 2016. | Series: Routledge advances in
internationalizing media studies; 16 | Includes bibliographical references
and index.
Identifiers: LCCN 2015036581
Subjects: LCSH: Mass media and culture. | Mass media and globalization. |
Mass media and language. | Television broadcasting—Social aspects. |
Dubbing of television programs. | Local mass media—Social aspects.
Classification: LCC P94.6 M395 2016 | DDC 302.23—dc23
LC record available at http://lccn.loc.gov/2015036581

ISBN: 978-1-138-80945-1 (hbk)
ISBN: 978-1-315-74998-3 (ebk)

Typeset in Sabon
by codeMantra

Contents

Introduction   1
ANDREA ESSER, MIGUEL Á. BERNAL-MERINO,
AND IAIN ROBERT SMITH

1 Defining 'the Local' in Localization or 'Adapting for Whom?'   19
  ANDREA ESSER

2 Transnational Holmes: Theorizing the Global-Local Nexus
  through the Japanese Anime *Sherlock Hound* (1984–)   36
  IAIN ROBERT SMITH

3 The Context of Localization: Children's Television in Western
  Europe and the Arabic-Speaking World   53
  JEANETTE STEEMERS

4 Audiovisual Translation Trends: Growing Diversity, Choice,
  and Enhanced Localization   68
  FREDERIC CHAUME

5 Transformations of *Montalbano* through Languages and Media:
  Adapting and Subtitling Dialect in *The Terracotta Dog*   85
  DIONYSIOS KAPSASKIS AND IRENE ARTEGIANI

6 Localizing *Sesame Street*: The Cultural Translation
  of the Muppets   99
  AARON CALBREATH-FRASIEUR

7 Television Formats in Africa: Cultural Considerations in
  Format Localization   113
  MARTIN NKOSI NDLELA

8 Exploring Factors Influencing the Dubbing of TV Series into
  Spanish: Key Aspects for the Analysis of Dubbed Dialogue   124
  ROCÍO BAÑOS

 9 Jerome Bruner and the Transcultural Adaptation of
   1970s Hollywood Classics in Turkey   141
   LAURENCE RAW

10 Tracing Asian Franchises: Local and Transnational
   Reception of *Hana Yori Dango*   151
   RAYNA DENISON

11 Fiction TV Formats in Poland—Why Bother to Adapt?   167
   SYLWIA SZOSTAK

12 Analyzing Players' Perceptions on the Translation of
   Video Games: Assessing the Tension between the Local
   and the Global Concerning Language Use   183
   ALBERTO FERNÁNDEZ COSTALES

13 Glocalization and Co-Creation: Trends in International
   Game Production   202
   MIGUEL Á. BERNAL-MERINO

   Glossary   221
   List of Contributors   229
   Index   233

Introduction

Andrea Esser, Miguel Á. Bernal-Merino,
and Iain Robert Smith

Introduction

The steady opening of world media markets for audiovisual entertainment over the past 30 years has shifted the focus from simple, mono-directional international distribution to more consumer-centric strategies, involving greater customization for specific target audiences. As a result, concepts such as localization, internationalization, and glocalization are gaining relevance in both academic and professional environments. The AHRC-funded Media Across Borders (MAB) network brings together experts on TV, film, and video game entertainment from around the world to highlight these trends, illustrating, with their analysis and case studies, the multi-directional flows of entertainment media and the rise in the quantity and significance of localization strategies.[1]

This collection is the first of its kind. It offers theoretical reflections on the transnationalization and localization of audiovisual entertainment and insights into the diversity of localization practices, the 'how-to' of localization, the reasons for localizing non-domestic content, and the transformative character of localization. It aims to create an understanding of the highly complex and multifaceted nature of localization, the plurality and fluidity of localization practices and audience demands and of the many diverse aspects that need to be considered by both localization researchers and practitioners.

Digital Technology: The Driving Force of Accelerating Localization and Diversification of Localization Practices

Digital technology plays a pivotal role in both the growth of content localization and the refinement of localization practices. Digitalization has led to a multiplication of distribution platforms. For instance, the number of television channels has grown substantially and keeps growing, and online distribution platforms continue to be established by new, often financially strong market players like Netflix or Amazon. Consequently, there has been a notable rise in the demand for audiovisual content but also in competition, which in turn has resulted in the growing demand for localization.

Digitalization also makes global distribution easy and inexpensive. Hence, it makes sense for content owners to exploit content globally. For a successful international rollout the content needs to be localized at least to a certain degree, though. It also needs to be localized and rolled out quickly to counter piracy. In today's world, wherever and whenever content is not available locally, or not easily obtainable, especially young people tend to find their own ways of accessing this content, for instance through peer-to-peer (P2P) sharing platforms or Virtual Private Networks (VPNs). Time-space compression in the distribution and consumption of audiovisual content, be it films, TV series or video games, put pressures on localizers to work with enormous speed. As a result, new ways of organizing localization are required.

Digitalization affects localization not just in terms of localization speed and the quantity of material localized. It also affects translation modes. Because of the above-mentioned multiplication of platforms and access routes there is a lot more choice in entertainment today, and this means we are seeing major transformations in consumption patterns. Traditional media markets are fragmenting, which both creates and reveals a substantial plurality and diversity in audience tastes and preferences. As far as localization is concerned, this leads to content providers offering audiovisual products in multiple translation modes. For instance, in countries that traditionally dub television programs, like Germany or Spain, viewers can now choose to watch a foreign TV series dubbed or subtitled or even dubbed and subtitled. The same applies to games and films. Consumers can choose dubbing, subtitling, or voice-over when watching foreign programs on the Internet, DVDs, or Blu-Ray discs, and between dubbing and subtitling when playing video games.

Finally, digitalization affects localization in that it allows localizers to adapt more elements than has been the case in the analogue past. It renders possible changes on all semiotic levels, from the textual to the acoustic to the visual; and with interactivity, even at the pragmatic level. More and more frequently, we see such enhanced forms of localization in animated films or TV series, like for example in the US version of the Japanese anime *Doraemon*, the Japanese version of the American cartoon *Powerpuff Girls*, or the *Spider-Man* comic book adaptations for the Indian market. Enhanced, multiple-level localization also takes place in video games. The Chinese edition of *World of Warcraft* is a good example, or the German edition of *Wolfenstein*. Some scholars (see, for example, Chaume in this collection) employ the term 'transcreation' to stress the enhanced, multi-level nature of this type of localization.

The most enhanced form of localization, of course, is a complete remake, something that has a long tradition in film. From shot-for-shot remakes such as Michael Haneke's 2007 US remake of his own Austrian thriller *Funny Games* (1997) to more divergent reworkings such as Sergio Leone's spaghetti western *A Fistful of Dollars* (1964) that borrowed the plotline and many of the set pieces from Akira Kurosawa's Japanese sword film *Yojimbo* (1960), there is an extensive history of transnational remaking practices within the film industry. This has only intensified in recent years. The increasing emphasis on reworking existing material within contemporary global cinema is exemplified by such recent examples as the Zhang Yimou film *A Simple Noodle Story* (2009) that remakes the Coen Brothers' *Blood Simple* (1984) and Spike Lee's *Oldboy* (2013) that remakes Park Chan-wook's 2003 Korean film of the same name. However, despite its prevalence and cultural significance, this phenomenon is only starting to be addressed within academic scholarship (see Smith and Verevis, 2016).

It is in television, though, where the increase in remakes is particularly stark. Since the new millennium, the trade in television programs has seen the systematization and rise of the so-called 'TV format' business (Bourdon, 2012; Chalaby, 2012; Moran, 2013). This type of trade implies factual entertainment shows, such as *Big Brother* or *Come Dine with Me*; game and talent shows, like *Who Wants to be a Millionaire?* or *Next Top Model*; but increasingly also TV drama series like *Betty, La Fea (Ugly Betty)* or *BeTipul (In Treatment)*, being sold around the world for local adaptation. 'Copying' across borders has always existed, of course, but before the turn of the millennium, it was ad hoc, usually unlicensed, and hence often constituted no more than a loose adaptation. Today most of this copying is licensed, and the production of local versions is tightly controlled by license holders.

TV formats are sold in the form of a 'production bible', accompanied by consultancy services. So-called 'flying producers', senior production staff of the company that owns the license, support licensees with their local adaptation. At the same time they ensure that no harm is done to the brand.

The Economic Value of Media Entertainment Localization

The economic value of these various forms of localization is substantial and continues to grow. Since the turn of the millennium, the production volume of the format trade—almost non-existent in the twentieth century—has reportedly grown from an estimated €2.1 billion a year (between 2002–2004) to €3.1 billion a year (2006–2008). The number of internationally franchised shows broadcast globally rose from 259 titles for the period 2002–2004 to 445 titles (2006–2008) (Jäger and Behrens, 2009). There has been no recent estimation for the global market, but trade journal literature suggests that format sales and revenues continue to rise. In 2012 it was reported that the top 50 European formats had generated a value of €1.56 billion in 2011, up 8.4% on the 2010 total (Stephens, 2012). The value of formats developed in the UK—the largest format exporting country in the world—in 2013/14 had risen to £1.28 billion, a 5% increase from the year before (TRP, 2015). This is only the new business concerning remakes. The old-fashioned trade in television programs, which are sold across borders and then dubbed, subtitled, or furnished with voice overs, continues and, due to growing demand for content, too, rises.

For the North American film business, international markets are indispensable. The *Theatrical Market Statistics Report for 2014*, released by The Motion Picture Association of America (MPAA), shows that in 2014 the global box office receipts for all US and Canadian films released around the world reached $36.4 billion, with 72% of revenues coming from outside Canada and the US. Ticket sales in the US and Canadian home markets had fallen by 5%. Even so, there was a slight rise compared to the 2013 total, driven by a 12% expansion in the Asia Pacific region. A diachronic comparison between home and international sales (2010–2014) demonstrates the enormous and growing significance of the international film market:

Table I.1 Global Box Office Receipts, all MPAA member films in billions of US$

	2010	2011	2012	2013	2014
Home box-office sales	10.6	10.2	10.8	10.9	10.4
International sales	21	22.4	23.9	25	26
Total box office sales	31.6	32.6	34.7	35.9	36.4

Source: MPAA, *Theatrical Market Statistics Report for 2014*.

Whereas in 2010, international box office sales already accounted for two thirds of all box office sales, by 2014 the international share had increased to 72%—rising continuously from 66% in 2010, to 69% in 2011 and 2012, and 70% in 2011. The five top international markets in 2014 for the US cinema industry were China (with $4.8bn), Japan ($2bn), France ($1.8bn), UK ($1.7bn) and India ($1.7bn). In sum, North American films have long ceased to be financed domestically; they are funded by global audiences. This makes film localization hugely important both qualitatively and quantitatively.

It is the video games market, though, that today has the largest share in international sales of audiovisual entertainment, and it is this sector that sees the most rapid changes and the biggest growth in localization. For the video games market, reports estimate that global revenues for 2014 reached $80+ billion. By the end of 2017, it is estimated that revenues will reach $100 (Newzoo, 2015). A substantial and growing slice of this business comes from foreign sales. Zynga, a leading, online-only game company, reports that international (i.e., non-US) revenue as a percentage of total revenue is now over 40% (Zynga, 2014: 50); and a report published in 2014 by Activision-Blizzard, the most important developer/publisher in the game industry, states that half of its revenues come from outside the US (Activision-Blizzard, 2014). Not surprisingly, both companies state that international sales are a fundamental part of their business looking into the future. International sales imply localization.

We want to note that this book does not claim that the localization of audiovisual products is new. The cartoon series *Heidi*, based on the novel of the same name by Swiss author Johanna Spyri (1880), for instance, was created in Japan in 1974, and its localized versions proved hugely popular in both Europe and America. What is new, and what this collection tries to demonstrate, is the volume and significance of localization and the expansion of both audiovisual production and translation companies into new territory. Film and TV production companies grow their revenues through international license sales and often also the actual production or co-production of local adaptations for foreign markets. Audiovisual translation companies are expanding into video game localization and even the co-creation of new game content. Additionally, what is new is the multiplicity and diversity of media flows, the speed with which audiovisual products cross borders, the multifaceted approach needed to manage international distribution, and the attendant growth and refinement in localization modes and strategies.

Aims of this Collection

The objective of this edited collection is threefold. First, it aims to illuminate the diversity of localization practices within the entertainment industries and the new trends we see in the localization of audiovisual entertainment (i.e., internationalization, co-creation, glocalization, transcreation, and the sale of TV programs in the form of franchise licenses). Second, our ambition is to reveal the enormous significance and complexity of catering to non-domestic consumers in the audiovisual sector today and in the foreseeable future. Through case studies and market analysis, members of the Media Across Borders network highlight some of the stakeholders, processes, difficulties, outcomes, and benefits of localizing audiovisual entertainment.

Finally, we have placed emphasis on the theoretical grounding for this collection. It is the first of its kind, and we want to make a start to developing a new frame of reference for studying, understanding, and planning the international flow of entertainment media in the twenty-first century and for addressing the intricacies, challenges and implications—positive and negative—that the 'glocalization' of audiovisual products entails. By bringing together scholars from a range of countries and disciplines, we have aimed to work toward a global comprehensive perspective; one that is non-reductive—neither in cultural, legal, or economic terms—but does justice to the multifaceted reality we find in today's media landscape.

The contributors in this collection come from Germany, Greece, Italy, Norway, Poland, Spain, Turkey, the UK, and Zimbabwe, from translation, film, television, and video games studies. Even though localization has gained increasing attention in translation studies, video games, film, and television scholarship, there has been little exchange between these disciplines to date. But in the age of media convergence, we believe, academics and media professionals working in historically separated media need to cross borders, embrace convergence, and learn about other entertainment media. With this collection, we want to break down disciplinary boundaries.

An interdisciplinary adventure inevitably opens up knowledge gaps and poses some communication difficulties. At the end of this collection, the reader will therefore find a glossary, offering short explanatory notes for the key concepts to be found within the book. The following will provide a brief overview of the localization and adaptation research carried out in the various disciplines that this book draws on: audiovisual translation, video games translation, film adaptation, and TV format studies.

Localization and Adaptation Research in the Various Disciplines

The study of the translation of audiovisual media claimed independence from the broader discipline of Translation Studies (TS) in the last decade of the twentieth century prompted by the exponential increase in translational complexity presented by the addition of acoustic and visual information to traditional text-only translation practice. Entertainment media are polysemiotic products that require further theoretical frameworks and new professional guidelines in order to generate translated products that are corresponding in nature and quality to the source material. The first Audiovisual Translation (AVT) studies focused initially on the stresses imposed on TS by AVT (Mayoral et al., 1988; Luyken et al., 1991; Zabalbeascoa, 1993; Gottlieb, 1997) and then expanded on the theoretical framework with the description of cinema and TV dubbing, subtitling, and voiceover professional practice (Agost, 1999; Karamitroglou, 2000; Diaz-Cintas, 2001, 2007; Ivarsson, 2002; Chaume, 2003, 2012). Media accessibility gained importance early in the new millennium, partly due to new legislation making it compulsory in some countries, and several researchers focused on subtitling for the deaf and audio-description for the blind (Neves, 2005; Orero and Matamala, 2007; Diaz-Cintas et al., 2007).

Game localization places itself within AVT but differentiates itself from the wider concept due to the new challenges the translation multimedia interactive entertainment software (TMIES) brings into the AVT framework. The most relevant publications in game localization have come out only in the past 10 years. The first considerable attempt belongs to Chandler (2005), who describes game localization from her US producer viewpoint, detailing the organizational processes that are necessary to help games be linguistically enabled for entry in more countries. Later she sought the collaboration of other authors for her second edition in Chandler and Deming (2012), which completed this industry handbook. Academic research into game localization started with O'Hagan and Mangiron (2006–2013) who highlighted transcreation (a form of translation that maximizes the characteristics of the target language) as the main characteristic of game localization, and Bernal-Merino (2006–2015) who integrates the translation and localization of video games into the context of previous media and professional practices and proposes shared-authorship and playability as key concepts in game localization theory. Other essential publications from the industry are by Edwards (2011) who applies the concepts of geo-cultural and geopolitical to game localization from her industry consultant viewpoint, and Bartelt-Krantz (2011) who highlights financial efficiency as an essential variable in game localization in her role as head of localization at Electronic Arts, one of the biggest publishers in the game sector. It is also worth mentioning that Game Localization SIG (Special Interest Group) created a basic whitepaper for the industry with practical advice for game developers (Honeywood et al., 2012).

Meanwhile, recent significant works on film remakes (and other serial forms, such as sequels) include: Lucy Mazdon's *Encore Hollywood: Remaking French Cinema* (2000), Jennifer Forrest and Leonard R. Koos's edited collection *Dead Ringers* (2001), Constantine Verevis' *Film Remakes* (2006), Carolyn Jess-Cooke and Constantine Verevis' *Second Takes: Critical Approaches to the Film Sequel* (2010), and Kathleen Loock and Constantine Verevis' *Film Remakes, Adaptations, and Fan Productions: Remake/Remodel* (2012). These studies provide numerous perspectives on the various industrial, textual, and critical strategies that inform remaking practices. While much of the scholarship draws upon the more established tradition of adaptation studies, there has been a concerted effort within the discipline to move beyond textual comparisons of source and adap-tation and to start to integrate other methodological approaches. Indeed, the 'transnational turn' within film studies has shifted scholarship away from considerations of the national in order to investigate the transna-tional dimensions of cinema, and this has impacted the ways in which film remakes are now being approached. Contemporary scholarship on film remakes is building on the pioneering work of Verevis, Mazdon, and others to better engage with the fluid and dynamic ways films are adapted and reworked across national borders.

In television studies, localization is a fairly young field of research and—like film—focuses nearly exclusively on remakes. 'Format research' began in the 1990s, with an article by Skovmand (1992) on game show adaptation, a monograph by Cooper-Chen on globally franchised games (1994), and Moran's seminal book, *Copycat TV: Globalization, Program Formats and Cultural Identity* (1998). It then grew as a result of the TV Format trade, which became systematic and visible at trade fairs and in trade literature around the turn of the millennium and has accelerated since (Chalaby, 2011; Esser, 2013; Moran, 2013). Format research is concerned with the origins, flows, and patterns of internationally distributed TV Formats (Chalaby, 2012; Esser, 2013), with their local-global texture (Kraidy, 2009; Esser, 2014), and with format adaptations as expressions of national identity (for example, Adriaens and Biltereyst, 2012; Ferrari, 2012; Bochanty-Aguero, 2012). Moreover, format scholarship is interested in the ways in which, the extent to which, the reasons adaptations differ from the originals and from one another (for example, Jensen, 2009; Moran, 2009; Mikos and Perrotta, 2012), and how the socio-cultural, political, and industrial context impacts on both the format business and concrete format adaptations and vice versa (Jensen, 2009, 2012; Chalaby, 2010; Esser 2010, 2013).

Some scholars have critically reflected on the potential impact formats may have on local television production (Moran and Keane, 2009; Keane, 2012) and—as in film scholarship—on the value of adaptations as opposed to original creations (Waisbord, 2004; Brennan, 2012). Some have highlighted the very different ways formats can be adapted (Jensen, 2009; Esser and Jensen, 2015; Calbreath-Frasieur in this book); others the different ways formats have been appropriated (for example, Kraidy, 2012). Academics from television studies who research dubbing and subtitling are much rarer (see, for example, Barra, 2009; Adamou and Knox, 2011); the latter is usually undertaken by scholars of audiovisual translation.

The Collection: Content and Structure

The chapters in this book are roughly organized in three sections, illustrating what we consider the essential pillars of our interdisciplinary project aimed at advancing our understanding of global entertainment media. These are 1) the theoretical and methodological implications of today's multiple, diverse, and fluid media provision and consumption, 2) the concrete localization practices, considerations, and transformations that need to be considered by both localization researchers and practitioners, and 3) the identification and exploration of new critical insights, new trends, and new approaches to entertainment media localization. Many chapters fall in more than one of these categories.

Multiplicity, Diversity, and Fluidity: Theoretical and Methodological Reflections

In the opening chapter, Esser critically explores common conceptualizations of 'the local' and resulting assumptions about what 'local'ization means. The chapter draws on globalization theories, which question the prevailing notion that the local is bound to territory, usually the nation state, and on empirical findings that reveal the diversity, multiplicity, and fluidity of television audiences. The chapter challenges several influential, foundational theories, concepts, and assumptions in television studies, particularly the 'national audience', 'adapting for a national market', 'cultural discount' and 'preference for the local'. This is important, Esser argues, because the reductionism and almost mythological nature of these concepts create blind spots that impede an advanced theoretical and practical understanding of 'local'ization. A careful audience analysis shows that, more often than not 'the local' cannot be equated with a nation or with a nation state market. It needs to be defined much more carefully, on a case-by-case basis.

Another attempt to enhance our theoretical understanding of the local in localized internationally distributed content is that by Smith, who interrogates the cultural politics of transnational localization processes through a study of the Japanese-Italian anime *Sherlock Hound* (1984–). Drawing on Morley and Robins' theorization of the 'global-local nexus' (1995: 116), his chapter investigates the ways in which forces of both globalization and localization impacted upon the production and reception of the series, in which all the central characters from the Arthur Conan-Doyle stories become anthropomorphized canines. Like Esser, Smith challenges reductionist models of localization. Moving away from an explanatory framework that privileges the local within the global, Smith instead draws attention to the complex and intersecting nexus of global and local forces that necessarily complicate our theorization of cross-cultural adaptations.

Steemers, in Chapter 3, explores the role that the wider context plays in the production and localization of children's television. By contrasting the localization of children's programming in Western European and Arab countries, she reveals how the balance between the global and the local differs in each region and how this is the result of differences in expertise, history, policy, and regulatory environment. The findings are important, Steemers argues, in that they demonstrate the continued need to examine regulatory and cultural factors on a country-by-country basis. Even though we see a seismic shift toward convergent digital media and multiplatform distribution and a move away from mass communications to communications placing greater emphasis on individual participation and engagement, Steemers rightly contends that state regulation and cultural differences still matter and need to be paid adequate attention in research concerned with localization and content provision more generally.

Chaume, an internationally renowned audiovisual translation scholar and practitioner, introduces two important trends that can currently be observed in audiovisual translation. The first is a new tendency for content providers to offer audiovisual products in multiple modes of translation. Increasingly, consumers can choose dubbing, subtitling, or voice-over when watching foreign programs on television, the Internet, DVDs, or Blu-Ray discs and between dubbing and subtitling when playing video games. What we see thus is an increase in the diversification and choice of translation modes for audiences. The second trend is the growing localization practice of 'transcreation', which can be observed particularly in animated films or series. It is an enhanced form of localization that takes place at an increasing number of textual levels and sites and is aimed at enhancing local meaning and appeal. Both trends, Chaume argues, are the result of digitalization and have far-reaching consequences for the future of audiovisual translation and the localization business.

Localization Practices, Considerations, and Transformations

Chapters 5 to 8 provide an in-depth analysis of concrete localization practices and considerations, exemplified through case studies. Moreover,

Calbreath-Frasieur and even more so Kapsaskis and Artegiani illuminate the notable textual transformations that can result from adaptation, advancing our understanding of the nature and meaning of localization further. Kapsaskis and Artegiani compare the English versions of the internationally successful Italian TV crime series *Il Commissario Montalbano* with the originals in an effort to demonstrate the substantial transformations cultural products can experience through translation. With their detailed analysis of the adaptation and translation of the Sicilian dialect in *The Terracotta Dog*, the two translation scholars and practitioners reveal how the main protagonist, Montalbano, undergoes a metamorphosis in each version, from the novels, to the Italian series, to the English subtitles. Montalbano, they convincingly conclude, cannot be understood as possessing any authentic or essential features carried over in each transformation. This is because the protagonist exists primarily in the modes of translation and intertextuality. Artegiani and Kapsaskis' findings are hugely important for our understanding of translated media products: They may be internationally distributed and consumed, but the stories and characters transform in the process of adaptation across media and language borders. In other words, there is not just one but many Montalbanos.

Calbreath-Frasieur, in Chapter 6, explores some of the strategies used by Sesame Workshop, the non-profit organization behind the *Sesame Street* franchise, to adapt the show for different countries and regions. He demonstrates how the localization of *Sesame Street* (first launched in the US in 1969) can range from fairly minor to substantial. Adaptation in *Sesame Street* above all takes place through the replacement of Muppet characters with local creations that are believed to fit with the importing culture. Additionally, new scripts can be commissioned to deal with local issues. Rejecting academic claims that international franchising, or formatting, is bad *per se*, Calbreath-Frasieur uses this lively, historical case study to argue and show that formatting can be used both effectively and ethically. In the case of *Sesame Street*, licensable characters are used to address educational and social needs worldwide, and Sesame Workshop producers work in close collaboration with local producers and creators.

In the next chapter, Nkosi Ndlela explores the localization of two popular entertainment formats, *Idols* and *Big Brother*, in sub-Saharan Africa. The case studies, which also consider the formats' audiences, are employed to examine the range of cultural factors that were considered in the adaptation process and to identify the concrete localization needs in sub-Saharan Africa. Ndlela contends that not only language but the adaptation of cultural and aesthetic elements as well as viewer perceptions within the wider international landscape, too, are vital for creating a positive resonance between a format and its audiences. His work provides welcome insights into the under-researched African television market(s) and illuminates an important aspect for international media research: As his examples show, African adaptations are based on multiple cultural affiliations that both divide states and transcend linguistic and politico-legal borders. Moreover, due to the extensive use of various digital platforms, there are different 'levels', different sites of localization. As a consequence, the final, overall 'local'ization picture is highly complex. These findings, critically explored in more detail by Esser in Chapter 1, are crucial, suggesting that a local adaptation cannot automatically be assumed to be a national adaptation. Instead, it must be carefully delimited on a case-by-case basis.

Turning to dubbing again, translation scholar Baños looks at text and context to advance our understanding of, first, the variety of factors influencing the dubbing of English-language television series into Spanish and second, how the resulting dubbed product may be perceived by audiences. Focusing on the translation of dialogue and the selection of orality markers in both Spanish dubbed and domestic sitcoms, she shows how translated texts are confined not just by the source text but also by numerous extratextual constraints. These extratextual constraints, she argues, differ from those of dialogue written in Spanish for domestic television sitcoms, with the result that the latter may appear much more spontaneous and natural than the dialogue of translated sitcoms. Baños's findings suggest that the appeal of a show written in the native language may be greater than the appeal of a dubbed show because of the latter's lack of orality or naturalness in actors' utterances. Paying closer attention to the extratextual factors identified in this chapter is important not just for translators, actors, and dubbing artists, but also for TV program buyers and audience researchers. The latter, especially, may benefit from studying the importance of authentic speech in the appeal of sitcoms.

Critical Reflections, New Avenues for Research, and New Approaches to Entertainment Media Localization

The final five chapters of the book offer critical reflections on past adaptation and localization research, its theoretical foundations and assessments, and internationalization and localization approaches taken by the entertainment industry. The authors suggest avenues for future localization research and, in the case of Bernal-Merino, a new approach for the video games industry to improve the efficiency, speed, and quality of localization, the experience of players' globally, and ultimately the international sales potential of game developers.

In Chapter 9, Raw argues that there is little use in comparing source and target texts if we want to understand how and why a text changes across cultures. He notes the significant impact that socio-cultural context has on adaptation and concludes that it would be much more fruitful to consider transcultural adaptations of cinematic texts in terms of 'stories'. Stories, according to psychologist Jerome Bruner, define cultures. They are the narratives people construct to make sense of the world and to determine their positions within it. Raw argues that to understand adaptations, we need to first understand the narratives that shape a culture and then look closely at how such narratives shape the adaptive process—a process of complex negotiations between the many creative talents involved, each with its own particular narratives that it brings to bear on the source text and the production of the target text. Adaptations of various popular Hollywood classics into popular Turkish films during the *Yeşilçam* (or Green Pine) era are used to demonstrate his argument. The opposition between local and global, Raw concludes, is a Western idea that perpetuates notions of cultural difference and consigns non-Western cinemas to the margins.

Returning to television format scholarship, Szostak challenges the concern that international franchising may undermine the local research and development capacity of young television markets (Moran and Keane, 2009), arguing instead that broadcasters in developing television markets can benefit from licensing and adapting international fiction formats. Drawing on numerous interviews with Polish TV executives, this young scholar shows how internationally franchised scripted formats, such as Colombian *Betty, La Fea* or Hungarian *Barátok közt* (*Between Friends*), have contributed to today's 'healthy state' of domestic television production in Poland. In parts, she argues, this is because format acquisition implies training for local scriptwriters and directors who through the adaptation process develop their craft of creating compelling television content. Her contention that formats in Poland have assumed an important developmental role is likely to resonate beyond Poland, and it seems to support earlier claims about television markets going from heavy importation in their early developmental years to healthy domestic production as they mature (Buonanno, 1999; Sinclair, 2000). The chapter also reveals, however, that learning is not always quick and that formats are used to fill gaps the broadcaster is unable to fill with domestic fare long-term.

Denison's chapter advances our understanding of the conditions under which adaptations, translations, and remakes take place. The film scholar looks at how Asian media franchises traverse cultural borders by unpacking the network of texts that are associated with *Hana Yori Dango*, a truly transnational media franchise that started as a girls' manga in Japan in 1992. *Hana Yori Dango*, Denison argues, has exceeded its Japanese origins and has taken on numerous transnational connotations through its remakes in China, Taiwan, India, South Korea, and the US. By closely interrogating the discourse surrounding these various adaptations, she demonstrates the complexities underpinning the processes of transnational borrowing and makes a convincing case for a more holistic and contextually nuanced appreciation of the global distribution of cultural brands and their diverse localized products.

In Chapter 12, Fernández Costales offers insights into global, localized video games and their paratexts from an audience perspective—a perspective that is rare in game, or in fact any localization research but, as this contribution suggests, is much needed. As Esser at the start of this collection notes, only by taking audiences into account can we verify or falsify the long held generalizing assumption about the 'preference for the local'. Fernández Costales' exploratory study, concerned with how players in the Spanish region of Asturias perceive matters around translation in video games, reveals some surprising findings. Other than expected by most media and localization scholars, there is a notable acceptance of (and at times even preference for) English-language video games and attendant paratexts amongst competent players. Fernández Costales' findings are supported by a larger games study, which has revealed a clear tendency that today many users in Spain enjoy English multimedia products (Orrego, 2015). More research of this kind is clearly needed.

Staying with video game localization, Bernal-Merino's concluding chapter reveals both new trends and the importance of localization in today's video games market, an economically highly significant industry, with a reported value of $81 billion globally in 2014. The expansion of video game companies into multinational corporations has been accelerated by the steady growth of the video game fansphere. These devoted fans from around the world, hyperconnected by digital technology, Bernal-Merino says, demand quality products on the day of release. Consequently, he argues, 'the foreign' should no longer exist in the global business paradigm. Whilst many companies have not yet accepted the implications of today's global media landscape, the leading game corporations have embraced a global simultaneous shipment distribution model. In doing so, they have also been forced to change their approach to game design and development. They now integrate internationalization in pre-production with the result that for the leaders in the game industry, localization is no longer an afterthought, as it has been from the 1980s, until recently, but is an essential part of their strategy to expand their user base in more regions around the world. Glocalization and co-creation, Bernal-Merino says, are important new trends for interactive entertainment companies, signaling a dramatic shift in the creation, marketing, and distribution of video games, new strategies that contribute to market penetration, player satisfaction, and brand permanence in all countries of distribution.

To conclude this introduction: Digitalization has brought many changes to the international distribution of entertainment media products in the new millennium, and it will continue to do so. We can expect the internationalization, proliferation, and convergence of entertainment media to proceed and audiences to continue to fragment. The options given to media consumers are likely to continue to grow, and they will also include modes of translation.

Both academia and industry seek to understand audiences and their preferences, the latter so they can cater to the diversity of preferences to keep or extend their market positions or open up new markets. Unfortunately, much of both academic and industry thinking pertaining to the internationalization of media content and its localization to date has been characterized by generalizations and simplifications. As we hope the contributions in this collection show, generalizations are impossible, though. Localization is highly context bound. Socio-cultural, political and economic context matters and media-specific sites and levels of localization, too, matter. Moreover, there are no fixed, standard markets. In today's age, it seems more and more sensible for localizers to target smaller markets within national and/or country borders or to transcend them. In some cases, it appears that the still common geographical space approach ceases to be meaningful altogether.

Localization is far from straightforward and simple, and we need to make greater efforts to acknowledge the diversity, multiplicity, and fluidity of today's localization practices and today's media consumers. We need to acknowledge complexity. Different media and genre bear different viewer motifs, investment, and pleasures. Media consumers differ in their preferences, and these preferences can change over time for a whole range of socio-cultural, technological, and economic reasons. The industry is significantly involved in shaping markets and preferences. Audiences and industry are mutually influencing and need to be researched if we want to understand the meaning of localization processes and outcomes, preferences for different modes of translation or even no translation, and future avenues of media entertainment localization.

Acknowledgment

The editors would like to express their deep gratitude to the British Arts and Humanities Research Council (AHRC) for the launch funding of the Media Across Borders network in 2012. It is this funding that brought together the contributors to this collection and many more who have since joined the network.

Note

1. The network also has an interest in the increase of interactive features to engage with the hyper-connected consumers of audiovisual entertainment in today's world and the growing number and importance of paratexts (for example, websites, music and toys) in today's 'attention economy', where consumer eyeballs have become the scarce good, desperately sought by producers of media content and consumer goods alike. In this collection, however, our primary focus is on issues of localization.

References

Activision-Blizzard. (2013). Annual Report. Available online at: http://investor.activision. com/common/download/download.cfm?companyid=ACTI&fileid=746096& filekey=2205B72D-1007-4DCB-A5F1-2D121D8EC95C&filename=Activision_ Blizzard_2013_AR.1.pdf. (Retrieved November 9, 2014).
Adamou, C. and Knox, S. (2011). Transforming television drama through dubbing and subtitling: Sex and the Cities, *Critical Studies in Television*, 6(1), 1–21.

Adriaens, F. and Biltereyst, D. (2012). Glocalized telenovelas and national identities: A "textual cum production" analysis of the "telenovela" Sara, the Flemish adaptation of Yo soy Betty, la Fea, *Television & New Media*, 13(6), 551–67.

Agost, R. (1999). *Traducción y doblaje: palabras, voces e imágenes*. Barcelona.

Barra, L. (2009). The mediation is the message. Italian regionalization of US TV series as co-creational work, *International Journal of Cultural Studies*, 12(5), 509–525.

Bartelt-Krantz, M. (2011). Game localization management: Balancing linguistic quality and financial efficiency. In M. Á. Bernal-Merino (Ed.), *TRANS. Revista de Traductología*, 15, 81–86.

Bernal-Merino, M. Á. (2006). On the translation of video games. *The Journal of Specialised Translation*, 6, 22–36. Online www.jostrans.org/issue06/art_bernal.pdf.

Bernal-Merino, M. Á. (2015). *Translation and Localisation in Video Games. Making Entertainment Software Global*. New York/Oxon: Routledge.

Bochanty-Aguero, E. (2012). We are the world: *American Idols* global self-posturing. In T. Oren & S. Shahaf (Eds.), *Global Television Formats* (pp. 260–81). London: Routledge.

Bourdon, J. (2012). From discrete adaptations to hard copies: The rise of formats in European television. In T. Oren and S. Shahaf (Eds.), *Global Television Formats* (pp. 111–27). London: Routledge.

Brennan, E. (2012). A political economy of formatted pleasures. In T. Oren & S. Shahaf (Eds.), *Global Television Formats* (pp. 72–89). London: Routledge.

Buonanno, M. (2009). A place in the sun: Global seriality and the revival of domestic drama in Italy. In A. Moran (Ed.), *TV Formats Worldwide: Localising Global Programs* (pp. 255–271). Bristol: Intellect.

Chalaby, J. (2012). At the Origin of a Global Industry: The TV Format Trade as an Anglo-American Invention, *Media, Culture and Society*, 34(1), 36–52.

Chalaby, J. (2011). The Making of an Entertainment Revolution: How the TV Format Trade Became a Global Industry, *European Journal of Communication*, 26(4), 293–309.

Chalaby, J. (2010). The Rise of Britain's Super-Indies: Policy-Making in the Age of the Global Media Market, *The International Communication Gazette*, 72(8), 675–693.

Chandler, H. (2005). *The Game Localization Handbook*. Massachusetts: Charles River Media.

Chandler, H. M. and Deming, S. O. (2012). *The Game Localization Handbook*, 2nd edition. Sudbury/London: Jones and Bartlett Learning.

Chaume, F. (2001). La pretendida oralidad en los textos audiovisuales y sus implicaciones en traducción. In R. Agost and F. Chaume (Eds.), *La traducción en los medios audiovisuales* (77–88). Castellón: Publicacions de l'Universitat Jaume I.

Chaume, F. (2004). *Cine y Traducción*. Madrid: Cátedra.

Chaume, F. (2012). *Audiovisual Translation: Dubbing*. London and New York: Routledge.

Cooper-Chen, A. (1994). *Games in the Global Village: A 50-Nation Study*. Bowling Green, Ohio: Bowling Green University Popular Press.

Díaz-Cintas, Jorge. (2001). *La traducción audiovisual: el subtitulado*. Salamanca: Almar.

Díaz-Cintas, J. and Remael, A. (2007). *Audiovisual Translation: Subtitling*. Manchester/New York: St. Jerome Publishing.

Edwards, K. (2011). Culturalisation: The geopolitical and cultural dimensions of game content. In M. Á Bernal-Merino (Ed.), *TRANS. Revista de traductología* 15. Málaga: Universidad de Málaga, 19–28.

Esser, A. and Jensen, P. M. (2015). The use of international television formats by public-service broadcasters in Australia, Denmark and Germany, *International Communication Gazette*, 77(4), 359–383.

Esser, A. (2014). European television programming: Exemplifying and theorizing glocalization in the media. In R. Robertson (Ed.), *European Glocalization in Global Context* (pp. 82–102). Basingstoke: Palgrave.

Esser, A. (2013). The format business: Franchising television content, *International Journal of Digital Television*, 4(2), 141–158.

Esser, A. (2010). Television formats: Primetime staple, global market, *Popular Communication*, 8(4), 273–292.

Ferrari, C. (2012). "National Mike": Global Host and Global Formats in Early Italian Television. In T. Oren and S. Shahaf (Eds.), *Global Television Formats: Understanding Television Across Borders* (pp. 128–147). London: Routledge.

Forrest, J. and Koos, L. R. (2001). *Dead Ringers. The Remake in Theory and Practice*. Albany: SUNY Press.

Gambier, Y. and Gottlieb H. (2001). (Eds.), *(Multi) Media Translation. Concepts, Practices, and Research*. Amsterdam/Philadelphia: John Benjamins Publishing Company.

Honeywood et al., (2012). IGDA Localization SIG (Special Interest Group).

Ivarsson, J. (1992). *Subtitling for the Media. A Handbook of an Art*. Stockholm: TransEdit.

Jäger, E. and Behrens, S. (2009). The FRAPA Report 2009 – TV Formats to the World, Cologne: Frapa.

Jensen, P. M. (2012). How media system rather than culture determines national variation: Danish and Australian Idols compared. In K. Zwaan & J. de Bruin (Eds.), *Adapting Idols: Authenticity, Identity and Performance in a Global TV Format*. Farnham: Ashgate Publishing.

Jensen, P. M. (2009). How media systems shape the localization of TV formats: A transnational case study of The Block and Nerds FC in Australia and Denmark. In A. Moran (Ed.), *TV Formats Worldwide: Localizing Global Programs* (pp. 163–186). Bristol: Intellect.

Jess-Cooke, C. and Verevis, C. (2010). *Second Takes: Critical Approaches to the Film Sequel*. Albany: SUNY Press.

Karamitroglou, F. (2000). *Towards a Methodology for the Investigation of Norms in Audiovisual Translation: The Choice Between Subtitling and Revoicing in Greece*. Amsterdam/Atlanta: Rodopi.

Keane, M. (2012). A revolution in television and a great leap forward for innovation? China in the global television format business. In T. Oren and S. Shahaf (Eds.), *Global Television Formats* (pp. 306–23). London: Routledge.

Kraidy, M. (2012). The social and political dimensions of global television formats: Reality television in Lebanon and Saudi Arabia. In T. Oren & S. Shahaf (Eds.), *Global Television Formats* (pp. 285–305). London: Routledge.

Kraidy, M. (2009). Rethinking the local-global nexus through multiple modernities: The case of Arab reality television. In A. Moran (Ed.), *TV Formats Worldwide. Localizing Global Programs* (pp. 27–38). Bristol: Intellect.

Loock, K. and Verevis, C. (2012). *Film Remakes, Adaptations, and Fan Productions: Remake/Remodel*. Basingstoke: Palgrave Macmillan.

Mayoral, R., Kelly, D. and Gallardo, N. (1988). Concept of constrained translation. Non-linguistic perspectives of translation, *Meta* 33(3), 356–367. Online www.erudit.org/revue/meta/1988/v33/n3/003608ar.pdf.

Mazdon, L. (2000). *Encore Hollywood: Remaking French Cinema*. London: BFI.

Mikos, L. and Perrotta, M. (2012). Traveling style: Aesthetic differences and similarities in national adaptations of Yo Soy Betty, La Fea, *International Journal of Cultural Studies*, 15(1), 81–97.

Moran, A. and Keane, M. (2009). (Eds), *Continuum: Journal of Media and Cultural Studies*, 23(2).

Moran, A. (2013). Global television formats: Genesis and growth, *Critical Studies in Television*, 8(2), 1–19.

Moran, A. (2009). (Ed.), *TV Formats Worldwide: Localizing Global Programs*. Bristol: Intellect.

Moran, A. (1998). *Copycat TV: Globalization, Program Formats and Cultural Identity*. Luton Press.

Morley, D. and Robins, K. (1995). Spaces of Identity. Global Media, Electronic Landscapes and Cultural Boundaries. London: Routledge.

MPAA (The Motion Picture Association of America). (2015).The Theatrical Market Statistics Report for 2014. http://www.mpaa.org/wp-content/uploads/2015/03/MPAA-Theatrical-Market-Statistics-2014.pdf.

Newzoo. (2015). The Global Growth of Esports. Available online at: www.gamesindustry.biz/articles/2015-02-17-report-esports-revenues-to-hit-usd465m-in-2017 (Retrieved May 17, 2015).

Neves, J. (2005). Audiovisual Translation: Subtitling for the Deaf and Hard-of-Hearing. PhD thesis. University of Surrey Roehampton.

O'Hagan, M. and C. Mangiron. (2013). *Game Localization: Translating for the Global Digital Entertainment Industry*. Amsterdam/Philadelphia: John Benjamins.

Orero, P. and Matamala, A. (2007). Accessible opera: Overcoming linguistic and sensorial barriers. *Perspectives: Studies in Translatology*, 15(4), 262–277.

Orrego-Carmona, D. (2015). The Reception of Non-professional Subtitling. PhD thesis (unpublished). Universitat Rovirai Virgili.

Sinclair, J. (2000). Geolinguistic region as global space: the case of Latin America. In G. Wang, J. Servaes & A. Goonasekera (Eds.), *The New Communications Landscape: Demystifying Media Globalization* (pp. 19–32). London: Routledge.

Skovmand, M. (1992). Barbarous TV International: Syndicated "Wheels of Fortune". In M. Skovmand & K.C. Schrøder (Eds.), *Media Cultures. Reappraising Transnational Media* (pp. 84–103). London: Routledge.

Smith, I. R. and Verevis, C. (2016). *Transnational Film Remakes*. Edinburgh: Edinburgh University Press.

Spyri, J. (1880–1946). *Heidi*. Cleveland, Ohio: World Publishing.

Stephens, J. (2012). New report offers 'snapshot' of buoyant European market, Frapa Newsletter Archive, 07.06.12. https://www.frapa.org/2012/06/07/new-report-offers-snapshot-of-buoyant-european-market/.

TRP Research. (2015). UK Television Exports Survey 2014/2015. London: Pact, http://www.thecreativeindustries.co.uk/media/311154/tv-exports-survey-fy-14-15.pdf.

Verevis, C. (2006). *Film Remakes*. Edinburgh: Edinburgh University Press.

Waisbord, S. (2004). McTV – Understanding the Global Popularity of Television Formats, *Television and New Media*, 5(4), 359–383.

Zabalbeascoa, P. (1993). Developing Translation Studies to Better Account for Audiovisual Texts and Other New Forms of Text Production, PhD Thesis, Universidad de Lleida.

Zynga. (2014). Annual report 2013. Available online at: http://investor.zynga.com/annual-proxy.cfm (Retrieved November 11, 2014).

1 Defining 'the Local' in Localization or 'Adapting for Whom?'

Andrea Esser

This chapter aims to enhance our understanding of 'the local' in localization. It looks at how audiences are constructed by broadcasters and considers the appeal, the consumption, and the reception of 'locally' adapted audiovisual entertainment. The chapter was prompted by findings from interviews with format producers and broadcasters (Esser, 2013, 2014; Ndlela, 2012, 2013), textual analysis of TV program adaptations (Jensen, 2009, 2012; Barra, 2009), and a number of qualitative and quantitative audience research projects (Kuipers and de Kloet, 2009; Klaus and O'Connor, 2010; Stehling, 2013; Esser, Keinonen, Jensen, and Lemor, 2016). All raised questions and doubts about the commonly unspecified use of the term and the widespread underlying assumption that formatted television programs, like *Big Brother* or *Who Wants to be a Millionaire?*, which are sold internationally for local adaptation, are localized for a national audience.

The reflections offered are furthermore inspired by theoretical arguments advanced by globalization theorists (Appadurai, 1996; Beck, 2006; Hannerz, 1996; Robertson, 1994, 2014; Tomlinson, 1991, 1999) and scholars with a specific interest in transnational media consumption and diasporic audiences (Aksoy and Robins, 2008; Harindranath, 2005; Athique, 2008, 2011; Kuipers and de Kloet, 2009; Robins, 2014a, 2014b). These arguments—whilst coming from such diverse fields as sociology, anthropology, cultural studies, and media and film studies—all question, on epistemological and political grounds, conceptualizations of national/ethnic culture and the attendant notion of cultural difference. Harindranath (2005), Aksoy and Robins (2008), and Athique (2011) contend such notions are the result of the extensive and abiding ideological work undertaken to create national cultures and identities. As such they are extremely powerful and persistent, but they also create methodological and theoretical gaps and obstruct understanding, new insights, and avenues of research.

There is a dissonance between the findings of the above-mentioned empirical studies and theories based on notions of 'national culture', 'cultural difference', and the resulting assumption that adaptation is carried out mainly to take account of 'national sensibilities'. Furthermore, there is an unresolved, irrefutable clash between these latter theories and the people refuting them and calling for non-identitarian and communitarian conceptualizations of audiences instead, like Harindranath, Athique, and Aksoy and Robins. These important frictions raise questions that are highly relevant to localization research: Who belongs (or does not belong) to the 'local audience' that media content is to be adapted for? What are the aspects of 'local'ization we should consider when adapting audiovisual content for 'local' audiences? And which concepts and theoretical perspectives require refinement?

To explore these questions I will draw particularly on TV Format adaptation. It is here that the local is most often equated with the national (see, for example, Moran, 2005; Beeden and de Bruin, 2009; Negra, Pike, and Radley, 2012; Moran and Aveyard, 2014; Keinonen, 2015), and it is the nation-centric thinking in particular I want to challenge in this chapter. But literature from film and video games studies, as well as television studies more generally, suggests that scholars here, too, tend to take 'national markets' and 'national audiences' for granted. It seems in all these disciplines that only a minority grapple with questions of how and how not to conceptualize media audiences and markets in a globalizing world.

In the first section, I will summarize the theoretical basis of my thinking, addressing the yet-prevalent assumption underlying much television scholarship that the local is bound to territory and that the TV audience is (still) defined by national culture and state borders. The second section will illuminate these abstract ideas with concrete examples from the perspective of broadcasters and format producers. That is, how do industry executives conceptualize their audiences when 'local'izing an internationally franchised show? In the third section, the nation-centric fallacy will be revealed through a range of audience research projects, all demonstrating that audiences of TV formats are on the one hand comprised of diverse, fluid, and multiple factions of a country's television market and on the other are much more transnational than TV scholars commonly assume.

In the final section, the widely accepted and cited theses of 'cultural discount' (Hoskins and Mirus, 1988) and 'preference for the local' (Straubhaar, 1991, 2007) will be critically scrutinized. It will be argued that the persistent and unquestioned dominance of these theories is the result not just of empirical findings but, importantly, of deeply engrained cultural essentialism, where space-based conceptualizations of place and the national imaginary reign. Just as empirical proof exists to suggest a preference for local content, there is also much evidence for the appeal of the foreign, the exotic, for what is perceived as 'global popular culture', as new and innovative, and/or simply as of better quality. What is in fact a highly complex picture, I contend, has been obstructed by the plausibility, catchiness, and part-truth of the 'cultural discount' and 'preference for the local' theses.

Overall, I hope with this chapter to open up avenues for more nuanced thinking and for research that takes into account the immense diversity, plurality, complexity, and fluidity we find in today's media consumption and reception. For practitioners working in localization this means that approaches to 'local'ization will become more intricate and varied and that localization strategies should be carefully mapped out on a case-by-case basis.

Theorizing National Culture and Cultural Identity

In their seminal work of the early 1980s Anderson and Hobsbawm argued that we should conceive of national culture not in essentialist terms but as something socially or culturally constructed, 'imagined' (Anderson, 1983) and 'invented' (Hobsbawm, 1983). Hall (1990) subsequently noted that cultures constantly change and are hybrid at any point in time. With specific reference to geography, Tomlinson (1991, 1999) astutely remarked "[c]ulture is entirely—even definitively—the work of human beings" and thus cannot, like flora and fauna, "naturally belong" to a geographical area (1991: 23). Tomlinson, Hannerz (1996), and Massey (1994) in particular queried space as a marker of culture and as the key element in the construction of 'place'— here understood as a unique community, landscape, and moral order, creating identity and a sense of belonging.[1] In other words, they were not convinced that people who occupy a particular space together—be it a pub, a city, or a country—all experience this space in the same way, feel the same, identify with each other. At the same time, people who live hundreds of miles apart from each other can feel a great togetherness, religion being a good example.

Of course people can also feel they belong to more than one group, which made Hannerz conclude that if people can belong to "differently distributed communities of intelligibility with regard to different kinds of meaningful forms", the notion of a bounded culture "as a self-evident package deal, with a definite spatial location" (1996: 21–22) becomes questionable. Massey therefore proposed an alternative interpretation of place as "articulated moments in networks of social relations and understanding" (1994: 154). Places, she argued, need to be conceptualized as processes, not as something frozen in time. Processes, however, cannot easily be bounded, divided off into simple enclosures. Boundaries may be needed at times for research purposes, but this does not mean they are necessary for the conceptualization of place (ibid: 155). Furthermore, Massey argued, we must acknowledge that places do not have single unique identities but are full of internal conflicts. None of this, she convincingly concluded, denies the importance of place. In short, place is what provides us with identification and feelings of belonging but unlike space, which has a geographical aspect, place is unbounded and fluid and can be entirely virtual.

In addition to these important epistemological insights, contemporary trends imply that retaining 'national culture' as the key analytical unit and outlook is even more problematic today than it already was in the past, due to its implications of space and fixedness. Appadurai (1996) rightly noted how accelerating globalization during the last four decades has put further pressure on the national. Transnational flows of people, technology, finance, media images, and ideologies, he argued, make it ever harder to pinpoint national cultures and identities. Robertson (1994, 2014) astutely pointed out how the market is actively engaged in constructing and advocating cultural difference, as this is what drives sales and profits. The market, Hannerz (1996) mused, seems to have become more powerful than the state when it comes to managing culture; and international marketing scholars Rittenhofer and Nielsen (2009) contend that in today's globalizing world it is producers and consumers (not states) who create markets (see chapters from Chaume, Bernal-Merino, Costales, Denison, and Ndlela in this collection). These markets are ever shifting, they rightly note, and differ from product to product. The traditional standard equation of (both producer and consumer) markets with countries does not fit the reality of today's world.

Focusing on media audiences specifically, important insights have come out of media diaspora research and its proposed shortcomings. Aksoy and Robins (2008), Robins (2014a, 2014b), and Athique (2008, 2011) warn against the prevalent tendency within diaspora studies to engage in the rhetoric of cultural essentialism and consequently turn diaspora into a site of reductive classifications and cultural homogenization. From the perspective of mainstream diaspora studies, Robins remarks critically, the media consumption of a young Turk living in Germany is approached and analyzed on the basis of her assumed 'essential Turkishness'. As a result of this, it is further assumed that she must have an identity crisis, caught between the norms and demands of 'her' culture (i.e., the 'Turkish' culture of her parents and grandparents) and the 'German' culture she currently resides in. Her media consumption of Turkish television programs or music is then interpreted as causing 'acculturation stress' and/or as evidence of her 'essential Turkishness' (Robins, 2014a: 29). What we have here, Robins rightly notes, is a reductive and circular argument, an argument that does not constitute sociology but rather mythology. "For, in reality, the considerable differences within 'the community' are perhaps more evident and significant than assumed commonalities" (ibid: 28). He refers to both the assumed 'Turkish' and 'German' communities here.

Cultural essentialism is not just a problem in diaspora studies, though. As Harindranath shows, proponents of media imperialism theories and their opponents, interested in audience reception, too, fall prey to "cultural nationalism riding on conceptions of a putative national culture" (2005), ignoring the vexed question of what constitutes a culture. In both discourses, he says, cultural difference is privileged as an immutable, defining, and essential category of presumed difference, wrongly and dangerously collapsing race/ethnicity/nationality into culture. In contrast, all the above authors call for the recognition of unique and complex cultural experiences. Leaving these highly important but abstract lines of thought, I now want to turn to more illustrative and television-specific arguments about why, when it comes to television consumption and reception, we also need to make greater efforts to recognize complexity. Why assumptions of a 'national TV audience', despite various historically grown and at times still evident justifications, are also problematic.

The 'Local' Television Audience—Defined by State Borders?

Historically, television in most of the world is nationally determined. In Europe, the stronghold of public-service broadcasting with its remit to reflect and build the nation, this is especially true. Public-service broadcasters were set up to produce television content for the nation, and to address audiences as national citizens. Media policy has been and to a considerable extent still is nationally and/or state oriented, and broadcast rights are historically traded on a country-by-country basis. Audiences' viewing habits and expectations have been shaped over decades by national terrestrial broadcasters, and industry executives use the nation label for marketing purposes at international TV markets, speaking of 'Danish drama', 'Israeli or British formats', or 'Japanese animation'. All of this is the result of the abiding ideological work undertaken to create and sustain national cultures and identities, and it may hence not be surprising that many television scholars still have a national outlook and use the 'national market' as their default unit of analysis. This may also explain why the vast majority of scholars exploring TV format adaptations think of these in terms of 'national adaptations' (for example, Waisbord, 2004; Moran, 2005; Larkey, 2009; Beeden and de Bruin 2009; Sharp, 2012; Mirrlees, 2013; Negra, Pike, and Radley, 2012).

But there are multiple problems with this line of analysis. On a general level, there is the common but persistent conflation of state and nation. If not for the aforementioned national mythology, this conflation would be quite surprising. After all, the world is full of multi-nation states and nations without states. It is also surprising considering that language is strongly associated with culture and is a notable force in determining television consumption. However, more often than not, language does not correspond with state borders: because multiple languages can be found within the boundaries of the state (as is the case in most African countries, India, China, and several European countries) or because the dominant language is shared with other countries (as is the case with English, Spanish, German, French, Portuguese and Arabic). Despite this messy reality, television scholarship dealing with this complexity is rare (see for example, Dhoest, 2011; Sun, 2013; Harindranath, 2013). But if we carefully look at the *de facto* situation of TV markets from above, the 'national' is rarely a useful concept, and if we look at broadcasters' audience constructions and actual TV consumption more concretely, as I will do next, the notion of 'national audiences', too, becomes questionable.

Broadcasters' Audience Constructions: Reflecting Complexity

If we look at broadcasters' audience constructions for internationally formatted TV programs—despite what many television scholars assume—very often the 'local' adaptation is not carried out with a national or nation state audience in mind. Ndlela's work on TV Formats in Africa (2012, 2013) demonstrates how on the African continent we find adaptations based on multiple cultural affiliations that both divide states and transcend state borders. The musical talent show *Idols*, for instance, has been produced in three different versions: *South African Idol*, which is produced in English to deal with the multiple languages spoken in South Africa; *Afrikaans Idol*, for the South Africans, Namibians, and small populations across Southern Africa that speak Afrikaans; and *West African Idol*, which seeks to incorporate diverse countries throughout the West African region, using English again as a lingua franca (Ndlela, 2012).

Ndlela's subsequent study of *Big Brother* provided further insights into both the transnationality and complexity of localization in Africa. The first adaptation of this originally Dutch format for the African continent was *Big Brother Africa*. Launched in 2013 and watched by audiences in 47 African countries, the program saw participants from 12 countries compete against each other. The program enjoyed "enormous popularity across the continent and beyond the countries represented" (Ndlela, 2013: 57). Its success, Ndlela argues, "derives on the 'transculturality' and cultural hybridity of its audiences, found in the different African countries" (ibid: 64).

As was the case with *Idols*, the localization of *Big Brother Africa* was not national but tailored to an English-speaking transnational audience found in Southern Africa, East Africa, and West Africa. Moreover, because the program's target audience was dispersed across multiple platforms, including mobile, internet and social media sites, further 'local'ization— through, for example, the editing out of certain scenes—occurred on these platforms. Here, too, Ndlela says, differing "cultural sensibilities" were taken into account, for instance, for religious reasons. Again though, he notes, many of the additional platforms were not confined to national, or in fact any geographical space, and neither are the cultural sensibilities catered to with the localization carried out for the online distribution platforms (ibid: 65).

It is not just the cultural complexity of postcolonial countries and/or the nature of developing television markets, however, that makes broadcasters and TV format producers adapt programs for target audiences that divide states and/or transcend state borders. Research by Jensen (2009, 2012), Barra (2009), and Esser (2014) in well-developed Western television markets shows how the choice of television channel and scheduling slot impacts the adaptation. Researching audiovisual translation in Italy, Barra (2009) notes how the adaptation and dubbing of *The Simpsons'* first two seasons (1991), which targeted an adult audience and were aired late at night, were "particularly gross and vulgar". Subsequent seasons, however, were scheduled in the daytime for a younger audience. As a result, "'bad words' [present in the original lines] were now censored, cut or masked directly in the adaptation step" (Barra, 2009: 516).

Regarding TV formats specifically, producers interviewed by me highlighted that a program is adapted in light of its specific target audience. The

German adaptation of the telenovela *Betty La Fea* (*Verliebt in Berlin*, Sat.1 2005–2007), for example, was produced for a pre-primetime slot on free-to-air channel Sat.1. To make the format more attractive to young people, who make up a large proportion of viewers for this slot, three young characters were added to the original Columbian storyline (Esser, 2013). It was not an aspect of 'national cultural difference', thus, that effected this change but a scheduling decision implying a target audience, which constitutes only a small fraction of Germany's inhabitants and which exists in every country. Even more revealing is the case of *Germany's Next Top Model* (Pro7, 2006-present), produced for a primetime slot on one of Germany's other major terrestrial channels, *Pro7*. Here channel identity was named as the most important aspect for the 'local adaptation'. Channel identity is closely linked to a channel's overall target group. *Pro7* defines theirs as "young adults of the media generation" (Pro7). Holger Rettler, the producer of *GNTM*, said he would have adapted the show very differently for Germany's other major commercial channel, *RTL*. It would have been a much less international, young, and glamorous look, he told me, than that chosen for the *Pro7* adaptation (in Esser, 2014).

All of the above examples show that in these five instances the broadcasters did not conceive of their audiences as 'national' and/or state-wide audiences, and this was the case even in Italy and Germany, where the cultural situation seems comparatively straightforward. Even though both countries are comparatively young and have strong regional identities, both are (mostly undisputed) nation states with a unified language. There is not room for more detail here, but for localizers and those interested in understanding localization it is important to note: Adaptation includes considerations to modify content in ways that take into account the specific audiences targeted by the broadcasters with the programs in question. Additionally, we need to consider: the overall channel identity, the "specific *media systemic conditions* (such as media policies, funding, market competition and broadcasting history)" (Jensen, 2009: 165) and the specific aims and enabling or constraining forces the broadcaster has to contend with at the time of the format acquisition and adaptation (see chapters from Baños, Ndlela and Szostak in this collection).

De Facto Audience Consumption and Reception: Fragmented, Fluid, and Border-Crossing

What about actual audiences? Let us turn from how producers and broadcasters conceive of, and in the process create, temporary audiences both within and beyond state borders to empirical findings that deal with actual audience consumption and reception. Quantitative audience analysis shows how fragmented and fluid the composition of the supposedly national television audience is in reality. According to audience ratings analysis from TV channel *Living*—the British-based channel on which all English-language versions of *Next Top Model* (NTM) are shown—the American franchise has three British audiences:

- Women who like the *NTM* format as such and watch the British, the American, the Canadian, and the Australian versions,
- Women who watch only the British version, which they seem to prefer for the local feel and the (presumably greater) opportunities for identification, and
- Women who prefer the US version, which has a much higher production budget (Rufaie in Esser, 2014).

This example with its three distinct audiences reveals the mistaken assumption of a national audience, or even one reduced to 'young British women'. In addition, it demonstrates the notable engagement with television content across state borders, here facilitated through the common language.

Academic audience research on formatted talent shows (O'Conner, 2012; Stehling, 2013; Esser et al., 2016), too, has uncovered notable evidence of cross-border television consumption. Young people, who have a strong interest in popular entertainment (much of which is global) and who make much use of the Internet and social networks, seem particularly eager and willing to engage with multiple versions of a format they like. Interestingly, awareness of, and engagement with international versions was not considered special or worth highlighting by the participants in the research on musical talent shows three European colleagues and I carried out (Esser et al., 2016). It seems that, as Beck (2006) has argued, everyday life has become cosmopolitan in banal ways. It unfolds beneath the surface of persisting national spaces, transforming them from within.

Cosmopolitanization occurs especially where the significance of language is diminished, as is the case in most talent shows. Moreover, the role of English as lingua franca and growing English language competencies worldwide, as suggested by Costales (Chapter 12 in this collection), fosters cross-border engagement on a global scale. But the role of technology, too, is crucial in this respect. It showed in our research (Esser et al., 2016), where significant differences in consumption became much more evident among different age groups than among the four European cities of Aarhus (Denmark), London (UK), Saarbrücken (Germany), and Tampere (Finland), in which our focus groups were held. It also showed in Ndlela's (2013: 68) research on *Big Brother*, revealing how dramatic changes in information and communication technologies have fundamentally altered media consumption patterns in Africa. These new technologies, and particularly the mobile phone, Ndlela says, enable M-Net to engage with different *Big Brother Africa* audiences on multiplatform outlets, including mobile, Internet and social media sites (Facebook and YouTube) in addition to the provider's conventional Multichoice TV channels. In Africa and around the world, audiences have ceased to be confined by geographical space.

This also influences the reception of programs consumed across borders. Both my own research (Esser et al., 2016) and that conducted by Klaus and O'Connor (2010), O'Connor (2012), Grüne (2013), and Stehling (2013) reveal that people across borders talk about talent shows in very similar ways. Themes brought up by focus group participants in all locations, for instance, included the starkly commercial and commodified nature of talent competitions, their stagedness and inauthenticity, the excessive use of 'weepy stories', and the (feared) negative effect fame may have on children especially but on older contestants, too. The findings of shared modes of viewing and reception across state borders are supported by film research (Kuipers and Kloet, 2009; Athique, 2011). Kuipers and de Kloet, who were part of a large-scale global reception study, note how "in the case of global blockbusters like *The Lord of the Rings*, national 'repertoires of evaluation' are superseded by more global repertoires" (2009: 101).

Neither cross-border consumption nor similarities in reception are new, of course. However, accelerating globalization processes seem to lead to a growing pool of globally shared cultural products and this in turn transforms cultures from within, including the mythological national cultures. It transforms expectations, tastes, and discourses concerning television content, and with this it may also evoke changes in adaptation practices, as noted by Barra (2013) in Italy. According to Barra, the extent of textual modifications has decreased in recent years. In the nineties, he says, there was a push in Italy toward 'domestication', often resulting in changes to entire storylines. Thus, the Jewish New Yorker and main character Fran Drescher in *The Nanny* was turned into an Italian American from the Ciociaria region and *The Simpsons'* characters spoke in southern regional dialects. Today, Barra says, Italian viewers have a greater appreciation of the cultural value of such TV series, and the general Italian audience has a better comprehension of the Anglo-Saxon world. This has helped localizers maintain original references without risking incomprehension and has led them to move away from the 'domestication' approach and adopt that of 'foreignization' instead (see also Costales, Chapter 12 in this collection).

There is no doubt that an increasing number of cultural references (e.g., to Hollywood films, cult TV shows or celebrities) today are marked by 'transnationality', and the same is true for the reception of globally formatted talent shows and the 'gossip communities' that Ndlela has identified in Africa. Gossip or fan communities are crucial in creating 'local meaning'. However, 'local' must be understood not as bound to space, but in Massey's sense as "articulated moments in networks of social relations and understanding" (1994: 154); as an unbounded, fluid place. Cult film fan communities and gaming and other YouTube communities forming around global popular culture create such networks across state borders without thinking—a sign of everyday, "banal cosmopolitanism" and of the intensification of popular culture's "cosmopolitanization" (Beck, 2006), networks where place and space are disconnected; networks that are multiple, diverse, complex and highly fluid.

'Cultural Discount' and 'Preference for the Local': Two Attractive but Reductive Concepts

So if place and space are increasingly disconnected (and never have been connected in absolute terms), how should we understand the 'cultural discount' and 'preference for the local' theses? In the 1990s, the localization of TV channels and TV programs became a key growth strategy for international broadcasters (Chalaby, 2005; Esser, 2001). Most media scholars came to agree that 'national television markets' would remain strong, followed in importance by geo-linguistic or geo-cultural markets offering close 'cultural proximity' (Straubhaar, 1991, 2007; Sinclair, Jacka, and Cunningham, 1996; Keane, Fung, and Moran, 2007). An article by Hoskins and Mirus (1988), which a few years earlier had theorized that the appeal of foreign TV programs is diminished by a 'cultural discount', was highly influential in this. In an attempt to explain international flows in television programs, the two management scholars concluded that a program developed in a specific context has its value diminished when introduced into a new market, because people there lack (they presumed) the cultural capital to properly understand and relate to the imported program. Straubhaar (1991, 2007), equally interested in TV program flows, subsequently developed the theses of 'cultural proximity' and 'preference for the local'. He argued that "audience preferences lead television industries and advertisers to produce more programming nationally and to select an increasing proportion of what is imported from within the same region, language group, and culture, when such programming is available" (1991: 39). Straubhaar gradually revised his concept of cultural proximity, adding to the national level of cultural proximity by including local, class or gender identities that may divide national audiences, historical transnational ties like those Latin American countries have with Spain and Portugal, and proximities based on genre, values, and themes that may be shared transnationally. Together with the actual localization trends that could be observed in the 1990s, these influential theories led the vast majority of television scholars to accept and perpetuate Straubhaar's 'preference for the local' thesis. Both in academic and industry circles the belief that audiences prefer local to imported programs, especially when of roughly similar value, became firmly cemented and widely accepted. Nevertheless, while empirical evidence exists to support this, there is also empirical evidence suggesting that the theories of cultural discount and preference for the local do not hold in many cases.

No systematic study of this has yet been conducted, but I want to give a few examples. For instance, our above case of *Next Top Model* challenges the preference for the local thesis. In the UK, both the domestic and the original versions are shown in the same primetime slot on *Living*. In light of the preference for the local thesis, we would expect the British adaptation to attract the larger audience. This is not the case, however. In 2008, the average audience size of *America's Next Top Model (ANTM)* on *Living* was 553,000 adults, whereas *Britain's Next Top Model (BNTM)* only attracted 412,000 viewers (Rufaie in Esser, 2014: 93). In other words, a notably greater number of viewers in the UK found the American version more appealing than the domestic production. In parts, this may be explained with the fact that the US version has a higher production value and hence is more glamorous. Qualitative audience research is needed to provide a fuller picture and sound empirical evidence for why the non-domestic version is preferred by certain viewers and a greater number of viewers.

Qualitative audience research not on *NTM* but on internationally franchised musical talent competitions offers some interesting insights. Some of the above-mentioned qualitative academic research found that not all focus group participants favored their home countries' productions (O'Conner, 2012; Esser et al., 2016). O'Connor found that the Irish working-class teenagers participating in her focus groups "expressed an admiration for the contestants from other cultures that were perceived to be more relaxed and expressive than the Irish" and criticized the "[Irish] contestants' accents, choice of songs, and singing abilities" (2012: 575). Their clear preference for the US and British versions, was mirrored by some of the participants in the focus groups carried out in our own research (Esser et al., 2016). A few of the Danish passport holders in the Aarhus groups found the American and British versions of *Idols* and *The X Factor* to be superior to the Danish versions in terms of entertainment and production value and in terms of contestants' abilities. Several participants, British and non-British, in the London focus groups made similar observations about the US versions in comparison to the British versions.

Overall, the responses in our nine focus groups were more varied than those that O'Connor received. This is not surprising, considering that her focus groups were much more homogeneous, consisting of Irish teenagers from a working-class background, whereas our focus groups were conducted in four different European cities and had a broader socio-demographic range. Whilst O'Connor found a nearly unanimous preference for British content, in our case responses varied; we could not find clear links between responses and respondents' age, gender, socio-economic background, nationality, or current geographical location. Despite this, our focus groups clearly confirmed what O'Connor had posited as a result of her findings, namely that those familiar with British and US shows "were being educated into aesthetic judgments of performance based on the rules of the talent show/game set by international/global standards" (2012: 579). This aspect could explain, at least in part, why *ANTM* attracted a larger audience in Britain than the domestic version or why the original British version of the globally popular auto show, *Top Gear,* "has been far more popular than either of the two attempted local remakes in Australia" (Moran and Aveyard, 2014: 21).

The above examples are particularly revealing as they allow us to compare the appeal of highly similar programs. Nevertheless, as shown, even in cases of strong similarity, many viewers do *not* prefer the domestic version. Particularly in cases where the production value, the overall look and feel and/or the contestants' abilities of a non-domestic show are seen as superior, the non-domestic is preferred by some, and in some cases even the majority of viewers.

'Quality'—to a certain degree considered in the cultural discount thesis—can only be part of the explanation. It does not explain empirical findings from non-format television research showing that the Brazilian poor and working class turn away from national channel TV Globo because they prefer Mexican to Brazilian telenovelas (Straubhaar, 2007). A 'preference for transnational TV programs' is also true for the other end of the socio-economic scale. Both Straubhaar (ibid: 247) and Ndlela (2012) note that the Brazilian and African elites respectively show a high preference for international pay-TV channels.

Recognizing Complexity

As far as the nation state is concerned, the above suggests that a noteworthy number of people do not see themselves in what is offered domestically or do not like what they see there for multiple reasons. Different people watch programs for different reasons, and they interpret them differently; even for individuals viewing motives and pleasures change, across genres, across individual programs, and even concerning the same program. Our research on musical talent shows revealed, for instance, that long-term viewers of those programs watch very differently today than they did 10 years ago, when musical talent shows became highly popular in many countries around the world. They have turned from dedicated, unquestioning fans to occasional viewers who have adopted a more distant and cynical mode of viewing.

Highlighting the complexity and the mistaken assumptions that audiences can easily and justifiably be classified as national audiences, who as a rule prefer domestic (i.e., national) over imported content, is not to say that language is insignificant. It is vital. It is also not to say that localization in geographical respect is insignificant or that audiences do not appreciate it. Familiarity, in terms of, for instance, ethnic appearance, dress, shared topical knowledge, or music traditions, clearly has its appeal. It is part of the construction of place, and even in a globalizing world, there is often a geographical element to familiarity. Neither does any of the above imply that feelings of national belonging or identity play no role on television and in the minds of television audiences.

In pan-regional talent competitions, such as *Asian Idols* or the *Eurovision Song Contest*, or for international sports events, producers consciously and deliberately "play on the audience's sense of national pride" (Tay, 2011: 331). In some countries, and this is especially true for newly created countries and/or those experiencing inner friction, broadcasters seem more likely to play on nationalism (see, for example, Volčič and Zajc, 2013). National identity, no doubt, strongly comes to the fore at these times. Additionally, it appears at moments when viewers engaging with multiple format adaptations adopt a 'comparative mode of viewing' (Esser et al., 2016), contrasting, for instance, the talent in the British version of *The X Factor* with the talent of the contestants in the US version. Very quickly—and not surprisingly, considering the extensive and abiding ideological work undertaken to create national cultures and identities—the comparative mode of viewing puts viewers into a 'them' and 'us' state of mind. But, as our empirical research suggests, at least in stable European democracies, neither the deliberate play on audiences' feelings of national identity nor audiences' adoption of a national identity position or of a comparative mode of viewing when watching entertainment programs is frequent.

Thus, the point I want to make with the above examples and this chapter overall is not that we must discard all aspects pertaining to the national and/or the nation state; there are still many relevant aspects. My aim is to show and to argue that we must not fall prey to reductive and essentialist assumptions and theorizing as a result of engrained cultural essentialism and reductionism. We need to aim for a more nuanced understanding that takes into account the complexity, diversity, multiplicity, and fluidity of television consumption and reception. An understanding that acknowledges that consumption and reception are based on multiple cultural affiliations that both divide states and transcend state borders. An understanding that acknowledges that no generalizations can be made, that there are many instances where familiarity is not space-based and/or where close familiarity and especially nationality are not the explanation for the appeal of a program. An understanding that we need to pay attention to highly specific contextual impact factors regarding the socio-demographic and socio-cultural make-up of the country, the diverse audiences to be found within it, the overall media provision, and the constraining and enabling factors of each broadcaster and its aims at any given point in time. Also, we must not generalize across genre. The focus of this chapter was on television entertainment programs. A focus on audiences of news and current affairs, on the other hand, would yield very different findings and insights. In short, what I want to suggest is that particularity matters.

Conclusion

This chapter has been critical of television scholarship working on assumptions of 'national audiences', 'national cultural adaptations', and cultural enclosure, community, and identity more generally. The "hegemonic national paradigm that stubbornly continues to prevail in media and cultural research" (Robins, 2014a: 33) is the result of the history of nation states, which "for the most part, [has] been about the denial, and often strategic erasure, of complexity" (2014b: 264). The empirical evidence provided throughout this chapter suggests a reality—at least pertaining to entertainment programs—that is not characterized largely by national and space-bound communitarian belonging and identification and therefore by national orientation in provision, national consumption, and reception. The reality is characterized by complex, diverse, manifold, and ever-shifting audiences, viewing preferences, and modes of reception, by audience configurations that both divide and transcend state borders.

If we leave behind culturally essentialist and reductive thinking and shake off our captivity to the national imaginary, if instead we adopt more advanced conceptualizations of 'local' and 'local culture', we will open up new fruitful avenues for research and gain new insights about what should be adapted, how, in which aspects, to what extent, and for whom. Adequate consideration of the immense complexity, diversity, plurality, and fluidity we find in today's media consumption and reception will open our eyes to localities and places that are not space-based. It will reveal preferences for places that are not geographically local or culturally proximate due to historical (for example, colonial) ties. We may find viewing preferences for content that is consumed and enjoyed outside of any known place, outside any known "networks of social relations and understanding" (Massey, 1994: 154). These networks may be new, a consequence of advanced digital technologies (see Chaume in this collection). They also may have existed for a long time, lingering in a blind spot formed as a result of our engrained national outlook.

Neither transnational places nor the immense cultural diversity, plurality, and complexity we find in nation states are new. They have always existed but remained hidden behind "abstract and closed systems of thought" (Robins, 2014a). However, in today's globalizing world with its accelerating transnational flows of media images, ideas, and people, we can expect the diversity, plurality, fluidity, transnationality, and complexity of media consumption and reception to increase. For those interested in localization this means that assumptions (even if only implicit) of monolithic viewer categories, whether based on nationality, ethnicity, or other socio-demographics must be discarded. Viewers' modes of consumption and reception are shaped by multiple factors, including geographical and social location, life experiences, age, gender, and many others. They are inevitably diverse, manifold, and fluid, and this is true even for each individual viewer. Contemporary marketing caters to this fluid multitude, creating ever smaller and constantly shifting markets. Localization strategies hence have to be carefully mapped out on a case-by-case basis.

Note

1. According to Agnew (2011), who has provided a helpful overview, space and place are two fundamental geographical concepts, which have been subject to long-standing academic controversy and variable use. In the simplest sense, space is general, place is specific. Place is usually understood in terms of one of the following three dimensions: as a site in space where an activity or object is located and that relates to other sites; as a series of locales or settings where everyday-life activities take place; or as 'sense of place' or identification. Place in the latter sense, and the one of most interest to us here, is expressed through a sense of 'belonging' either consciously or as displayed through everyday behavior such as participating in place-related affairs. Alternatively, Agnew says, we could say it is identification with a place as a unique community, landscape, and moral order. A revival of interest in the concept of place during the 1980s and '90s continued to produce different positions and uses, making it impossible to provide a short definition that has common currency today. But the overall focus and interest in place has been on its mediating role in both social relations and the acquisition of meaning, and there is a shared understanding that 1) place is constructed through social practices; 2) is fluid and dynamic as is responds to interconnections with other places and people's movements; and 3) is unbounded because of its constant shifts and transformations, yet relational since it is located in a variety of extensive economic, political, and cultural networks with differing geographic scopes.

References

Agnew, J. (2011). Space and place. In J. Agnew & D. Livingstone (Eds.), *Handbook of geographical knowledge*. London: Sage.

Aksoy, A., and Robins, K. (2000). Thinking across spaces: Transnational television from Turkey. *European Journal of Cultural Studies*, 3(3), 343–365.

Aksoy, A., and Robins, K. (2008). Banal transnationalism: The difference that television makes, Working Paper, WPTC-02-08, available online at: http://www.transcomm.ox.ac.uk/working%20papers/WPTC-02-08%20Robins.pdf (Retrieved July 2, 2010).

Anderson, B. (1983). *Imagined Communities: Reflections on the Origin and Spread of Nationalism*. Verso: London.

Appadurai, A. (1996). *Modernity at large: Cultural dimensions of globalization*. Minneapolis, MN: University of Minnesota Press.

Athique, A. (2008). Media audiences, ethnographic practice and the notion of a cultural field, *European Journal of Cultural Studies*, 11(1), 25–41.

Athique, A. (2011). Diasporic audiences and non-resident media: The case of Indian films. *Participations: Journal of Audience and Reception Studies*, 8(2), 1–23.

Barra, L. (2009). The mediation is the message. Italian regionalization of US tv series as co-creational work. *International Journal of Cultural Studies*, 12(5), 509–525.

Barra, L. (2013). Invisible mediations. The role of adaptation and dubbing professionals in shaping US tv for Italian audiences. *VIEW*, 2(4), available online at: http://www.viewjournal.eu/index.php/view/article/view/JETHC048/81 (Retrieved January 13, 2015).

Beck, U. (2006). *Cosmopolitan Vision*. Cambridge: Polity.

Beeden, A., and de Bruin, J. (2009). The office: Articulations of national identity in television format adaptation. *Television & New Media*, 11(1), 3–19.

Bielby, D., and Harrington, C. L. (2008). *Global tv: Exporting television and culture in the world market*, New York: New York University Press.

Billig, M. (1995). *Banal Nationalism*, London: Sage.

Bruin, de J. (2013). NZ idol: Nation building through format adaptation. In T. Oren & S. Shahaf (Eds.), *Global Television Formats* (pp. 223–241). London: Routledge.

Carini, S. (2013). Recreating Betty's world in Spain. In J. McCabe and K. Akass (Eds.), *From Telenovela to International Brand. TV's Betty Goes Global* (pp. 115–125). London: I.B. Tauris.

Chalaby, J. (2005). *Transnational Television Worldwide: Towards a New Media Order*. London: I.B. Tauris.

Dhoest, A. (2011). When regional becomes national: The production and reception of Flemish tv drama in a culturally divided country. *Critical Studies in Television*, 6(2), 13–23.

Esser, A. (2001). *The Transnationalisation of Television in Europe*, 1985–1997. Unpublished PhD thesis.

Esser, A. (2013). Interviews with tv executives involved in the German adaptation, *Verliebt in Berlin*, in J. McCabe & K. Akass (Eds.), *Betty goes global* (pp. 72–82). London: I.B. Tauris.

Esser, A. (2014). European television programming: Exemplifying and theorizing glocalization in the media. In R. Robertson (Ed.), *European Glocalization in Global Context* (pp. 82–102). Basingstoke: Palgrave.

Esser, A., Keinonen, H., Jensen, P. M., and Lemor, A. (2016). The duality of banal transnationalism and banal nationalism: Television audiences and the musical talent competition genre. In A. Moran, P. M. Jensen & K. Aveyard (Eds.), *Global television formats. State of the art.* Bristol: Intellect.

Grüne, A. (2013). *Skeptical readers and indifferent cultural identification in the context of formatted television.* (Paper presented at the IAMCR Conference, 25–29 June). Dublin.

Hall, S. (1990). Cultural identity and diaspora. In J. Rutherford (Ed.), *Identity: Community, Culture, Difference* (pp. 222–237). London: Lawrence and Wishart.

Hannerz, U. (1996). *Transnational Connections. Culture, People, Places.* London: Routledge.

Harindranath, R. (2005). Ethnicity and cultural difference: Some thematic and political issues on global audience research. Particip@tions, 2(2), available online at: www.participations.org/volume%202/issue%202/2_02_harindranath.htm (Retrieved December 13, 2014).

Harindranath, R. (2013). The cultural politics of metropolitan and vernacular lifestyles in India. *Media International Australia*, 147, 147–156.

Hobsbawm, E. (1983). Introduction: Inventing Traditions. In E. Hobsbawm & T. Ranger (Eds.), *The Invention of Tradition* (pp. 1–14). Cambridge: Cambridge University Press.

Hoskins, C., and Mirus, R. (1988). Reasons for the U.S. dominance of the international trade in television programs. *Media, Culture & Society*, 10, 499–515.

Jensen, P. M. (2009). How media systems shape the localization of tv formats: A transnational case study of *The Block* and *Nerds FC* in Australia and Denmark. In A. Moran (Ed.), *TV Formats Worldwide: Localizing Global Programs* (pp. 163–186). Bristol: Intellect Ltd.

Jensen, P. M. (2012). How media system rather than culture determines national variation: Danish and Australian idols compared. In K. Zwaan & J. de Bruin (Eds.), *Adapting Idols: Authenticity, Identity and Performance in a Global Tv Format* (pp. 27–40). Farnham: Ashgate Publishing Limited.

Keane, M., Fung, A. and Moran, A. (2007). *New Television, Globalisation, and the East Asian Cultural Imagination.* Hong Kong: Hong Kong University Press.

Keinonen, H. (2016). Cultural negotiation in an early programme format: The Finnish adaptation of *Romper Room*. In A. Moran, P. M. Jensen, & K. Aveyard (Eds.), *Global Television Formats. State of the Art.* Bristol: Intellect.

Klaus, E., and O'Connor, B. (2010). Aushandlungsprozesse im Alltag: Jugendliche Fans von Casting Shows. In J. Rose, T. Thomas & C. Peil (Eds.), *Alltag in den Medien. Medien im Alltag* (pp. 48–72). Verlag für Sozialwissenschaften.

Kuipers, G. and Kloet, J. de. (2009). Banal Cosmopolitanism and *The Lord of the Rings*: The Limited Role of National Differences in Global Media Consumption, *Poetics*, 37, 99–118.

Larkey, E. (2009). Transcultural Localization Strategies of Global TV Formats: *The Office* and *Stromberg*. In A. Moran (Ed.), *TV Formats Worldwide* (pp. 187–201). Bristol: Intellect.

Massey, D. (1994). *Space, Place and Gender.* Cambridge: Polity.

Mirrlees, T. (2013). *Global entertainment media. Between cultural imperialism and cultural globalization.* New York: Routledge.

Moran, A. (2005). Global franchising, local customizing: The cultural economy of tv program formats. *Continuum: Journal of Media & Cultural Studies*, 23(2), 115–125.

Moran, A., and Aveyard, K. (2014). The place of television programme formats. *Continuum: Journal of Media & Cultural Studies*, 28(1), 18–27.

Ndlela, M. N. (2012). Global television formats in Africa: Localizing *Idols*. In T. Oren & S. Shahaf (Eds.), *Global Television Formats* (pp. 242–259). London: Routledge.

Ndlela, M. N. (2013). Television across boundaries: Localisation of *Big Brother Africa*. *Critical Studies in Television*, 8(2), 57–72.

Negra, D., Pike, K., and Radley, E. (2012). Gender, nation and reality tv. *Television & New Media*, 14(3), 187–193.

O'Connor, B. (2012). Spaces of celebrity: National and global discourses in the reception of tv talent shows by Irish teenagers. *Television & New Media*, 13(6), 568–583.

ProSieben. (2015). ProSieben - We Love to Entertain You, (Company website) available online at: https://www.sevenonemedia.de/plattformen_tv_prosieben (Retrieved April 12, 2015).

Robertson, R. (1994). Globalization or glocalization? *Journal of International Communication,* 1(1), 33–52.

Robertson, R. (2014). Situating glocalization: A relatively autobiographical intervention. In G. Drori, M. A. Höllerer, & P. Walgenbach (Eds.), *Global Themes and Local Variations in Organization and Management* (pp. 25–36). London: Routledge.

Robins, K. (2014a). Transcultural Research as Encounter, and a Possible Creative Modality of Its Dialogue. In *Transculturality and Interdisciplinarity Challenges for Research on Media, Migration and Intercultural Dialogue*. Proceedings of the Training Workshop on Methodologies for Research on Media, Migration and Intercultural Dialogue. Barcelona: United Nations University & CIDOB.

Robins, K. (2014b). Europe and Its Complexity. What Would Like to Be Said? *Cultural Politics*, 10(3), 262–274.

Rittenhofer, I. and Nielsen, M. (2009). Marketscapes. Market between Culture and Globalization, *Journal of Language and Communication Studies*, 43, 59–95.

Sharp, S. (2012). Global Franchising, Gender and Genre: The Case of Domestic Reality Television. In T. Oren & S. Shahaf (Eds.), *Global Television Formats* (pp. 346–365). London: Routledge.

Sinclair, J., E. Jacka and Cunningham, S. (1996). Peripheral Vision. In J. Sinclair, E. Jacka & S. Cunningham (Eds.), *New Patterns in Global Television* (pp. 1–32). Oxford: Oxford University Press.

Stehling, M. (2013). From localisation to translocalisation: Audience readings of the television format Top Model. *Critical Studies in Television*, 8(2), 36–53.

Straubhaar, J. (1991). Beyond Media Imperialism: Asymmetrical Interdependence and Cultural Proximity, *Critical Studies in Mass Communication*, 8, 1–11.

Straubhaar, J. (2007). *World television*. London: Sage Publications.

Sun, W. (2013). Scaling lifestyle in China: The emergence of local television cultures and the cultural economy of place-making, *Media International Australia*, 147, 62–72.

Tay, J. (2011). The Search for an Asian Idol: The Performance of Regional Identity in Reality Television, *International Journal of Cultural Studies*, 14(3), 323–338.

Tomlinson, J. (1991). *Cultural Imperialism. A Critical Introduction*. London: Pinter Publishers.

Tomlinson, J. (1999). *Globalization and Culture*. Chicago: University of Chicago Press.

Volčič, Z., and Zajc, M. (2013). Hybridisation of Slovenic public broadcasting: From national community to commercial nationalism. *Media International Australia*, 146, 93–101.

Waisbord, S. (2004). McTV. Understanding the global popularity of television formats. *Television & New Media*, 5(4), 359–383.

2 Transnational Holmes

Theorizing the Global-Local Nexus through the Japanese Anime *Sherlock Hound* (1984–)

Iain Robert Smith

On February 23, 2012, BBC Worldwide released a YouTube promo video titled 'Sherlock in five languages', featuring a sequence from the English-language BBC series *Sherlock* (2010–) dubbed into Italian, Russian, Spanish, and French. The video was evidently designed to showcase the transnational reach of *Sherlock*, emphasizing its presence beyond the English-speaking world and drawing attention to the fact that the series has been sold to over 200 territories worldwide (BBC Worldwide, 2012). Prestigious drama series such as *Sherlock* are a key strategic component utilized by the commercial arm of the BBC to extend the global reach of British television. Indeed, *Sherlock* was one of the principal BBC titles highlighted within the subsequent BBC Worldwide Annual Review 2013/2014, "Inspiring Global Audiences", and central to their vision outlined therein to "build the BBC's brands, audiences, commercial returns and reputation across the world" (BBC Worldwide, 2014). This strategy to stimulate further interest in British drama production within global markets has been particularly successful in East Asian territories such as Japan. While *Sherlock* was initially seen as relatively niche programming in Japan, originally broadcast in a late night slot on NHK's BS Premium satellite channel, there was a concerted effort with subsequent series to develop the Japanese audience for the show. This included personal appearances from star Benedict Cumberbatch in Tokyo and a media campaign in which Cumberbatch wore a yukata kimono and was dubbed 'King of the Magazines' (Morimoto, 2014). Inspired by this growing popularity, the monthly manga collection *Young Ace* began publishing a manga adaptation of the show in October 2012 featuring likenesses of Cumberbatch and co-star Martin Freeman, while NHK Educational TV launched a Sherlock Holmes puppet series *Sherlock Gakuen* in March 2014 that focused on a teenage Holmes attending a London boarding school. As Lori Morimoto has noted, a significant factor within the reception of the BBC *Sherlock* in Japan was the perceived 'Britishness' of the show and the framing of Cumberbatch as an "elegant English gentleman" within wider critical reception (Morimoto, 2015). While *Sherlock* is a show that is clearly designed to appeal to an international audience and to help fulfill the commercial strategy of extending the global reach of the BBC, it is simultaneously marked as an unambiguously 'British' production in many ways, and this national specificity forms a key part of its transnational appeal.

The complex relationship here between constructions of national identity and transnational processes of media consumption is representative of the broader tensions underpinning notions of media globalization. While we live in a world that is increasingly defined by processes of cross-border flow and transnational exchange, the role of national identity is far from being subsumed between the dual forces of global homogenization and heterogenization. Perceptions of national and cultural difference still play a crucial role within media circulation, and this is particularly acute when cultural products come to be seen as representative of a national culture. Sherlock Holmes is an especially useful character with whom to explore these issues, given his position as one of the most adapted characters of all time (Leitch, 2009: 207). Although numerous film and television adaptations have appeared around the world—from the Danish silent film *Sherlock Holmes i Bondefangerkløer,* produced by the Nordisk Film Company in 1910 to the recent Russian mini-series *Шерлок Холмс,* broadcast in 2013—Sherlock Holmes is often perceived as a "quintessentially English" character (Döring, 2006: 73). There is a productive tension here between his situatedness in relation to notions of Englishness and the fact that he has become a transnational figure appearing in a range of different literary cultures worldwide. Within Japan itself, Sherlock Holmes has formed part of the local literary culture since at least 1894 when an abridgement of *The Man with the Twisted Lip* was released under the title *Kojiki Doraku.* The character has subsequently formed the basis of a diverse range of adaptations from 1899's *Chizo no Kabe,* in which Holmes and Watson were replaced by the Japanese duo Homma and Wada, to the manga series *Tanteiken Sherdock* (2011–), in which a young Japanese boy discovers that his dog is the reincarnation of Sherlock Holmes. The position of Holmes in Japan, therefore, offers a privileged site for exploring the ways in which popular characters are adapted around the world and the broader cultural implications this has for our understanding of national and transnational flows and exchanges.

To interrogate these complex cultural dynamics, this chapter will focus its attention on a specific Japanese adaptation of Sherlock Holmes: the anime series *Meitantei Holmes* (*Famous Detective Holmes,* 1984–1985), best known in English as *Sherlock Hound.* Produced jointly by the Japanese TMS Entertainment and the Italian public broadcaster RAI, the series began broadcasting on the Japanese TV channel Asahi on November 26, 1984, and ran for 26 episodes in total. Designed to follow other successful co-productions between Japanese anime studios and European broadcasters such as the Franco-Japanese series *Ulysses 31* (1981–1982) and the Spanish-Japanese series *Dogtanian and the Three Muskehounds* (1981–1982), *Sherlock Hound* took an established European literary property and populated it with anthropomorphic animals in an attempt to create a children's TV series that could travel internationally. The series functions as a particularly resonant case study for examining what Morley and Robins term the global-local nexus: the "new and intricate relations between global space and local space" (1995: 116). By investigating the ways forces of globalization and localization impact the production and reception of the series, this chapter will demonstrate that *Sherlock Hound* is not only illustrative of what Susan Pointon has described as the "constant cross-pollination and popular cultural borrowing that complicate and enrich anime texts" (1997: 44) but also provides a useful lens for analyzing the cultural politics of transnational processes of localization.

As I have written about elsewhere, there has been a tendency within academic scholarship on cross-cultural adaptation to frame these kinds of texts through a limited model of localization whereby international circulating texts are seen to be adapted to conform to local cultural practices and traditions (Smith, 2016). Within such a framework, the process of adaptation across geographical and cultural borders is understood primarily through reference to the local context—an Italian adaptation is framed through its Italianness or a Japanese adaptation is framed through its Japaneseness. However, a limited model of localization that frames cross-cultural adaptations as primarily 'local' versions of 'global' texts misrepresents the complex and contradictory ways texts are actually adapted across borders. *Sherlock Hound* may be an adaptation of the stories of Arthur Conan Doyle by a Japanese anime studio, but a model of localization that centers upon the Japaneseness of the adaptation would misrepresent the multifaceted cultural processes at play. As Amy Shirong Lu has argued, anime is a cultural form that privileges internationalization, with texts often designed to be exported and consumed around the world and local specificity often downplayed (2008: 170). Moreover, there are underlying assumptions about the kinds of local specificity that need to be downplayed, and these assumptions need to be interrogated. It is essential that our models of localization are able to adequately address the transnational processes at work within cultural forms such as anime, especially when they are designed for export. Implicit within the term localization is the idea that a text is somehow being made 'more local', yet, as I will explore in this chapter, the cross-cultural adaptation of a text across borders can involve the opposing pressure to reduce local specificity. While often framed and understood as local versions of globally circulating texts, it is important that we remember that these adaptations are themselves functioning within a transnational media landscape in which the local is not necessarily what is being produced or valued.

To situate this investigation within its wider historical context, the chapter will begin with an account of the history of Sherlock Holmes adaptations within Japan. Supplementing this historical frame, the chapter will then interrogate the internationalization of anime and the processes of transnational reworking and exchange that underpin its development. This will allow me to position *Sherlock Hound* in relation to the broader discourses surrounding anime, before investigating the specific ways in which the series engages with the global-local dynamics I have been describing. Ultimately, by investigating the precise ways in which the anime series adapts and reworks elements from the Sherlock Holmes canon, this chapter will interrogate the wider implications of processes of cross-cultural adaptation. Taking us beyond an explanatory framework that privileges the local within the global, I will instead draw attention to the ways cross-cultural adaptations themselves function within a complex and intersecting nexus of global and local forces that complicate any straightforward model of localization.

Sherlock Holmes in Japan

The French film theorist Andre Bazin famously said of characters like D'Artagnan from *The Three Musketeers* that they have been adapted so often that they "enjoy in some measure an autonomous existence of which the original works are no longer anything more than an accidental and almost superfluous manifestation" (1967/2005: 53). We can see this phenomenon reflected in the history of Sherlock Holmes adaptations within Japanese literary culture. From his first appearance in a four-part story in the magazine *Nihon-jin* in January 1894, Holmes has appeared in a range of Japanese adaptations far removed from the Conan Doyle stories. As Keith Webb outlines in his book, *Sherlock Holmes in Japan*, the early adaptations were often marked by their deliberate attempts to modify the text for the Japanese market (1998: 18). These include adaptations that relocate the characters and stories from their London setting. An 1899 *A Study in Scarlet* entitled *The Bloodstained Wall* casts all of the characters as Japanese, and in a 1910 story titled *The Adventure of the Golden Pince-nez* Holmes is renamed Honda and depicted as a silver-haired old man. These attempts at localization often betray certain assumptions about what would need adapting for a Japanese readership, such as an adaptation of *The Red Headed League* that was changed to *The Bald Headed League* to account for the fact that red hair is so rare within Japanese culture (Webb, 1998: 19). Yet, while there were numerous adaptations, spin-offs, and pastiches that attempted to localize and adapt the text for the Japanese market, we should note that there were also many attempts to translate the official canon with textual fidelity[1] in mind. These include an eight volume set of Doyle's works published by Kaizo-sha in 1931–1933 and a later more extensive 13-volume series published by Getsuyo Shobo from 1951 to 1952. Though Holmes has appeared in so many adaptations and reworkings that he has been freed largely from his roots in an original text, there was nevertheless an established interest in Japan for the Conan Doyle stories and a wider cultural awareness of Sherlock Holmes as an iconic character.

Furthermore, while Sherlock Holmes has enjoyed a lengthy and varied afterlife within Japanese literary culture, it is clear that the most significant and lasting presence of Sherlock Holmes has been in the realm of manga and animation. Beyond the *Sherlock Hound* series, there are numerous manga and anime adaptations of Holmes—from relatively straight adaptations of the canon (such as the Kodansha series of 16 manga *Meitantei Holmes* that ran from 2010 to 2012) to texts that exhibit a more tangential relationship to the character. The most famous example of the latter is *Detective Boy Conan*, a long running manga series featuring a child detective who adopts the name 'Conan' in a knowing tribute to Arthur Conan Doyle. Selling over 140 million volumes, it is the fifth bestselling manga of all time and has been adapted into a long running anime series, numerous feature films, a range of video games, and even a trading card game. While the series adopts some of the recognized tropes from the Holmes universe including having detectives wearing the distinctive inverness cape and deerstalker hat,[2] its status is closer to a knowing homage than a direct adaptation of the Conan Doyle canon. Moreover, this is consistent across the majority of manga and anime adaptations of Holmes, including examples such as *Tanteiken Sherdock* (2011–), which features a talking dog named 'Sherdog', and *Christie High Tension* (known in English as *Young Mrs. Holmes* 2007–), which follows the adventures of Holmes' 10-year-old niece Christie, who has inherited his skills of deduction.

Throughout these numerous cross-cultural interactions with Conan Doyle's stories, there have been attempts to localize and adapt Sherlock Holmes to fit with the prevalent trends and tropes of Japanese popular culture at that historical moment. In her book on *Adaptation*, Linda Hutcheon proposes a biological analogy to these kinds of cross-cultural processes. Drawing on Richard Dawkins notion of 'memes' (1989: 192), which function as cultural equivalents to genes, Hutcheon argues that stories get "retold in different ways in new material and cultural environments; like genes, they adapt to those new environments by virtue of mutation—in their 'offspring' or their adaptations" (2006: 32). This can be a useful way of thinking about processes of localization—focusing on how texts travel across cultures and tracing how they have been adapted to thrive within their new contexts. Using this model, we can trace how Holmes has been appropriated and transformed across Japanese literary and popular culture, with characters such as Detective Conan far removed from the Conan Doyle stories from which he takes his name, but integrated effectively within the dominant trends of manga storytelling. Nevertheless, while certain adaptations were clearly marked by attempts to localize and transform content for the Japanese context, there is something more complicated happening in my main case study in this chapter: *Sherlock Hound*. As we will see, this series is not so much adapting Holmes to the local cultural environment of Japan as adapting to the specific material and cultural environment of anime production in the early 1980s—a key distinction—and this has broader implications for our understanding of cross-cultural processes of adaptation.

Sherlock Hound and the Global/Local Nexus

Sherlock Hound was a co-production between the Japanese studio Tokyo Movie Shinsha (TMS) Entertainment and the Italian public broadcaster Radiotelevisione italiana (RAI). It began production in 1981, although due to an unanticipated copyright negotiation with the Conan Doyle estate[3], there was a suspension in production and the series was not completed and broadcast until 1984. While it would screen as *Meitantei Holmes* within Japan, it would be titled *Il Fiuto di Sherlock Holmes* for the Italian market, *Sherlock Koira* in Finland, *Sherlock Holmes, a mesterkopó* in Hungary, *Sherlock Holmes* in France and Spain, and *Sherlock Hound* on British and American television. Of the 26 episodes, Kyosuke Mikuriya was to direct the majority of the series, although his contribution is often overshadowed by the six episodes that were directed by Studio Ghibli co-founder Hayao Miyazaki. As I will discuss later, it is this auteurist link with the early work of Hayao Miyazaki that has helped *Sherlock Hound* achieve a certain level of international fame and longevity beyond its initial circulation. While the series has rarely been discussed in depth within English language writing on anime, the few mentions that appear in sources such as Fred Patten's *Watching Anime, Reading Manga* (2004: 211) and Trish Ledoux's *The Complete Anime Guide* (1997: 149) tend to frame it largely in relation to Miyazaki's career and the broader history of Japanese animation.

Indeed, the majority of English language criticism on anime has tended to situate it principally through the prism of Japanese society and culture. Often contrasted with other forms of animation around the world, especially works produced by Hollywood, anime is framed within this reception as a distinctly Japanese product that reflects the distinctiveness of Japanese culture more broadly. As Thomas LaMarre has argued, such an approach "easily slides into cultural determinism or culturalism, inviting a view in which animation produced in Japan directly and inevitably reproduces Japanese values" (2009: 89). The problem with such an approach is that it risks essentializing an intrinsic Japaneseness and neglects the fact that anime is so often designed to reach a global market. As Otsuka Eiji asks, in response to the US fandom surrounding Hayao Miyazaki: "Why do so many Americans see Miyazaki's films as distinctively Japanese, as receptacles of Japanese values, when they are so clearly globally targeted entertainments?" (as cited in LaMarre, 2009: 89). A culturalist approach that focuses on cultural specificity is plainly inadequate when faced with forms such as anime that are distributed globally. In recent years, the academic scholarship on anime has attempted to resolve this tension and move beyond the national as an explanatory framework. Rayna Denison, for example, has advocated paying attention to the transnational dimensions of anime in "an attempt to move beyond discussions of how Japanese anime are, and to open up a space in which to discuss their relevance beyond their home nation" (2011: 221).

Sherlock Hound is a valuable case study, therefore, not primarily because of its relationship to the local, national context, but rather for its relationship with the transnational dimensions of anime production and circulation. Given that this was a co-production between a Japanese animation studio and an Italian broadcaster that was specifically designed for export, it is necessary to go beyond a limited textual analysis that focuses on the

Japaneseness (or lack thereof) of the text and instead interrogate the wider global contexts of cross-cultural exchange within which this adaptation took place. The following section therefore will take a tripartite structure to interrogate these underlying transnational dynamics, focusing on 1) the production context, 2) the text itself, and 3) the subsequent circulation. As I will outline, anime has a particularly complex relationship with national identity, and it is important that we address the ways in which processes of cross-cultural adaptation and reworking function in relation to these composite constructions of national identity.

First, it is important to acknowledge the role that the co-production arrangement with Italy had on this production. Like Japan, Italy has an extensive history of adaptations of Sherlock Holmes, including the live-action RAI productions *La valle della paura* (1968) and *L'ultimo dei Baskerville* (1968). It also has a history of importing anime after the success of *Heidi of the Alps* (*Alps no shojo Heidi*, 1974), a co-production between the Japanese animation studio Zuiyo Eizo and the German Taurus Film. As with *Sherlock Hound*, this was a significant series in the development of what would later become the anime studio Studio Ghibli—directed by co-founder Isao Takahata and featuring scene design and layout by Hayao Miyazaki. Inspired by the success of *Heidi* and other similar co-productions between European production companies and Japanese animation studios, the Italian producer Marco Pagot and his company Rever Cinematografica proposed an agreement with TMS Entertainment to produce a Sherlock Holmes adaptation for the Italian broadcaster RAI. This was to lead to a long-lasting relationship between Pagot and Hayao Miyazaki,[4] although the initial production was disrupted by a copyright claim from the Conan Doyle estate, and this delay would lead to Miyazaki leaving the production and ultimately leaving the animation studio in November 1982. Miyazaki recounts in his biography *Starting Point 1979–1996* that this was a challenging period in his career, admitting, "After *Heidi*, I didn't have my whole heart in my work" (2014: 331). While he worked on *Sherlock Hound* throughout late 1981 until summer 1982, he ultimately wanted to move away from telling 'simple stories' like *Sherlock Hound* and *Lupin III: The Castle of Cagliostro* (2014: 334). He wanted to attempt something more ambitious—resulting in the serialized manga and film adaptation *Nausicaa of the Valley of the Wind* (1984) that was to launch his career as a feature film director.

Unlike some of the other Japanese adaptations of Holmes discussed earlier in this chapter, therefore, this was not a case of Japanese producers attempting to localize Holmes for a domestic audience but an attempt to produce a series for an Italian production company wanting to reach an international audience. The timing here is crucial. As Rayna Denison has observed, historically "anime have had an important cultural presence in mainland Europe" (2011: 223). This reached a peak in the early 1980s with interactions of European and Japanese studios producing *The Adventures of Tom Sawyer* (1980), *Dogtanian and the Three Muskethounds* (1981),

Around the World with Willy Fog (1981), and *Ulysses 31* (1981) in addition
to *Sherlock Hound*. This cycle of co-productions came during a period in
the history of Japanese animation when there was a prevalent assumption
that to reach an international audience, animators would have to collaborate with non-Japanese production partners and downplay the national
specificity of Japanese culture. This assumption relied upon the notion of
cultural discount—a concept employed by Colin Hoskins and Rolf Mirus.
They argue that "a particular program rooted in one culture and thus attractive in that environment will have a diminished appeal elsewhere as viewers
find it difficult to identify with the style, values, beliefs, institutions and
behavioural patterns of the material in question" (1988: 500). The Hoskins
and Mirus model has subsequently been applied to an extensive range of
exported cultural products. However, it is important to note that in the initial article they were arguing that Japanese films and TV programs tend to
have a high cultural discount and that this has meant that Japanese exports
have been focused on more 'culturally neutral' consumer technologies.
There are a number of problems with the cultural discount model—not least
its reliance on problematic notions of cultural neutrality. Nevertheless, the
Japanese TV industry itself seemed to share this assumption, believing that
Japanese programs would struggle in international markets since "the imag-
ery of TV programs and popular music is inescapably represented through
living Japanese bodies" (Iwabuchi, 2002: 95).

   Building on Hoskins and Mirus' observations regarding the use of cultural
discount within the Japanese media industries, Koichi Iwabuchi proposed
that the major audiovisual products that Japan exports could be characterized as the "'culturally odorless' three C's: consumer technologies (such as
VCRs, karaoke, and the Walkman); comics and cartoons (animation); and
computer/video games" (2002: 27). While cultural odor can at times be the
principle appeal of a product internationally—Iwabuchi mentions the exot-
icized image of the Japanese geisha girl—there was a tendency throughout
the 1980s for the Japanese media industries to produce 'culturally odorless'
products that would avoid signifying Japaneseness to a global audience.
Key to this kind of internationalization strategy is an attempt to produce
"cultural artefacts in which a country's bodily, racial and ethnic characteristics are erased or softened" such that their cultural odor is diminished
(Iwabuchi, 2002: 27). It is no coincidence that the leading character in the
Japanese video games of this period was Super Mario, an Italian-American
plumber who first appeared in the game *Mario Bros* in 1983. We can see this
emphasis on downplaying Japaneseness throughout the anime and video
games produced during this period. Sandra Annett notes that many anime
creators were quite open about their strategy to soften the Japaneseness
of their works, including Yoshiyuki Tomino—best known for the *Mobile
Suit Gundam* franchise. Tomino explains that he "always tried to make his
characters as standard and as universal as possible by not giving them local
colour or national colour or ethnic colour" (as cited in Annett, 2011: 179).

The politics of this position have been hotly contested within scholarship on anime. As Amy Shiron Lu observes, the predominant explanations frame this either negatively, with scholars like Kenji Sato speculating that this phenomenon results from "Japanese people's deeply entrenched sense of self-loathing, extending even to their own ethnic traits" (1999) or positively, as a subtle 'cultural imperialism' where distinctive cultural traits are downplayed to reach a wider global market. I agree with Lu that neither of these is a sufficient explanation for the ways anime "looks the way it does and why it has achieved such global popularity" (2008: 172). The wider implications of the assumption amongst Japanese TV producers that "the suppression of Japanese cultural odor is imperative if they are to make inroads into international markets" (Iwabuchi, 2002: 94) needs to be interrogated further if we are to truly understand the multifaceted nature of this strategy. As we will see, this kind of conjecture clearly had an influence on the production choices underpinning *Sherlock Hound*, yet this was only one part of a diverse set of determinant factors influencing the ways in which this anime series was produced and circulated.

Turning to the text itself, we can see this attempt to soften racial and ethnic characteristics in what is perhaps the defining adaptation choice made by the producers of *Sherlock Hound*—the decision to depict the central characters as anthropomorphic animals. By embodying Holmes as a red fox, Lestrade as a bulldog, and Moriarty as a wolf, the producers were purposely making a show that could easily be dubbed and localized in other countries. As Bradley Stephens notes, there is a well-established tradition of using anthropomorphized animal characters within animation. The key factor that helps these texts travel is that "Their bodies lack the racial distinctions that mark human beings and their voices can be dubbed into any language, enabling them to connect with numerous audiences at once without offering privileged identification for any one group of viewers" (Stephens, 2014: 199). In other words, the animals in *Sherlock Hound* are not seen to be racially distinctive and do not signify Japaneseness to the global audience and can therefore be dubbed into a variety of languages without privileging a particular national audience. Moreover, it should be noted that this internationalization strategy was not solely limited to anime featuring non-human protagonists. As Susan Napier argues, "the characters in anime often do not look particularly Japanese" and instead "participate in what might be called a nonculturally specific anime style" (2000: 24). This relates to a term that is often used within discussions of anime—*mukokuseki*. Literally meaning 'something lacking nationality', the term is used to evoke the ways anime producers attempt to create works that are non-culturally specific in order to allow their series to travel internationally. Furthermore, the potential for a lack of cultural specificity embedded within visual style is a significant part of what marks out animation from live action films and TV series more broadly. As Napier notes:

> Unlike the inherently more representational space of conventional live-action film, which generally has to convey already-existing objects

within a pre-existing context, animated space has the potential to be context free, drawn wholly out of the animator's or artist's mind. It is thus a particularly apt candidate for participation in a transnational, stateless culture. (2000: 24)

Of course, this kind of strategy is not unique to Japanese animation. David Stuart Davies (2007) outlines in his survey of Holmes adaptations that Conan Doyle's stories have formed the basis for a diverse range of animated TV episodes and films. It is significant just how many of these shows feature anthropomorphized animals as leading characters—including Mickey Mouse, Daffy Duck, Snoopy, Felix the Cat, The Chipmunks, Chip 'n' Dale, Winnie the Pooh, Garfield, and Count Duckula, among others. A focus purely on the Japanese context of anime may suggest that the choice of anthropomorphic animals for a Holmes adaptation was primarily a local strategy that could be tied to an ideology of self-loathing or, indeed, cultural imperialism. However, I would contend that it is the potential transnationalism of animation as a medium, especially within programs aimed at young viewers, that is the primary factor here.

While it may seem a relatively benign strategy to remove national signifiers to produce an animated show that can easily be dubbed and sold internationally, it is important to recognize that while Japaneseness was downplayed, the show did not remove national signifiers entirely. Indeed, the show retained the Victorian London setting of the Conan Doyle stories and incorporated a particular vision of Victorian Englishness into its world of anthropomorphic animals. This can be understood as a form of what Rayna Denison refers to as "positive Occidentalism" (2011: 226). While Occidentalism traditionally involves stereotypical and negative depictions of Western characters, there is a more admiring form of representation that we often find in anime where *Nihonjinbanare* (non-Japanese cultural elements) are integrated positively into the stories, and Western locations provide an "easily nostalgised, romanticised and 'othered' space" (Denison, 2011: 228) for the central narrative to take place. This is clearly the case in *Sherlock Hound*, which depicts a nostalgized England through a number of recognized landmarks in episodes such as 'The White Cliffs of Dover', 'The Bell of Big Ben', and 'The Adventure of the Thames Monster'.[5] It is no coincidence that a significant proportion of the episodes are focused on these iconic landmarks, especially given that these are 'original' stories and not adaptations of specific Conan Doyle stories. Moreover, episode 19 'The Rosetta Stone', which is one of the most international episodes given that it features French, Egyptian, Greek, and even Japanese characters, is still largely set within the confines of the British Museum [Figure 2.1]. As Denison notes, "England is often narratively represented as a locus for tourism (perhaps particularly London), with famous English sites deployed as sites to be toured by anime characters" (2011: 227). *Sherlock Hound* clearly reflects this tendency with its touristic gaze on Victorian London.

Figure 2.1 Sherlock Hound (1984–1985).

Moreover, the episode 'The Rosetta Stone' contains a number of additional resonances with the wider issues of cultural translation I have been discussing. The episode centers on a plan by Moriarty to steal the eponymous stone from the British Museum, and while much of the story is a relatively simple heist narrative focusing on Moriarty's attempts to steal the stone and Holmes's efforts to foil him, it nevertheless raises some important issues in thinking through processes of cross-cultural adaptation and translation. While housed in the British Museum, the ownership of the Rosetta Stone is under dispute, and several nations including France, Greece, and Egypt have made claims to have it returned to their country. There are no easy ways of ascribing national provenance to the stone— especially given that it contains a decree in three scripts (Ancient Egyptian, Demotic, and Ancient Greek). The plot follows Moriarty's attempts to steal the stone on behalf of the French given that it was initially redis- covered during a Napoleonic expedition to Egypt. Quite apart from the clear symbolic value of the Rosetta Stone as a physical representation of translation for a series that is itself bringing together various national cultures, it is important to note how the episode goes on to represent the national specificity of its various characters. As we have seen, anime pro- ducers often claim to make their stories 'universal' by removing national or ethnic characteristics, yet it is significant just how much of this episode makes use of stereotypical national signifiers in telling its story. This is most clearly embodied in the Frenchman who invites Moriarty to steal the stone. As we can see in Figure 2.2, he is depicted in an outfit clearly modeled on Napoleon with the characteristic bicorne hat and epaulettes. Furthermore, Holmes first meets with him in a French restaurant where he is singing 'La Marseillaise', and when we see him again he is singing Jacques Offenbach's 'Orphée aux enfers', a song best known for its use during can-can dancing, before finally chanting "Vive La France!" Despite claims to the *mukokuseki* nature of anime and its lack of cultural odor, we see here the ways in which stereotyped representations of national identity persist within shows like *Sherlock Hound*. Meanwhile, Holmes and Watson enlist the help of Japanese author Natsume Sōseki, best known in Japan for his novel *I Am a Cat* (1905), to help track down the stone. In real life, Sōseki spent time in London from 1900 to 1901, so there was some historical evidence to make this link. It is significant that this is the only character identified as Japanese in the entire series. As Jonathan Clements has outlined in his production history of the series, even this inclusion was opposed by the Italian producer Luciano Scafa until the Japanese writer Keishi Yamazaki suggested that he was only objecting "because Holmes sought the help of an Asian" (as cited in Clements, 2011: 314).

Figure 2.2 Sherlock Hound (1984–1985).

It is important that this was the point of contention for the Italian studio. Assumptions about cultural discount here go beyond any notion of ethnic self-loathing or cultural imperialism on behalf of the Japanese production company. They reflect wider assumptions about the transnational

Figure 2.3 Sherlock Hound (1984–1985).

potential (or otherwise) of specific national representations. The series may be downplaying certain racial traits and removing signs of Japaneseness, but this is clearly not in the service of a benign '*mukokuseki*' universalism given that the series is otherwise filled with nostalgized and often stereotypical representations of European nations. This instead reflects problematic assumptions about which national representations can travel and which aspects of local culture need to be downplayed. There is a clear hierarchy here; some national representations are privileged above others within the global circulation of media content. The assumption is that certain forms of Europeanness can travel—from the Victorian England of *Sherlock Hound* to the seventeenth-Century France of *Dogtanian and the Three Muskehounds*—while other forms of national specificity, such as the inclusion of identifiably Japanese characters, would need to be removed or downplayed.

Significantly, and somewhat ironically, this strategy to downplay Japaneseness has encountered quite a different reception in subsequent years. After the initial airing in the mid-1980s, *Sherlock Hound* has had a limited yet varied presence on home video,[6] including a number of VHS and DVD releases in Japanese, English, French, and Italian. The first UK release was a Manga Entertainment DVD box set in 2010, in response to increased interest in the work of Hayao Miyazaki, in the wake of the box office successes: *Princess Mononoke* (1997) and *Spirited Away* (2001). This reflects a shift in the Western reception of Japanese popular culture more broadly and an increase in what Henry Jenkins terms 'pop cosmopolitanism', where the transcultural flows of popular culture are inspiring "new forms of global consciousness and cultural competency" (2006: 156). There is growing cross-cultural fandom within both the UK and US devoted to anime. Often this fan reception celebrates these works precisely for their perceived Japaneseness. As Iwabuchi has noted, since the late 1980s, "Japanese animation and computer games have attained a certain degree of popularity and become recognized as very 'Japanese' in a positive and affirmative sense in Western countries as well as in non-Western countries" (2002: 31). When shows from the 1980s are re-released on home video, therefore, they are received within a new context in which the cultural odor of Japaneseness has become a valued commodity. The distinctive cultural odor has become a significant part of the appeal for many fans—reflecting a historical shift from the original production context in the early 1980s to the present day, in which there are now "obsessively devoted fans of Japanese animation in both Europe and the United States" (Iwabuchi, 2002: 31).

Moreover, when Manga Entertainment released the UK DVD of *Sherlock Hound* it released the show without the Japanese language track, and there was a brief backlash where many fans were upset that they were losing some of the Japaneseness from the text. As we can see in the following excerpt from a DVD review at the time, there was disappointment that the release only contained the English language dub and a sense that this attempt to localize the text for the English market was not what this audience desired:

> Not that I doubt the quality of the English/American narration, but I feel the Japanese voice actors are much more suited to this Lupin-esque comedy/adventure, and despite the obvious British settings, the original voices were clearly developed to fit the mould of Miyazaki's anthropomorphic cast.
>
> (Fan, 2010)

As Laurie Cubbison (2005) reminds us, there is a wide variety of ways in which audiences watch anime. We need to be careful how we make generalizations about this reception, yet it is certainly evident that in recent years there has been an increased attention in the West to the national specificity of Japanese animation, and a growing interest in seeking out signs of that Japaneseness. This is one of the ironies underlying the processes of cross-cultural exchange that I have been describing. *Sherlock Hound* is an adaptation of a series of British novels made in co-production with an Italian production company that deliberately removed signifiers of Japanese national specificity—yet the predominant fan interest in the West has subsequently focused precisely on this Japaneseness. Indeed, in 2014, Discotek media brought a new DVD release of *Sherlock Hound* to the US market that was deliberately catering to fans who were upset by the lack of Japanese language in earlier releases—the front cover proudly declared that this was the "Complete & Unabridged" release that included all episodes in the "Japanese and English language". As we have seen, this is a show that had been designed primarily for export and that was intended for dubbing into various 'local' languages around the world, yet one of the primary selling points of the latest US home video release was the very fact that it included the 'original' Japanese language track. The seemingly contradictory histories of production and reception here offer an insight into the tensions underpinning processes of cross-cultural exchange. While there are a number of assumptions circulating about the necessary alterations that are required to create works that circulate globally—relying on notions of cultural discount and *mukokuseki* culture—these products are subsequently received in a variety of unanticipated ways that often dispel the very idea that nationally identifiable elements need to be downplayed for a text to travel.

Conclusion

To conclude, I would like to return to the BBC series *Sherlock* with which I opened this chapter. As we saw, a key element of the reception of the show was its perceived 'Britishness', and this formed a key part of its transnational appeal in Japan. From the fan publications to the promotional paratexts, there was an emphasis within Japan on framing this text through perceptions of a British cultural odor. Within this chapter, I have proposed that we can see a similar phenomenon in relation to *Sherlock Hound*. It is precisely its perceived 'Japaneseness' that has become part of its transnational appeal—despite the various attempts at the production stage to remove or downplay identifiably Japanese elements and the underlying assumptions about the kinds of local specificity that could travel.

Throughout this chapter, therefore, we have seen how forces of localization work in a dynamic and symbiotic relationship with forces of globalization, and using *Sherlock Hound* we have studied how these impact both the production and circulation of textual meaning. Often our models for understanding cross-cultural adaptation are based on culturally reductive models of localization—asking how a global television format has been adapted for the local market and offering an explanatory framework based on essentialized notions of cultural difference. Yet, as we have seen, cross-cultural adaptations often work toward a global audience, and this necessarily complicates the ways in which we frame these processes. Moreover, even when those products are geared toward a global audience and betray certain assumptions about what that necessitates, they are received in a variety of local ways that often contradict those very assumptions. Ultimately, then, perceptions of local specificity still play a crucial role within transnational processes of cultural exchange—even when those products are themselves designed to elide that very specificity—and if we are to truly engage with the complexity of these processes, it is essential that we are attentive to these tensions in our research.

Notes

1. It is important to note that I am not claiming that these texts are somehow more intrinsically 'faithful' to the Conan Doyle texts. Nevertheless, I am arguing that they clearly embody an attempt to avoid changing the source text in the process of translation.
2. Of course, as Thomas Leitch (2009) reminds us, these aspects of the iconography of Holmes were not themselves derived from the novels but from their presence in subsequent adaptations and illustrations–most notably the illustrations of Sidney Paget. The question of an 'original' source text here is complicated by the lengthy history of Holmes adaptations and the ways in which subsequent texts often use elements derived from these earlier adaptations rather than the Conan Doyle stories themselves.
3. As Clements (2011: 313) has outlined in his chapter on the series, it seems likely that the producers had assumed that the works of Conan Doyle would be out of copyright given that the Japanese law allows for works to come out of copyright 50 years after the death of their author, and he had died in 1930.
4. Indeed, this friendship would eventually lead to Miyazaki naming the lead character in his 1992 film *Porco Rosso* after Pagot.
5. Interestingly, this emphasis on Victorian Englishness became a model for other filmmakers to emulate. When the famed manga and anime artist Katsuhiro Otomo was working on the art for his film *Memories,* he admits he was paying close attention to *Sherlock Hound* as a model: "Not an exact copy, but we want to recreate the same sense of Englishness" (as cited in Clements, 2009: 37).
6. The Miyazaki fan site Nausicaa has an extensive list of home video releases at http://www.nausicaa.net/miyazaki/video/holmes/.

References

Annett, S. (2011). Imagining transcultural fandom: Animation and global media communities. *Transcultural Studies*, 2, 164–188.

Bazin, A. (1967/2005). *What is cinema? Volume 1.* Berkeley: University of California Press.

BBC Worldwide. (2012). Sherlock in five languages–BBC Worldwide showcase [Video], available online at: https://www.youtube.com/watch?v=jNzeuzYPiLc (Retrieved July 1, 2015).

BBC Worldwide. (2014). Annual review 2013/2014, available online at: http://www.bbcworldwide.com/media/100452/annualreview2014.pdf (Retrieved July 1, 2015).

Clements, J. (2009). *Schoolgirl milky crisis: Adventures in the anime and manga trade.* London: Titan Books.

Clements, J. (2011). The curious case of the dog in prime time. In. J. Steiff (Ed.), *Sherlock holmes and philosophy* (pp. 307–315). Chicago: Carus Publishing.

Cubbison, L. (2005). Anime fans, DVDs, and the authentic text. *Velvet Light Trap,* 56(1), 45–57.

Davies, D. S. (2007). *Starring Sherlock Holmes.* London: Titan Books.

Dawkins, R. (1989). *The selfish gene.* Oxford: Oxford University Press.

Denison, R. (2011). Transcultural creativity in anime: Hybrid identities in the production, distribution, texts and fandom of Japanese anime. *Creative Industries*, 3(3), 221–235.

Döring, T. (2006). Sherlock Holmes–He dead: Disenchanting the English detective in Kazao Ishiguro's *When we were orphans*. In C. Matzke & S. Mühleisen (Eds.), *Postcolonial postmortems: Crime fiction from a transcultural perspective* (pp. 59–86). Amsterdam: Rodopi Press.

Fan. (2010). At last. [Review of the DVD *Sherlock Hound*], available online at: http://www.amazon.co.uk/review/R1IY1RRSCBS7RV/ (Retrieved July 1, 2015).

Hoskins, C., and Mirus, R. (1988). Reasons for the U.S. dominance of the international trade in television pograms. *Media, Culture & Society*, 10, 499–515.

Hutcheon, L. (2006). *A theory of adaptation*. London: Routledge.

Iwabuchi, K. (2002). *Recentering globalization: Popular culture and Japanese transnationalism*. Durham: Duke University Press.

Jenkins, H. (2006). Pop cosmopolitanism: Mapping cultural flows in an age of media convergence. In *Fans, bloggers, and gamers: Exploring participatory culture* (pp. 152–172). New York: New York University Press.

LaMarre, T. (2009). *The anime machine: A media theory of animation*. Minneapolis: University of Minnesota Press.

Ledoux, T. (1997). *The complete anime guide*. Issaquah: Tiger Mountain Press.

Leitch, T. (2009). *Film adaptation and its discontents: From Gone with the Wind to The Passion of the Christ*. Baltimore: Johns Hopkins University Press.

Lu, A. S. (2008). The many faces of internationalization in Japanese anime. *Animation,* 3(2), 169–187.

Morimoto, L. (2014). Yukata! Batch goes global. *On/Off Screen*, available online at: https://onoffscreen.wordpress.com/2014/08/15/yukatabatch-goes-global/ (Retrieved July 1, 2015).

Morimoto, L. (2015). Rationalized passions: Sherlock and nation-branded boy booms in Japan. (Paper presented at the Society for Cinema and Media Studies Conference, Montreal, Canada March 27, 2015), available online at: https://www.academia.edu/11708514/Rationalized_Passions_Sherlock_and_Nation-branded_Boy_Booms_in_Japan (Retrieved July 1, 2015).

Morley, D., and Robins, K. (1995). *Spaces of identity: Global media, electronic landscapes and cultural boundaries*. London: Routledge.

Napier, S. (2000). *Anime: From Akira to Princess Mononoke*. New York: Palgrave.

Patten, F. (2004). *Watching anime, reading manga*. Berkeley: Stone Bridge Press.

Pointon, S. (1997). Transcultural orgasm as apocalypse. *Wide Angle,* 19(3), 41–63.

Sato, K. (1999). More animated than life: Ethnic bleaching in Japanese anime, *Kyoto Journal*, 41, 22–27.

Smith, I. (2016). Cowboys and Indians: Transnational borrowings in the Indian Masala Western. In A. Fisher (Ed.), *Spaghetti Westerns at the crossroads*. Edinburgh: Edinburgh University Press.

Stephens, B. (2014). Animating animality through Dumas, d'Artagnan, and Dogtanian. *Dix-Neuf,* 18(2), 193–210.

Webb, K. E. (1998). *Sherlock Holmes in Japan*. Bellevue: NextChurch Resources.

Yuichi, H., and Hall, J. (2013). *East wind coming: A Sherlockian study book*. London: MX Publishing.

3 The Context of Localization

Children's Television in Western Europe and the Arabic-Speaking World

Jeanette Steemers

Although localization practices are crucial for the adaptation of texts, just as significant are national policy initiatives and corporate strategies, which deliver the context for localization. This context is grounded in economics, policy, location, and culture and provides the terrain for the contestation, negotiation, and accommodation of local, regional, and national requirements. The children's television industry is particularly pertinent for observing these processes, because it is heavily globalized through international distribution, a business that is dominated by US corporations who develop, produce, and disseminate children's content globally across media platforms. The children's sector is also worthy of examination because it comprises abundant animation series that often "escape the limitations of their cultures of origin" (Havens, 2007). It is an industry encompassing a worldwide network of children's media professionals who engage at international markets, festivals, and screenings to appraise ideas and content for their markets. It also provides a setting for exploring the interplay between the global and the local, the connection between the 'micro contexts' of specific production sites and media practices, and the 'macro forces' of politics, economics, and culture that shape production (Mayer, 2009: 15). This is where universal interpretations of childhood, originating within 'industry lore' and perpetuated by international gatekeepers, are worked through, reinforcing "particular institutional practices and economic arrangements" (Havens, 2007), including ideas about what the 'universal child' likes.

This chapter explores the geographical, cultural, and policy contexts of children's television (Lustyik and Zanker, 2013a: 160), focusing on developments in Western European and Arab countries to explain some of the factors that have influenced localization and local content in a global landscape. The findings are drawn from industry analysis (press, industry, and regulatory sources), interviews with practitioners at the Prix Jeunesse Children's Media Festival in Munich (June 2014), and participant observation at a pre-summit workshop on 'Children's Media at the Core of Public Service Media in the Multiplatform Era' held at the September 2014 World Summit on Media for Children in Kuala Lumpur, Malaysia. The findings also utilize interviews undertaken as part of an Arts and Humanities Research Council project on pan-Arab children's television. The chapter first considers the global landscape for localization and the role of US players, before comparing and contrasting localization in Western European and Arab countries where the balance between the global and the local has been shaped by differences in expertise, history, policy, and regulatory environment. Attempts to balance these forces of localization and globalization raise interesting questions about the future political economy of children's media industries, particularly as television enters a transitional phase with the rise of video on demand (VOD) distributors (for example, Netflix or Amazon) and online content aggregators (YouTube).

The Global Landscape for Localization

In today's media business, children's television stands out as one of the most globalized forms of content. Globally, the sector has long been dominated by the world's largest media conglomerates. Disney, Time Warner (Cartoon Network), Fox Kids, and Viacom (Nickelodeon) sell content internationally and operate their own globally branded channels and electronic spaces, supported by large production, marketing, and distribution infrastructures that drive revenue streams in consumer products and entertainment across multiple platforms and multiple territories (Wasko, 2001; Banet-Weiser, 2007). In these international endeavors, US companies are sustained by the long shelf life of children's products, which can be targeted at new generations of children every three to four years.

As US-based entities, the strategies of US players are driven largely by the demands of the large, wealthy, and therefore lucrative US market. However, technological developments over the years (cable, satellite, online) and the desire to leverage profits internationally because of a more competitive domestic market have driven international expansion first of TV networks and more recently of VOD distributors (Netflix, Amazon). In Europe and the Middle East this growth has led to an abundance of largely US-sourced children's content on dedicated niche channels and on demand, a far cry from the scarcity associated with the monopolistic state and public service provision of the previous century.

Within this expanded market children are targeted according to gender and age (infants, preschool, tween, pre-teen), although those older than 12 are mostly ignored by broadcasters, because they are seen as a more commercially elusive audience that is shifting its media engagement toward other platforms and social networking (Ofcom 2014a; Lustyik and Zanker, 2013a: 162). According to White and Preston (2005), US corporations like Fox and Disney have encouraged children to see their channel brands and electronic spaces as "places" they can visit to develop identities they can share irrespective of regional or local cultural affinities. In these "corporate branded environments" where territories are "featureless" and "unmarked by familiar landmarks" and where characters are "carefully crafted and animated in such a way as to maximize the potential for identification in a global market" (White and Preston, 2005: 239), it would appear that children are being encouraged to recognize brand consumption as a marker of identity, community, and belonging (ibid: 253–54). This is a position at odds with the views of many national governments, broadcasters, and advocacy groups who argue for stories that reflect local cultures and for locally produced content specifically developed to give children a "sense of their own place in an increasingly complex world" (Lustyik and Zanker, 2013b: 179).

A critical approach assumes that US dominance has a homogenizing effect, effacing the local and promoting Western or more particularly US perspectives and values that serve US global capitalism and cultural domination (Dorfman and Mattelart, 1975; Schiller, 1969, 1991). Applied to children's media culture, children are seen as vulnerable to the harmful influences of advertising, violence, and consumer culture that manipulate their desires (Engelhardt, 1986; Kline, 1993), a view widely prevalent in international forums such as the World Summit on Media for Children in 2014 and among both Western and Arab commentators (Palmer, 2006; Tayie, 2008).

A more nuanced position suggests that cultural flow is not a 'one-way street' because of the prevalence of local production as well as cultural exchanges between countries other than the US (Fejes, 1981: 286) across geolinguistic (Sinclair, Jacka, and Cunningham, 1996) or geocultural regions (Hesmondhalgh, 2002: 180), with ties based on cultural and linguistic rather than simply geographical proximity. According to this view, audiences are not powerless but actively interpret content according to their own distinct cultures and experiences (Ang, 1985) in ways that often transcend physical and cultural boundaries. This bringing together of localizing, regionalizing, and globalizing factors is called 'glocalization' by Robertson and involves a process whereby homogenizing and heterogenizing forces (including advertising and consumerism) mix and assimilate the particular and the universal to make cultural products such as television programs more relevant to local markets (Robertson, 1995: 40).

From this perspective, the international impact of companies like Disney or Nickelodeon is neither automatic nor uniform. To flourish overseas they need national policy-makers and regulators to relax regulations (on advertising or local content, for example) that might curb their activities, and regulations vary throughout the world. For instance, while New Zealand offers a largely deregulated market that easily facilitates access (Lustyik and Zanker, 2013a), Chinese regulator SARFT exercises strict regulations on where and when foreign animation can air in order to protect the Chinese animation industry and Chinese children from harmful influences (Franks, 2014). It has been argued that for global strategies to work, media companies must work to customize their offerings in order to appeal to local cultures (Hall and Jacques, 1997: 35–36). Yet the degree to which this is necessary or even possible also depends on the distinctive characteristics of local markets including the strength of local competition, local preferences, and changing consumption habits. In this respect, the relationship between globalizing forces and local culture is less about opposites and more about the degree of balance between homogeneity and heterogeneity and different degrees of dependency.

This blurring of global, national, and local is reflected in tangible increases in co-productions, formats and international channels that feed into a more hybrid television culture that blends aspects of the global and local in respect to audience identities and media practices (Barker, 1999: 43). According to Boyd-Barrett local producers "draw on the codes and conventions (...) of the global popular to stamp their own product, channel, distribution network as 'professional', 'competitive' and attractive to audiences and, more importantly, advertisers" (1997: 16). This is also applicable to children's television. For example, at the 2014 World Summit on Media for Children in Kuala Lumpur, several workshop participants named US educational preschool show *Sesame Street* and its local versions in Bangladesh and Afghanistan (see Chapter 6 in this collection) as an example of a children's series that was both popular and high quality. They then went on to identify programs in the Philippines (*Batibot*), Pakistan (*Abu Bakr*), and Ethiopia (*Tsehai*) that copied elements of the popular US format, confirming the aspirational qualities of the show and its influence on local production in other parts of the world.

Conversely, overseas producers who wish to export to the US will adjust productions to fit US priorities, for example by including curricular elements for preschool shows (Steemers, 2010: 105–106). This argument is taken a step further by Bloch and Lemish (2003) who argue that many non-US texts, such as the UK pre-school series *Teletubbies,* the *Harry Potter* franchise, and the Japanese *Pokémon* phenomenon only became internationally popular once they were successful in the US, transforming "a local product into a global phenomenon" (ibid: 26). They suggest this is part of a *megaphone* effect: selecting a text and filtering it through the US before distributing it globally (ibid: 159). This "empowers" local voices to be heard worldwide "despite a strong American accent" (ibid: 160), but they note that this works best for texts from Western or industrialized countries that are culturally proximate (ibid: 171) or where "foreignness" is made "less apparent" through the avoidance of particular locations or culturally specific signs or characters. For example, in the *Pokémon* movie they claim that "a conscious effort was made (...) to eliminate Japanese elements so as not to interfere with fantasy for American audiences" (Bloch and Lemish, 2003: 181).

Opposing arguments suggest that trying to satisfy broader international tastes rather than local markets by stripping content of its 'otherness' comes at the expense of children's needs and identity formation, grounded in more narrowly defined geographical or cultural communities, "predicated on telling stories and hearing voices that reflect local cultures" (see Lustyik and Zanker, 2013b: 183). It should also not be forgotten that US children's programming still dominates the international trade in children's content, which can then be distributed cheaply on branded channels or sold below production cost to cash-strapped children's television departments (Steemers, 2010: 42–47). In this case, 'cultural discount' (Hoskins and Mirus, 1988: 500), where audiences prefer programming that is most proximate to their own culture, is less relevant because animation, the most heavily traded form of children's content, is often stripped of "anything that stands in the way of international sales" (Steemers, 2010: 51).

In overseas markets US corporations employ a range of localization strategies. They might start by localizing soundtracks, although in some markets there is no adaptation at all. Animation for younger children is usually dubbed; live action programs for older children may be sub-titled depending on the market. Channels may be further localized through locally targeted commercial breaks, program presentation links, and interstitials. The "local opt-out" (Chalaby, 2002: 194) is a separate country-specific channel operation, which adheres to the core brand values of the transnational network but operates its own schedules with some locally commissioned and acquired material.

At its most basic, localization is simply about selecting the most appropriate schedules to fit the daily routines of a specific territory. However, with recent changes in distribution and consumption, localization has been extended to include localized websites and on-demand operations that encourage "a potentially interactive local flow with the young local audience" (Sigismondi, 2009: 161). In economically more important markets, such as the UK and Germany, locally appointed executives run local channel operations, commissioning local content. In July 2014, Disney Europe announced that it would be commissioning long-form live action, sport, and factual entertainment from independent European producers, rather than producing these in-house (Parker, 2014). The ultimate level of localization involves producing local adaptations of internationally licensed formats. Yet this, with the exception of a small number of shows (most notably *Sesame Street*) is limited in the children's sector, because it has always been cheaper to buy in ready-made animation or drama than to invest in local content (Steemers, 2015).

Evidence from the UK suggests that international children's TV channel operators have consistently spent a small proportion, as little as 10% of their aggregate expenditure, on original programming (Ofcom, 2007). In the UK, first-run originated UK content on channels run by commercial children's channels (Nickelodeon, Turner, ITV, Baby TV, CSC Media Group, and Disney) actually declined from 283 hours in 2010 to 111 hours in 2013 (Ofcom, 2014b: 19) with total children's content expenditure of £43m on all content in 2013 (Ofcom, 2014c: 177). This compares with £94m spent by the BBC on 585 first-run originated hours during the same period (Ofcom, 2014c: 12).

Steemers and D'Arma's 2012 study of US owned channels in Germany, Britain, France, Italy, and the Netherlands showed that the vast majority of programs were sourced from US parent companies and that cultural and policy related factors influenced localization strategies. In aggregate, the proportion of locally originated programming on Cartoon Network, Disney Channel, Nickelodeon, Nick Jr, and Playhouse Disney was higher in the UK and France (19% and 17% respectively) than in Italy (5%), Germany, and the Netherlands (less than 5%) (2012: 150). No US player has consistently committed to localization across all five markets. Disney, which holds a license from the French regulatory authority, has been more engaged in localization in France, because of a combination of regulatory demands (local content and production quotas), production subsidies, and tax incentives (ibid). There is less investment in Germany, where the pay TV market is smaller and where there are no production quotas or significant subsidies and tax incentives. In 2014 Disney launched its own free-to-air childrens' channel in Germany, ending its 50% participation in German children's channel SuperRTL.

In sum, when US companies localize their offerings the reasons are complex and influenced by a "variety of connected country-related factors" including policy and regulatory environments that will vary from country to country. Consistently high levels of US animation and drama on US-owned channels reveal that in general adaptations to local cultures and languages take place only when "necessary and economically viable" and only when they "leverage the existing global structures of distribution of entertainment content" (Sigismondi, 2009: 157).

Comparing Localization Initiatives—Western European and Pan-Arab Approaches

The internationalization of television and the rise of US-owned children's channels and media brands, described above, have underpinned calls for more culturally relevant content because of fears about a loss of local culture and identity among children (Moran and Chung, 2008). In Western Europe, this is manifested in discourses about children's rights to access indigenous programs (see Messenger Davies and Thornham, 2007: 15–18; Von Felitzen & Carlsson, 2002) and claims about their importance for "children's cultural sense of themselves, or their identities and for the cultural life of the nation as a whole" (Brogan, 2007).

In Arab countries, restrictions on non-governmental advocacy groups and the lack of both credible audience research and a strong children's television production community place limits on the emergence of informed public debates about how media should best serve children to affirm their sense of self, community, and place (Steemers and Awan, 2015). When pan-Arab satellite television took off in the mid-1990s, there was an apparent paucity of attractive indigenous programming for children in most Arab countries (Lepeska, 2010). However, with the launch of pan-Arab children's satellite channels, Spacetoon in Dubai and MBC3 in Saudi Arabia in 2000 and 2004 respectively followed by Qatari-based JCC (Al-Jazeera Children's Channel) in 2005, there was an upsurge in provision for children. However, JCC (renamed Jeem TV in 2013), established by the Qatar Foundation for Education, Science and Community Development, was different from rival pan-Arab services Spacetoon and MBC3 because of its non-commercial goals and a clear commitment to 'local' production, produced specifically for Arabic-speaking children rather than a reliance on imported content (Lepeska, 2010). In this vein, the arguments made by Mahmoud Bouneb, former Executive General Manager of JCC, reveal similar concerns about identity. However, in this case local as promoted by JCC refers to Arab society as a whole rather than a specific geographic locality. According to Bouneb, the goal of establishing JCC was to build a "better tomorrow" in pan-Arab television for children, one that would plant "the seed of hope ... for a better Arab citizen" (Bouneb cit. in Lepeska, 2010) as well as one that would avoid "letting Western values be (seen as) the only ones" (2009). It was a view that recognized the integration of Islam into content "as part of our daily life" through special programming for Ramadan (Bouneb cit. in Lepeska, 2010), but that took little account of 'local' production that reflected the diverse nature of Arab culture.

The increasingly transnational nature of content production and distribution highlights the difficulties in defining concepts such as 'localization' and 'local' when they encompass a range of transnational collaborations. For example, popular animation series are made for the international marketplace. Even if they are commissioned in Europe or the Middle East they may be produced in cheaper (the Far East) or more tax-efficient locations (Canada, Ireland) (Steemers and D'Arma, 2012: 76). In the case of JCC, the only pan-Arab children's channel to make any significant investment in 'local' programming, local content was largely driven by an in-house team of non-Qatari Arabs and Western consultants as well as co-productions with partners based in the UK, France, Canada and Malaysia. According to Bouneb, there was "no experience of making kid's content for the Arab world" (cit. in Benzine, 2009), although there was a tradition of making some local children's productions for national channels in Egypt (including animation) and Lebanon.

Moreover, although arguments in favor of local content are voiced in both Europe and the Middle East, there is not much evidence about whether local or localized content is beneficial in respect of 'public value' (see Buckingham, 2009: 140). In cases where domestic production is so intertwined with overseas partnerships, any notion of the link between domestic production and identity is already weakened. What is more, even if children profess a preference for local content and variety, which can vary from country to country (Drotner, 2001: 290; Messenger Davis and Thornham, 2007), this is not, according to Buckingham evidence that "home-grown" programming is beneficial for children's "socialization and healthy cultural development" (2011: 203). Drotner, pointing to the rise of multicultural societies in Europe, also cautions against "simple analogies about domestic culture as a homogeneous and known domain of experience that may be neatly contrasted to foreign culture as an equally homogeneous unknown" (Drotner, 2001: 294).

Debates about children's media in Europe and the Middle East also take place with different conceptualizations and social constructions of childhood, which leave a mark on government policies and industry strategies. Western broadcasters, regulators, and researchers place emphasis on the child as an individual with agency. However, Arab media institutions focus more on the child's status within the framework of the family, an institution permeated by Islamic approaches to social values and cultural standards that sit uneasily next to Western notions of the empowered child uninhibited by authority (Steemers and Awan, 2015).

In Western Europe, there is a longer history of supporting local children's content based on public service institutions with a public service ethos founded on citizenship, which has been national in orientation. This compares to the Arab world where more recent pan-Arab initiatives for promoting 'local' content involve an interplay of national, regional, and international elements served by transnational Arabic language services for children, such as JeemTV/JCC. 'Local' in this sense stresses the particularities of Arab culture and children being "part of Arab society" rather than the particularities of a place or region (Sakr and Steemers, 2015). Moreover, Western European countries regulate for both positive outcomes that promote quality national or European content (public service broadcasting, quotas) and 'negative' interventions against harmful effects (of advertising, violence). However, in the world of transnational Arab satellite channels there are few regulations or laws that impact content for children, leaving interventions largely an internal matter for broadcasters, often exercised as internal censorship in matters relating to gender, relationships etc. (Sakr and Steemers, 2015).

In the two regions, there are differences in provision between small and large nations, although size is not always key to the ability to produce local content. In both instances, the ability to originate is shaped by wealth. In Europe, the most prolific producers of local content are national public service broadcasters in those countries where public service broadcasting has a strong institutional and financial base, the UK, Germany, and the Netherlands and across Scandinavia but less so in southern Europe (D'Arma, Enli, and Steemers, 2010). In the Arab world, despite a history of colonization by Britain and France, with their public service broadcasting experience, there is no home-grown tradition of public service broadcasting, and the production of local/regional content for children was limited in scope until the mid-2000s and the launch of pan-Arab JCC. The exceptions are local adaptations of *Sesame Street*, which can be traced back to Kuwait in 1979, followed by versions in Jordan, Palestine, and Egypt in the 1990s and 2000s. Attracted by its educational goals, the most recent Abu Dhabi-based *Sesame Street* production, *Iftah ya Simsim*, was being produced in 2014 with support from the Arab Bureau for Education in Gulf States (ABEGS).

Given the realities of transnational operations and the institutional arrangements for enhancing local content production, this raises the question of what policies are best suited to enhance local content. As discussed already, degrees of localization are contingent and vary according to the size and wealth of markets, levels of regulation, and the strength of domestic competition.

Interventions by some European governments to encourage local content include government subsidies, tax breaks, production, and investment quotas, seen most prominently in France. In the UK, the Treasury introduced animation tax credits in 2013, followed in 2014 by tax credits for live action children's programming, in an attempt to attract players such as Disney and Nickelodeon to produce in the UK. The same approach has been successfully deployed in Ireland and Canada, but there is no evidence that investment by US players in local production results in more 'local' programming for Canadian children (Bowen, 2014). In cases like this, transnational collaborations that invite 'local' investment may ultimately suppress the local if production is used to feed global appetites. This is also evident in the way that another oil-rich Arab emirate, Abu Dhabi, has sought to attract overseas media companies to its content creation hub, twofour54, with rebates of up to 30% on location, production, and post-production facilities (twofour54, 2013). Established within a free trade zone in 2008, twofour54 is part of a longer-term state plan to build "a sustainable media industry" in the UAE (Smith, 2014) with international aspirations. This is reflected in *Driver Dan's Story Train* (Karim wa Qitar al-Hekayat), a co-produced children's series, with UK based 3Line Media, which was animated in Abu Dhabi by the locally based Blink Studios. It was produced in two versions: the Arabic one is an original adaptation fully produced by Blink Studios that "reflects the culture of the Arabic-speaking world, with the live action sequences featuring children from the region". Airing on both the BBC's CBeebies channel and JCC's preschool channel, Baraem, it was promoted by twofour54 as an "English language series" that "was produced locally for the regional market and exported to the world" (twofour54, 2013).

The strongest intervention for local content within Western Europe has been public service broadcasting, although the impact is variable because of differences in market size, wealth, public support, and proximity to same-language markets. These differences are evident in responses from European public service broadcasting executives who attended the Prix Jeunesse in 2014. For all European public service broadcasters the provision of 'local' children's programming is regarded as an important part of their remit. For Dutch public service broadcaster, KRO, it is "always important that children can identify with the characters (...) That it's child-centred" (Snellars, 2014). For ZDF, one of the two large German public service broadcasters, co-productions are now essential to keep costs down for drama and animation. Yet these are regarded as positive, because although "keep[ing] cultural identity" is important "we don't want only German programming, because we live in an international world now" (Wellershof, 2014).

In German-speaking Switzerland, a much smaller multilingual territory, German-language public service broadcaster, SRG, has a different perspective as it contemplates a move away from scheduled broadcasting toward video-on-demand streaming with exclusive Swiss-German language content, because "we are surrounded by [German] competitors" whose ability to secure the best shows and pay for dubbing draws Swiss children away (Grond, 2014). By contrast, in the equally small, but linguistically unified Danish market, policy-makers have supported publicly funded DR in its decision to launch a second children's channel targeted at preschool children. Smaller, less well-resourced public service broadcasters, such as RTV Slovenia, focus on a small number of in-house productions but also invest in "high quality dubbing" to ensure an advantage over commercial rivals (Pestaj, 2014).

In the Arab world, public service broadcasting does not exist, but some aspects of public service broadcasting were adapted for JCC/Jeem and preschool channel, Baraem, in an attempt to establish a platform for local content in an environment where there was a "famine of genuine original programming" (Kuttab, 2010). Unlike European public service broadcasters whose activities are primarily focused within their own national boundaries, the JCC project owed its existence to wider Qatari policies for global visibility, regional influence, and national development (Sakr and Steemers, 2015). The guiding principles were educational and cultural with an emphasis on language (classical Arabic), but without the accountability and independent funding necessary for a functioning public service system. When JCC launched in 2005, it emphasized education through 'edutainment', allowing children to "learn about different environments and cultures" while helping them to "develop self-esteem, respect their traditions and values, appreciate people around them" (JCC Launch statement). With the launch of JCC's preschool channel Baraem in 2009, 'local' aspects were highlighted again, when the channel program director, called it "a channel of the homeland" (cit. in Buxton, 2009), suggesting that 'homeland' was more than a geographical place.

However, without enough skilled Qatari staff to run a children's production and broadcast operation, JCC relied on broadcast professionals from other Arab countries and Western consultants to fill HR, scheduling, management, commissioning, audience research, and finance roles. Local productions in Arabic grew, and there was a target of 60% local transmissions before 2011 (Anonymous, 2014; also Lepeska, 2010). Before 2011, there were co-productions with UK producers including game show format *Borj al-Jaras* (*The Buzzer*), animation series *Al-Dunia Rosie* (*Everything's Rosie*), preschool show (*Baas*), and cookery show *Al-Tabaq al–Taer* (*Flying Saucer*), as well as collaborations with Canadian (*Nan and Lili*), Japanese, and Malaysian partners (*Saladin*) (Sakr and Steemers, 2015). However, local and international co-productions were suddenly curtailed in September 2011 when the non-Qatari Arab management team at JCC was replaced by

Qataris (DigitalTVEurope, 2011). Subject to regulation influenced by the ruling family and with a shift in oversight from the Qatar Foundation to Al Jazeera Network in November 2013, JCC (renamed Jeem) has since been commercialized. This has taken place through the introduction of advertising and lessening of emphasis placed on educational local productions and co-productions, in favor of acquisitions. Large packages were bought from Disney and other overseas suppliers in 2013 in order to compete more effectively with MBC3 (Sakr and Steemers, 2015), as well as smaller animation acquisitions such as *Ella Bella Bingo* (Singapore's August Media Holdings and Norway's Kool Productions). These purchases underline the shift toward a less specific appeal to 'children all over the world … geographical and cultural barriers notwithstanding' rather than specific local or regional audiences (Jyotirmoy Saha, CEO August Media Holdings cit. in Hawkes, 2013). What remains constant is a content strategy based on special series, competitions, and animation that uphold Arab culture broadly as Islamic culture in the holy month of Ramadan and that, according to Saad al-Hudaifi, Deputy Executive General Manager and Acting Director of Channels, aim "at providing compelling and responsible programmes to Arab children and their families" (Anon, 2013). The target again is Arab society as a whole.

Conclusion

This chapter has shown that the balance between national policy initiatives and global corporate strategies has been an important factor in determining levels of local content and degrees of localization. In spite of frequent calls for more 'local content', children's television is a particularly difficult environment for local production, because of a surplus of attractive, cheap US programming from US players who see little economic advantage to investing in local originations. Producers from other countries are now also inclined to produce with an eye to the US market in particular, so the transnational aspect in children's audiovisual production is no longer limited just to US programming. US strategies that prioritize brand identification over identification with local culture present a challenge to campaigners and policy-makers who feel that children should have access to 'local' content that gives them a sense of place and belonging. Arguments about the beneficial impact of local content or the negative impact of imported content are neither clear-cut nor uniform. Reasons for this lack of clarity include different local circumstances related to regulation, the strength of local provision, local preferences and concerns, and the blurring of what is national, global, or local, as producers draw on the codes and conventions of the globally popular (including American tastes) to broaden appeal beyond local markets.

These differences are clearly evident in the regional markets of Western Europe and the Arabic-speaking markets of the Middle East. While concerns about US content are expressed in both, solutions are shaped by local circumstances and different conceptualizations of childhood. Although provision by Western European public service broadcasters is uneven, there is a regulatory framework and an expectation that children will be taken into account. In Arab countries, there is no strong legacy of providing quality local entertainment for children, and what is promoted as local by pan-Arab channels like Jeem is actually targeted at a transnational Arab audience, spread across many diverse countries. Even though JCC tried to build a children's production community from scratch to cater to a pan-Arab audience, it proved vulnerable to Qatari politics and the lack of a regulatory framework in 2011 when top management was removed and local co-productions were radically scaled back in favor of large scale overseas acquisitions.

The differences outlined here demonstrate the continuing need to examine regulatory and cultural factors on a country-by-country basis even with the shift toward convergent digital media, the rise of multiplatform distribution, and the shift away from mass communications to communications that place greater emphasis on individual participation and engagement (Flew, Iosifidis, Steemers, 2015). This chapter has focused on television delivered by channels; as children's media consumption shifts toward more on-demand consumption, it raises further questions about the future and nature of localization and local content. Producers try to balance the demands of domestic and international markets that are becoming even more fragmented and financially challenging with the rise of new players like Netflix and YouTube who operate on a transnational basis and seem relatively unencumbered by national regulations related to local content (Franks, 2013; Whittingham, 2014).

Acknowledgements

The Arts and Humanities Research Council (Grant No. AH/J004545/1) supported some of this research including data collected in collaboration with Naomi Sakr (University of Westminster).

References

Ang, I. (1985). *Watching Dallas*. London: Methuen.

Anon. (2013). JCC lines up special programmes. Saad al-Hudaifi: captivating and inspiring programmes for children and their families. *Gulf Times*, July 1, http://www.gulf-times.com/Mobile/Qatar/178/details/357996/JCC-lines-up-special-programmes (Retrieved April 24, 2015).

Anon. (2014). Arab media expert and journalist, former JCC employee, interviewed by Jeanette Steemers and Naomi Sakr, September 10, 2014.

Banet-Weiser, S. (2007). *Kids rule! Nickelodeon and consumer citizenship*. Durham, NC: Duke University Press.

Barker, C. (1999). *Television, globalization and cultural identities*. Buckingham: Open University Press.

Benzine A. (2009). Al Jazeera: Arab production 'Immature'. *C21*, October 4, 2009.

Bloch L-R., & Lemish, D. (2003). The megaphone effect: The international diffusion of cultural media via the USA. In P. Kalbfleisch (Ed.), *Communication Yearbook 27* (pp. 159–190). London: Routledge.

Bouneb, M. (2009). Interviewed by Naomi Sakr, Doha, April 20, 2009.

Bowen, C. (2014). Executive director, Youth Media Alliance, Canada, Interviewed by Jeanette Steemers, Munich, June 2, 2014.

Boyd-Barrett, O. (1997). International communication and globalization: Contradictions and directions. In A. Mohammadi (Ed.), *International communication and globalization* (pp. 11–26). London: Sage.

Brogan, A. (2007). Director, Kindle Entertainment, Interviewed by J. Steemers, London, March 27, 2007.

Buckingham, D. (2009). *The impact of the commercial world on children's wellbeing. Report of an independent assessment.* London: Department for Children, Schools and Families & Department for Culture, Media and Sport, UK.

Buckingham, D. (2011). *The material child: Growing up in consumer culture.* Cambridge: Polity.

Buxton. M. (2009). Meet the buyers: Al Jazeera. *C21*, November 3, 2009.

Chalaby, J. (2002). Transnational television in Europe; The role of pan-European channels. *European Journal of Communication,* 17, 183–203.

D'Arma A., Enli, G., & Steemers, J. (2010). Serving children in public service media. In G. Lowe (Ed.), *The public in public service media* (pp. 227–242). Göteborg: Nordicom.

D'Arma A., & Steemers, J. (2012). Localisation strategies of US-owned children's television networks in five European markets. *Journal of Children and Media,* 6(2), 147–163.

Della Carva, M. (2014). Google to revamp its products with 12-and-younger focus. *USA Today,* December 3. http://www.usatoday.com/story/tech/2014/12/03/google-products-revamped-for-under-13-crowd/19803447/ (Retrieved March 13, 2015).

Digital TV Europe. (2011). Al Jazeera dismisses kid's channel chief and senior staff. November 11, available online at: http://www.digitaltveurope.net/17567/al-jazeera-dismisses-kids-channel-chief-and-senior-staff/ (Retrieved February 10, 2015).

Dorfman, A., and Mattelart, A. (1975). *How to read Donald Duck.* New York: International General Editions.

Drotner, K. (2001). Global media through youthful eyes. In S. Livingstone & M. Bovill (Eds.), *Children and their changing media environment* (pp. 283–305). Hillsdale, NJ: Erlbaum.

Engelhardt, T. (1986). Children's television: The shortcake strategy. In T. Gitlin (Ed.), *Watching television* (pp. 68–110). New York: Pantheon.

Fejes, F. (1981). Media imperialism: An assessment. *Media, Culture and Society,* 3, 281–289.

Flew, T., Iosifidis, P., and Steemers, J. (2015). *Global media and national policies: The return of the state.* Basingstoke: Palgrave (in press).

Franks, N. (2013). On the fast track. *C21*, April 16, available online at: http://www.c21media.net/on-the-fast-track/ (Retrieved February 6, 2015).

Franks, N. (2014). Unlocking China. *C21* March 18, available online at: http://www.c21media.net/unlocking-china/ (Retrieved February 6, 2015).

Grond, T. (2014). Head of Children's Programming, SRG, Swiss Radio and Television. Interviewed by Jeanette Steemers, Munich, May 31, 2015.

Hall, S. and Jacques, M. (1997). Les Enfants de Marx et de Coca-Cola, *New Statesman,* November 28, 34–36.

Havens, T. (2007). Universal childhood: The global trade in children's television and changing ideals of Childhood. *Global Media Journal,* 6(10), available online at: http://lass.purduecal.edu/cca/gmj/sp07/gmj-sp07-havens.htm. No Pagination (Retrieved May 8, 2014).

Hawkes, R. (2013). Ella Bella Bingo travels to the Middle East. *Rapid TV News*, December 4, 2013, available online at: http://www.rapidtvnews.com/20131204 31157/ella-bella-bingo-travels-to-the-middle-east.html#ixzz3IfUelq8U (Retrieved April 20, 2015).

Hesmondhalgh, D. (2002). *The cultural industries*. London: Sage.

Hoskins, C., and Mirus, R. (1988). Reasons for the US dominance of the international trade in television programmes. *Media, Culture and Society*, 10(4), 499–515.

Kline, S. (1993). *Out of the garden: Toys, tv, and children's culture in the age of marketing*. London: Verso.

Kraidy M. (2012). The rise of Transnational Media Systems: Implications of Pan-Arab media for comparative research. In D. Hallin and P. Mancini (Eds.), *Comparing media systems beyond the Western world* (pp. 178–198). Cambridge: Cambridge University Press.

Kuttab, D. (2010). Author's transcript of contribution to conference on 'Children's Television in the Arab world', University of Westminster, London, June 4, 2010.

Lepeska, D. (2010). How Al Jazeera children's channel grew up. *The National*, January 8, 2010, available online at: http://www.thenational.ae/news/world/middle-east/how-al-jazeera-childrens-channel-grew-up (Retrieved April 20, 2015).

Lustyik, K., & Zanker, R. (2013a). Digital children's channels: A comparative analysis of three locally launched services. *International Journal of Digital Television*, 4(2), 159–176.

Lustyik, K., & Zanker, R. (2013b). Is there local content on television for children today? In A. Valdivia and E. Scharrer (Eds.), *The international encyclopedia of media studies* (pp. 179–202). Oxford: Blackwell.

Mayer, M. (2009). Bringing the social back in: Studies of production cultures and social theory. In V. Mayer, M. Banks, and J. Caldwell (Eds.), *Production studies: Cultural studies of media industries* (pp. 15–24). London: Routledge.

Messenger Davies, M., & Thornham, H. (2007). *Academic literature review: The future of children's television programming*. London: Ofcom.

Moran, K., & Chung, L. (2008). Global or local identity. Analysis of the role of Viacom on identity formation among children in an international context. *Global Media Journal*, 7(12), 1–29, available online at: http://globalmediajournal.com/open-access/global-or-local-identity-a-theoretical-analysis-of-the-role-of-viacom-on-identity-formation-among.pdf?aid=35191 (Retrieved January 31, 2015).

Ofcom. (2007). *The future of children's television programming*. London: Ofcom.

Ofcom. (2014a). *Children and parents; Media use and attitudes report*. London: Ofcom.

Ofcom. (2014b). *PSB annual report 2014 annexes 6.ii. Children's analysis*. December 15, 2014. London: Ofcom.

Ofcom. (2014c). *The communications market report*, August 7, 2014. London: Ofcom.

Palmer, S. (2006). *Toxic childhood*. London: Orion Press.

Parker, R. (2014). Disney: Indies to make all long-form shows. *Broadcast*, July 10, 2014, available online at: http://www.broadcastnow.co.uk/disney-indies-to-make-all-long-form-shows/5074018.article (Retrieved January 15, 2015).

Pestaj, M. (2014). Creator, RTV Slovenia, Interviewed by Jeanette Steemers, Munich, June 1, 2015.

Robertson, R. (1994). Globalisation or glocalisation? *The Journal of International Communications*, 1(1), 33–52.

Sakr, N., & Steemers, J. (2015). Co-Producing content for Pan-Arab children's tv: State, business and the workplace. In V. Mayer (Ed.), *Production studies, The sequel! Cultural studies of global media industries*. London: Routledge.

Schiller, H. (1969). *Mass communications and American empire*. Boulder: Westview, second edition.

Schiller, H. (1991). Not yet the Post-Imperialist Era. *Critical Studies in Mass Communication*, 8(1), 13–28.

Sigismondi, P. (2009). Global Ssrategies in the children's media market: The Jetix Case in Italy. *Journal of Children and Media,* 3(2), 152–165.

Sinclair, J., Jacka, E., & Cunningham, S. (1996). (Eds.), *New patterns in global television: Peripheral vision*. Oxford: Oxford University Press.

Snellars, G. (2014). Editor in Chief, KRO, Interviewed by Jeanette Steemers, Munich, June 4, 2015.

Steemers, J. (2010). *Creating preschool content. A story of commerce, creativity and curriculum*. Basingstoke: Palgrave Macmillan.

Steemers J. (2015). Formats and localisation in the children's audiovisual sector. In P. Jensen and A. Moran (Eds.), *Global television formats*. London: Intellect.

Steemers, J., & Awan, F. (2015). Arab and Western perspectives on childhood and children's media provision in T. Sabry, N. Sakr, and J. Steemers (Eds.), *Children's Television and Digital Media in the Arab World: Childhood, Screen Culture and Education*. Bristol: IB Tauris.

Steemers, J., & D'Arma, A. (2012). Evaluating and regulating the role of public broadcasters in the children's media ecology: The case of home-grown television content. *International Journal of Media and Cultural Politics*, 8(1), 67–85.

Tayie, S. (2008). Children and mass media in the Arab world: A second level analysis. In U. Carlsson et al. (Eds.), *Empowerment through media education: An intercultural dialogue* (pp. 67–87). Göteborg: Nordicom.

Twofour54. (2013). *Your gateway to new media business opportunities*. Promotional pamphlet. Abu Dhabi.

Von Feilitzen, C., & Carlsson, U. (2002). (Eds.), *Children, young people, and media globalisation*. Göteborg: The UNICEF International Clearinghouse on Children, Youth and Media.

Wasko, J. (2001). *Understanding Disney: The manufacture of fantasy*. Cambridge, MA: Polity Press.

Wellershof, I. (2014). Head of Fiction, ZDF, Germany, Interviewed by Jeanette Steemers, Munich, May 31, 2014.

White, C., & Preston, E. H. (2006). The spaces of children's programming. *Critical Studies in Media Communication*, 22(3), 239–255.

Whittingham, C. (2014). Amazon aims to bolster kids' originals, *C21* October 12, 2014, http://www.c21media.net/amazon-aims-to-bolster-kids-originals/ (Retrieved January 31, 2015).

4 Audiovisual Translation Trends

Growing Diversity, Choice, and Enhanced Localization

Frederic Chaume

Introduction

Audiovisual Translation is an academic umbrella term that covers all types of linguistic and semiotic transfers of audiovisual texts. At the end of the twentieth century, this activity was named after the main practices that it encapsulated at that time: dubbing, subtitling and voice-over. Both before and since then, scholars proposed other terms that either focused on one audiovisual translation mode or aimed to cover all transfers of audiovisual texts (Chaume, 2003). Some examples include film dubbing (Fodor, 1976), constrained translation (Titford, 1982), film translation (Snell-Hornby, 1988), screen translation (Mason, 1989), film and TV translation (Delabastita, 1989), media translation (Eguíluz et al., 1994), multimedia translation (Mateo, 2001), transadaptation (Gambier, 2003; Neves, 2005), and other hyponymic terms that refer to an actual practice or group of practices, such as revoicing, captioning, or sound synchronization. The same process was seen in languages other than English, with labels referring to film translation, subordinate translation, and the like, until the label audiovisual translation eventually became established once and for all in most languages.

The media industry is nowadays in transition. Digital technologies have accelerated the pace of change not only in film and TV production, but also in audiovisual translation. The industry is facing a turning point in consumer behavior. We are witnessing new approaches to advertising and branding, social networks, the blogosphere and impact of "citizen" journalism, intellectual property rights, digital cinema, video games, etc. In the realm of audiovisual translation, we are also witnessing new manifestations of translation activities such as crowdsourcing and community translation, the non-professional translation of (audiovisual) texts, fansubs and fandubs, new forms of free-commentary, such as the literal video versions, to mention only a few. Deuze (2007) claims that consumers' participation in the production process as co-creators has increased significantly in the last 10 years in fields as varied as journalism, TV and film production, advertising, and design and communication, among others. For example, citizen journalists reporting news through Twitter and Facebook have become a valuable source for TV news stations; "amateur photographers have the chance to offer royalty-free photos for sale through online photo stocks;

the crowdsourcing models of the fashion industry involve the consumers as part of the design process. The engagement of media consumers in media production highlights the emergence of user-generated content, not just as an addition to the industry-produced content but also as an important and necessary part of the industry's final product" (Orrego-Carmona, 2015). With all these possibilities available to the audience, some consumers have become active consumers or *prosumers* (Tapscott et al., 2006), since these changes have permitted them to assume part of the powers and responsibilities that traditionally fell in the hands of the producers. We are facing now, no doubt, the audience's turn.

This crucial role of digital technology carries with it a) more choice for audiences and a growing diversity in translation practices and b) enhanced forms of localization, such as transcreation. We are able to see these two simultaneous trends in audiovisual translation, both of which are a result of digitalization.

Therefore, in the age of digital technology, and in order to remain a valid theoretical concept, the notion of audiovisual translation needs to be wide enough to accept and include all new changes that arise in the audiovisual translation market. New changes in technology imply new audiovisual transfer modes or involve a combination of audiovisual transfer modes. In addition, classical audiovisual translation modes are sometimes so well defined that it is difficult to apply the same definition to new ways of transferring an audiovisual product. Audiovisual content crosses all borders thanks to audiovisual translation, but at the same time audiovisual translation keeps stretching its own borders to accommodate new ways of sending products abroad.

One interesting and completely new way of sending and selling audiovisual products abroad is transcreation. According to Fowler and Chozik (2007) in *The Wall Street Journal*, this new move consists of reinventing a character from a comic or an audiovisual product. But what does this reinvention involve? What really is transcreation? Is it not just another new label for simple translation? What is the difference between transcreation and domesticating translation? Does it have a hidden agenda to penetrate new markets as a kind of covert translation so that the audience does not realize that it is watching a translated foreign product? What is its distinctive feature, if indeed it has one?

Audiovisual Translation: New Audiences, New Demands

The term *audiovisual translation* is currently used as a hypernym that encompasses both well-established and new groundbreaking interlinguistic and intralinguistic screen translation practices such as dubbing, subtitling, surtitling, respeaking, audiosubtitling, voice-over and partial dubbing, simultaneous interpreting in film festivals, free-commentary, and Goblin translation, subtitling for the deaf and the hard of hearing, audiodescription for the blind and visually impaired, and fansubbing and fan dubbing (Chaume, 2012). Goblin translation, listed above, is a kind of domesticating voice-over named after the pseudonym of Dmitry Puchkov, an English-to-Russian movie and video game translator and script-writer, whose alternative voice-over translations of famous Hollywood movies are widely known both for their perceived profanity and humor. Some fascinating trends in the professional market indicate that dubbing countries are starting to take firm steps toward subtitling. Some subtitling countries are now beginning to experience the joy and ease of dubbing. European voice-over countries prefer to forget their recent past—which associates voice-over with Soviet regimes—in favor of dubbing and subtitling, whereas voice-over is knocking on the door of dubbing and subtitling countries and has won favor among teen audiences in Western countries, where it is increasingly used to translate reality shows. On the other hand, the same TV genres are translated differently in different countries (TV sitcoms dubbed or subtitled, depending on countries, or documentaries dubbed, subtitled, or voiced-over according to different countries). What is more shocking, the same TV genres are translated differently also in the same country: one can find the same films dubbed and subtitled according to different TV channels in many Latin American countries, and one can also find films dubbed and subtitled at the same time in the same language, in China, for example.

New genres, like videogames, comic books, corporate videos, infomercials, or webtoons, among others, are flooding the audiovisual market and also need audiovisual translation practices—and what is even more interesting, a combination of audiovisual translation practices—to cross country borders and reach audiences all over the world.

All of these audiovisual translation modes can be grouped into two big macro-modes: captioning and revoicing. This means that audiovisual texts are either translated by introducing a target text with the translation or reproduction of the dialogues and inserts on or next to the screen, (captioning) or by inserting a new soundtrack in a different language (revoicing), either canceling out the original soundtrack of the source language dialogues (dubbing) or leaving it in place (voice-over). In other words, the audiovisual text is either subtitled or revoiced.

The recent vigorous appearance of digital technology and the increase of digital telecommunication in the market and in our lives have forced audiences and market agents to reconsider the role of audiovisual translation modes in terms of audience appeal, choice, and commercial success. In addition to the new trends mentioned above, digital technology allows several audiovisual translation modes to be included in the same program: in dubbing countries on TV, for example, we can choose to watch a foreign film dubbed or subtitled (or dubbed and subtitled at the same time). We can also choose between dubbing, subtitling, and even voice-over when watching foreign programs on the Internet or between dubbing and subtitling when watching a DVD or Blu-Ray. Dubbing country audiences no longer need to complain that they cannot watch foreign films, TV series, cartoons, or documentaries in their original language, since nowadays almost everybody has the access and choice to watch most programs in their original languages and activate target language subtitles in almost all platforms.

Anyway, as happens with all major changes, there is still much to be done in order to fulfill the audience's needs. Great Britain, traditionally a subtitling country—although foreign cartoons and some other specific genres have always been dubbed for younger audiences—is beginning to face new challenges, as different audiences have started calling for new approaches to audiovisual translation. David Blunkett, a British labor party politician, was born blind due to a rare genetic disorder. He became an MP, Shadow Education Secretary, and eventually, in 2001, Home Secretary. In 2013, Blunkett accused TV executives of failing people with impaired vision (two million people in this country, according to RNIB) by not dubbing foreign dramas into English. Blunkett argued that in an aging population, people with hearing and sight impairments are increasingly part of the mainstream and are no longer a minority but a major sector of the public with the same rights as everyone else who pays the TV license fee. Blunkett also complained that old and blind people were frustrated with the lack of dubbing of foreign dramas and documentaries such as *The Killing* (Veena Sud, 2011–) and *Borgen* (Adam Price, 2010–), screened on BBC Four with English subtitles but not dubbed. Unfortunately, Blunkett's efforts haven't produced any change at all for the moment, but this is the first time that dubbing is urgently asked for in Great Britain.

Another significant example in the United Kingdom is the Royal National Institute of Blind People's (RNIB) claim that audiosubtitling (i.e., spoken subtitles) in addition to audio description would give greater access to blind or partially sighted people. Audiosubtitling is already successfully practiced in some European subtitling countries such as Finland, Norway, and The Netherlands, among others, and it could easily be introduced in the UK. The RNIB's statement in favor of audiosubtitling together with Blunkett's call for dubbing for the blind, the partially sighted, and the elderly population are two significant moves toward giving the audience the possibility to choose what to watch, when and where to watch it, and, especially, how to enjoy audiovisual creations.

In Great Britain too, in 2014, Lope de Vega's *Punishment without Revenge*, a tragedy written in 1631, was performed in Spanish with English surtitles. In many of these cases, the arrival of surtitles has made foreign-language productions truly accessible to those audiences who do not speak or understand enough to get by. Without surtitles many such shows would not attract an English-speaking audience.

These changes in cinema, theater, TV and DVD consumption, among others all over the world (Chaume, 2013), show that we are facing a new turn in the field of audiovisual translation: the audience's turn. The media broadcasters' monopoly is now over. What Pérez-González (2014) calls the demotic turn, a combination of the proliferation of participatory audiovisual translation and the democratization of access to digital technologies, has entered the world of audiovisual transfers. Broadcasters must pay heed to this shift, since the age of universal media broadcasting is gradually coming to a close. The choice between globalization and localization in translation activities is now not only in the hands of broadcasters and distributors, as it was in the past, but is also open to new audiences, valiantly demanding their rights and proclaiming their own tastes. On the one hand we have more choice thanks to digitalization. On the other hand we count on a strengthened audience, even able to interact with audiovisual products.

For example, according to a report by Nielsen Co. in 2015 there are already five million 'Zero TV' residences in the US, up from two million in 2007. The Nielsen Co started labeling people in this group 'Zero TV' households, because they fall outside the traditional definition of a TV home. A growing number of them have stopped paying for cable and satellite TV service and don't even use an antenna to get free signals over the air. According to the same report, youth as a whole are watching less TV, and the decline appears to be accelerating. These people are watching clips, shows, and movies on the Internet, sometimes via cell phone connections. And they now watch what they want to watch, when they want to watch it, and the way they want to watch it, something not permitted by traditional TV broadcasting. For example, in the field of audiovisual translation, young audiences may prefer to consume fansubs instead of traditional subtitles when watching a foreign video. Or voiced-over realities instead of dubbed ones. Or fandubs instead of dubbed cartoons. The days of decisions taken by just a few agents, used to dictating what audiences like and dislike, are progressively coming to an end.

Although this move *per se* does not entail a preference for localization, and although there is no explicit request for localization on behalf of local audiences, the fact that the power to choose is now in the hands of the audience obliges distributors and broadcasters to reinvent the approach to these new empowered audiences. Localization is simply one of these ways. One example of this is a kind of compromise between broadcasters and distributors on the one hand and audiences on the other: a new type of audiovisual translation known as transcreation.

Transcreation

A popular new term now on everyone's lips in the academic circles of Film Studies and Translation Studies is transcreation. As Bernal-Merino (2015: 88) puts it: "It is being increasingly used by a new wave of companies seeking to distance themselves from traditional translation firms. These new firms offer translation-like services that include not only translation but also creativity" (Yunker, 2005: 1). However, as this author also argues, creativity has always been a skill developed by translators and demanded by distributors and broadcasters. When translating cartoons, teen pics, and some comedies, for example, translators have traditionally used their creativity, intentionally moving away from literal renderings that would sign the death knell for these programs. Creativity is essential for effective audiovisual text transfers. The problem is the notion and the scope of the term translation: if one understands translation in a strict, straight-jacketed way, as it was understood in the past, then it is true that audiovisual translation in general, and transcreation in particular, go beyond the limits of this concept. But nowadays no one sticks to this narrow old-fashioned definition of translation: after all the research done in Translation Studies over the past 40 years, considering translation as a literal rendering can even be considered as an insult to our discipline. Creativity and translation, in particular in the audiovisual and literary fields, go hand in hand.

However, transcreation goes beyond linguistic creativity. It is a form of enhanced localization that encompasses the adaptation of non-linguistic codes to the supposed likes of the target audience, especially the musical code and the iconographic and graphic codes (Chaume, 2012). In 2014, the Disney XD channel ran the episodes of the third season of the famous Japanese anime *Doraemon* (Kozo Kusuba, 2005–), about an eponymous robotic cat who travels back in time from the 22nd century to help a preteen boy named Nobita Nobi. The anime was adapted, transcreated, for America's culture and customs—not for Europe and Australia, for example—according to its strict guidelines on violence, renderings of discrimination, and depictions of sexual content.

This adaptation involved reinventing some particular features of the cartoon, and these features belong to certain filmic codes. Which cinematic codes were reinvented, or manipulated, then, in this well-known transcreation? In the first place, from a narratological point of view, the adaptation moved the setting from Japan to a fictional town in America. Second, in order to explain the premise of the story, a preliminary narration explaining why Doraemon came from the future was added, maybe because the new producers felt that American children lacked the necessary background to understand the story, whereas it was clear to Japanese children.

Although the robot cat Doraemon kept his original name, some of the other names were changed: Doraemon's owner Nobita became Noby, the bully Gian became Big G (Gian's original name is a wordplay on the English word *giant*), and the spoiled kid Suneo was mutated into Sneech to recall the word *sneer*. Most of Doraemon's gadgets were translated literally: The magical portal Dokodemo Door is now the Anywhere Door; the flying Takecopter is called the Hopter; the memorization tool Anki Pan is now Memory Bread; and Honyaku Konnyaku was translated as Translation Gummy. Therefore, proper names were adapted slightly to make them easier to understand for American children and also to convey the characters' personalities (Sneech/Sneer), physical appearance (Big G), or simply by means of linguistic domestication—the affectionate form Noby is more American than the foreign word Nobita, because it sounds like an American nickname, a true hypocoristic. Interestingly enough from the perspective of polysystem theory, the recent English edition of the manga also has similar names. Therefore, the flow between systems goes from audiovisual to written texts in this case, in the opposite direction from what used to be typical in the past.

However, other changes and edits were also made to bring the show closer to an American audience, such as Japanese text being replaced with English text on certain objects like notices and graded exams. Written text on screen was adapted, and many Japanese signs were replaced; *Gōda Shōten* (Gōda's Shop) became *Goda's Goods*, for example. Elsewhere, a stand selling *ishiyaki imo* (sweet potatoes baked on stones) was replaced by a popcorn truck. Captions and texts on screen were therefore translated or adapted so children did not have to see incomprehensible Japanese letters and words. This can be considered as authentic domestication, moving toward self-protection and blocking out foreign influences and values. Under the premise that this kind of manipulation must take place in order to make it easier for American children to empathize with the original product, distributors shape foreign models and references into what they think the target audience will like to watch.

But the manipulation did not stop there, at the linguistic level. The transcreation process also involved on-screen edits and additions: yen notes were replaced by US dollar notes; om-rice (omelet with rice) was turned into pancakes, and chopsticks were changed to forks.

Figure 4.1 Doraemon, yen notes replaced by US dollar notes

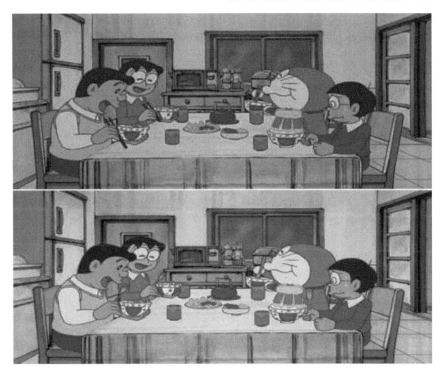

Figure 4.2 Doraemon, chopsticks replaced with forks

Iconicity is also a big issue in audiovisual translation. An audiovisual text is a semiotic construct woven by a series of signifying codes that operate simultaneously to produce meaning. A film, a cartoon, or a documentary is made up of a series of codified signs, articulated in accordance with conventional editing rules. The way the audiovisual text is organized and the meaning of all its elements results in a semantic structure that the spectator deconstructs in order to understand the meanings of the text. The interest for the translator, and especially for the researcher, lies in disentangling the meaning and functioning of each of these codes and the possible impact of all signs, linguistic and non-linguistic, on translation operations. But these translation operations would make sense in what has been considered, to date, to be a proper translation, an interlinguistic translation. In transcreation there is interlinguistic translation, but there is also intersemiotic translation, a kind of semiotic adaptation.

For example, in this new *American* Doraemon, as the webpage Anime News Network (2014) explains, Japanese check marks were replaced with American crosses to indicate mistakes in a test, and an 'F' letter grade was added to better explain the '0' mark.

In another episode, Nobita's waterfalls of tears were deleted from the image.

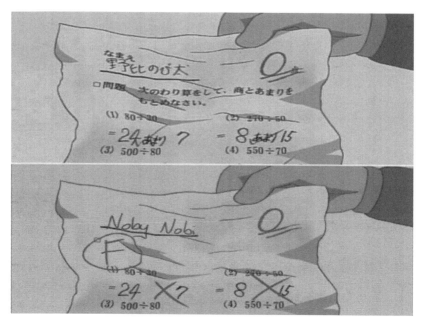

Figure 4.3 Doraemon, Japanese check marks replaced with American crosses

Figure 4.4 Doraemon, Nobita's waterfalls of tears deleted for the US version

Other food-related changes, such as fewer sweets and more on-screen fruit, were introduced to promote healthy eating in children's TV programs; even Doraemon's iconic and quintessential *dorayaki* was removed. Since Doraemon has no ears, he gets angry when people often mistake him for a raccoon dog in the original story. However, as raccoon dogs outside Japan do not look round and fat as they do in Japanese folklore, Doraemon is mistaken for a seal in the English transcreated version (Anime News Network, 2014).

The acoustic channel gives us access to dialogues (linguistic code) and particular suprasegmental features—intonation, stress, the various tones of voice, and features like whispering, breathiness, huskiness, and nasality that can be used by speakers to affect the meaning of utterances (paralinguistic code)—that constitute an important source of meaning for understanding the on-screen characters' intentions, ideology, and power relations. Paralinguistic features have been replaced in this new American Doraemon, and dialogue is also not just literally translated but adapted to make it more entertaining and to fit a natural speaking rhythm, as in the case of most audiovisual products. Therefore, linguistic and paralinguistic codes have been translated with a flair of creativity, not exclusive to transcreation, but part of all audiovisual translations.

Music (musical codes), however, can also convey substantial meaning and may be significant to the plot. Both songs and incidental music form part of the musical code, another meaning code transmitted through the acoustic channel. In this localized Doraemon, the theme song, other songs, and even sound effects have been adapted to make it easier for American children to empathize. For example, the American song sounds like fast-paced electronic music, and the opening sequence has many more frames and many more frames per second.

There are many examples of transcreation on today's screens and comic books all over the world. Spider-Man, a superhero from New York City, already well-known in India, was also transcreated as a young Indian hero. Peter Parker was renamed Pavitr Prabhakar, a phonetic distortion of Peter Parker. He lives in Mumbai—the whole city landscape has changed. He wears a traditional Indian dhoti, and he fights a demon from Indian mythology. All names in the Indian comic resemble those of the original version: Meera Jain is Mary Jane Watson, Auntie Maya is Aunt May, Uncle Bhim is Uncle Ben, Aadi is Eddie Brock, Hari Oberoi is Harry Osborn, and so forth. Like in the localization of Doraemon, names are adapted to the tastes and traditions of the target culture. But in this case, the flow has changed direction, going the other way from English to another language, Hindi in this case. Such a change might indicate cultural sensitivity on the part of Marvel at first sight. To take an American social icon and recontextualize him with an eye to local interests, themes, and issues may seem a progressive and sensitive move. However, there may be other reasons behind this move: when the first Spider-Man movie opened in India, it took 67m rupees (£940,000) in its first four days of release, and made more in its first weekend than any Hollywood movie yet released in India, according to BBC

News (24/06/2004). It is also therefore clearly part of a major effort to capitalize on its potential Indian audience.

As in the case of Doraemon, the localization or transcreation process is no guarantee of success. Spider-Man is not only a hero who constantly swings from one skyscraper to another. He is also an urban-dwelling American, and the topics of justice, individual responsibility and collective freedom the comic has always dealt with are particularly Western in nature, just as Doraemon's values have a totally Eastern background. Relocating him in a different culture is not so easy, and for many fans it can erode the foundations on which the essence of the character was built. In this sense, Marvel does not seem to be translating a comic but creating a new character out of the successful and well-known features of a previous one. Although it was a short venture in comic, it traveled to videogame format, under the name of Spider-Man Unlimited (Gameloft), a cross-media process worth analyzing.

Another example of transcreation, but now only from the aesthetic point of view, is the Japanese version of *The Powerpuff Girls* (Craig McCracken, 1998–2005), who are immediately recognizable to North-American audiences by their big round heads and small bodies. However, the Powerpuff Girls showed up in Japan with a totally new look: the heroines had grown up and developed long legs and wore mini-skirts. When the real Powerpuff Girls first aired in Japan, the cartoon failed to attract a wide audience. Producers therefore localized the characters to fit Japanese tastes.

The same happened with other animated TV shows, but some of them also have a didactic function, i.e., they are adapted in order to teach social skills and moral values. *Sesame Street* (Samuel Gibbon & Jon Stone, 1969–) in India swapped Big Bird for Boombah, an aristocratic lion fond of *bhangra*, a Bollywood dancing style. Producers and distributors are also creating new characters to connect with particular audiences: Takalani Sesame in South Africa, for example, features a five-year-old HIV-positive girl called Kami, orphaned by AIDS. In an area where AIDS is epidemic, Kami is intended to confront issues related to HIV-positive children in a way that helps them understand this terrible problem (see Calbreath-Frasieur in this collection for more). *Dora the Explorer* (Chris Gifford, 2000–), the Hispanic cartoon girl who teaches Spanish to American children, now teaches English around the world without being redrawn, other than the occasional wardrobe change typical of each country, as in China, for example. The world of merchandizing and publicity has produced transcreations of many popular cartoon characters, like the transcreation of Minnie Mouse in China, redrawn with smaller eyes, a tiny mouth, and a look that resembles Hello Kitty rather than the original Disney character.

Transcreation in the audiovisual world is normally linked with the world of publicity, with commercials, simply because there sometimes it is taken for granted that some advertisements have to be linguistically and semiotically manipulated to be effective in foreign cultures. A commercial can be dubbed, voiced-over and subtitled—and even not translated at all when the company behind it wants to explicitly show the foreignness of the product and wants the audience to feel that foreignness. Although there are numerous examples, they will not be dealt with here since the focus of this chapter is on fiction: films, TV series, and cartoons. But, for example, in Spain *L'Oréal* and *Ferrero Rocher* commercials are dubbed, products shown in teleshopping programs are voiced-over, *Nespresso* and *Volkswagen* commercials are subtitled, and *Jean Paul Gaultier* and *Dolce & Gabbana* perfume advertisements are usually not translated. On a graded continuum of the translation of commercials, the strategy known as *no translation* would be at the end of the foreignizing pole, followed by *subtitling*, then *voice-over,* and finally *dubbing* at the end of the domesticating pole. Transcreation goes a step further.

Sometimes the important question is not precisely to show the product's foreignness, but how close the product comes to the target audience's needs. In the past most adverts and commercials were locally, regionally, or nationally produced, and there were relatively few international brands that did not localize their ads but now do. It is here that transcreation plays its part in the world of advertising. As consumer behavior becomes more sophisticated (Gobé, 2001), it leads to a change in marketing strategy with a greater focus on emotional value—*emotional branding*. These changes in consumer behavior and marketing strategies have implications on translation as well (Ho, 2004), one of them being making a step further in traditional audiovisual translation modes toward transcreation (Pedersen, 2014).

Thus, creative agencies are increasingly being commissioned to localize the products to the target culture and environment through new transcreated adverts. These new commercials shift away from the form and content of the original. Sony, Nestlé, BP, Costa, and Harrods are just some of the big companies to commission transcreations for their adverts. And transcreation in the world of publicity is not restricted to audiovisual products. It also involves print advertising, outdoor advertising, TV commercials and videos, radio spots, in-store promotion, packaging, websites, content marketing, publishing, and major presentations: a whole world of new transfer modes in new and old kinds of media, conveyed through visual and acoustic channels and written and oral registers.

Following the same line of thought, but in a different audiovisual genre, Mangiron and O'Hagan (2006:20) postulate the term transcreation to describe what takes place in videogame localization, because "localisers are granted *quasi* absolute freedom to modify, omit, and even add any elements which they deem necessary to bring the game closer to the players and to convey the original feel of gameplay". This is really enlightening, because by adding elements the authors mean adding icons and written text to the images. This gives us leeway to connect transcreation with the semiotics of film. The theory of filmic codes comes into play.

A Semiotic Approach to Transcreation: The Relationship Between Linguistic and Non-Linguistic Codes

The filmic codes theory, that is an approach to audiovisual translation based on filmic narrative and the semiotics of film, is founded on the writings of Christian Metz (1974), among others, and the so-called Film Semiotics School. A pioneer in the field, Christian Metz applied insights from structural linguistics to the language of film. A film is considered to be an instance of a structured language, arranged in codes and sub-codes, within the universe of signs. In the field of audiovisual translation, some scholars, such as Chaume (2004 and 2012), Ramière (2006 and 2010), Martínez Sierra (2008), Chapado (2010), and Martínez Tejerina (2012), among others, claim that the linguistic code, despite its predominant role in any audiovisual text, is but one more code at work in the construction and later transfer of meaning in audiovisual texts. It is of special interest for the translator to observe the interaction between all the signifying codes, since this interaction singles out the semantic potential of the audiovisual text and its texture or grammaticality. Awareness of all the filmic codes involved in the audiovisual text is extremely helpful, especially when the linguistic code is no longer the only code that can be manipulated—transcreation goes beyond traditional audiovisual translation because in digital files all codes can be manipulated. A translation that does not take all the codes into account can only be regarded as a partial translation, and that is why transcreation can be equated to translation in its ideal, originally intended sense.

The relationship between image and word—the interplay of the signification systems of audiovisual texts—materializes in terms of cohesion and coherence between the two simultaneous narratives, the visual and the acoustic, in such a way that the translator is obliged to employ translation strategies that can transmit not only the information contained in each narrative and each code—as noted throughout this chapter—but the meaning that emerges as a result of this interaction. This results in an added value (Chion, 1993) or an extra meaning (Fowler, 1986: 69) that goes beyond the mere sum of the two narratives. In transcreation, translated words match translated images, they are coherent; target language dialogues are uttered by target characters, with target culture names, wearing target culture clothes, eating target culture food, and paying with target culture money.

Translation problems emerge when the meaning conveyed by all acoustic and visual codes and the linguistic (or paralinguistic) code interact, either because they do match or because they do not. This is the true nature of audiovisual translation: code interaction. Problems arise when we hear, see, or hear and see, simultaneously, two or more signs that refer to each other. In the case of two signs transmitted by means of different codes, the track containing the dialogues is usually modified. Transcreation overcomes this constraint, since it minimizes this kind of problem generated by code interaction. The manipulation of images and sounds smooths out the semiotic noise that some dubbings and subtitlings produce. Transcreation puts all codes at the same level: all codes can now be manipulated in order to localize the product. The term translation is wide enough to include what transcreation means and implies.

Conclusions

The advent of digital technology has provided ubiquitous entertainment, communications, and online connectivity. This radical change has also implied more choice for audiences and a growing diversity in translation practices. Digitalization has also promoted what can be labeled as enhanced forms of localization, such as transcreation. Transcreation, then, goes beyond traditional audiovisual translation because it includes iconic manipulation. In the early nineties, Zabalbeascoa (1993) claimed that visual manipulation is also sometimes advisable when translating texts with images. He mentioned *The Benny Hill Show* (Benny Hill, 1955–1991) as one of the audiovisual texts that needed localization in some target cultures. Benny Hill also composed and sang patter songs and often entertained his audience with lengthy high-speed double-entendre rhymes and songs, which he recited or sang in a single take. In the period when the show was aired in Spain, for example, comedy monologues were not so popular as they are nowadays. Zabalbeascoa argued that Hill's lengthy monologues were not funny for the Spanish audience simply because Spaniards were not used to this genre—as they are now—and advocated removing them from the Spanish dubbing, a somewhat daring suggestion for the time. Seeing how transcreation has now spread across the globe, Zabalbeascoa's proposals were the germ of contemporary transcreation in the realm of audiovisual translation.

  In conclusion, transcreation is the translation of almost all meaning codes of an audiovisual text. Traditional audiovisual translation modes were limited to the transfer of dialogues (linguistic code), the transfer of human sounds (paralinguistic code), the transfer of some lyrics in songs (musical code), and especially in the past and in the case of dubbing, the transfer or addition of some special effects (special effects code). Translators could not manipulate images. It was not done. It was forbidden. It was an offence to a work of art. Creativity was reduced to the manipulation of sound codes conveyed through the acoustic channel. Transcreation now allows translators to be part of the creative process and constitutes a step beyond traditional audiovisual translation, as it includes the translation—the transfer, the manipulation—of visual codes. Readers and spectators see and watch new icons, new indexes, new symbols, new lighting, new body movements, new shots, new text on screen, even new editing in a transcreated product. It is an extreme case of domestication, a good example of localization, a target-oriented translation that does not limit itself to the rendering of the linguistic code, but that is open to changing the whole product, while maintaining the basic features of the original one, those features that the distributor is not willing to sacrifice so that the product can still be fully recognized in the target culture. Audiovisual translation theory can accept the term transcreation when it is applied to those translations where visual codes are also adapted to the target culture.

According to Bernal-Merino (2006):

> [...] we could even say that all translations are transcreations since they require a certain degree of creativity on the translators' part, although they are not creating anything from scratch but from a very clear source. 'Transcreation' might be a good term in the sense that it acknowledges the fact that it is consciously replacing text and references deemed too culturally specific. It is a translation that completely tilts the balance towards the target audience but claims to be the same product, despite those differences. From the developers' point of view, they are maximizing their investment in the form of one basic design and multiple different finishes depending on the local taste. It is the same basic principle that companies apply to cars, computers, or magazines. So, could Translation Studies accommodate 'transcreation'? It seems to me that there is a lack of consistency. I do not think we can establish a clear definition or that, indeed, Translation Studies would gain anything by embracing this term.

In fact, Bernal-Merino equates transcreation with translation. If scholars can broaden out the concept of translation quickly enough, then the term transcreation will not be necessary. When subtitling for the deaf was welcomed into academic circles as an intralinguistic practice, and audiodescription for the blind as an intersemiotic practice, in the realm of audiovisual translation, the whole discipline had to admit that translation was no longer an interlinguistic exchange. Now, if we react quickly to these new market processes that include visual code manipulation in order to make the product even more acceptable to target audiences, our discipline will not need the term transcreation as a new concept, because the term translation, in itself, would embrace the translation of icons, of indexes, of symbols, of body language, of shots, etc. For the time being, though, transcreation is a useful term to indicate translations that involve visual manipulation, the localization of visual codes, the adaptation of costumes, food, money, body language, physical appearance, and any other cinematic code to the likes and cultural background of the target culture.

References

Anime News Network. (2014). Doraemon's anime visual & script changes for U.S. TV detailed, available online at: http://www.animenewsnetwork.com/news/2014-05-11/doraemon-anime-visual-and-script-changes-for-u.s-tv-detailed (Retrieved July 13, 2015).

BBC News. (2004). Spider-Man gets Indian make-over, available online at: http://news.bbc.co.uk/2/hi/entertainment/3836797.stm (Retrieved July 13, 2015).

Bernal-Merino, M. A. (2006). On the translation of videogames. *Jostrans,* 6, 22–36, available online at: http://www.jostrans.org/issue06/art_bernal.php (Retrieved April 6, 2015).

Bernal-Merino, M. A. (2015). *Translation and localisation in video games.* London and New York: Routledge.

Chapado, M. (2010). La audiodescriptibilidad del film: una nueva perspectiva de análisis fílmico. *Frame,* 6, 159–195, available online at: http://fama2.us.es/fco/frame/frame6/estudios/1.9.pdf (Retrieved April 6, 2015).

Chaume, F. (2003). *Doblatge i subtitulació per a la TV.* Vic: Eumo Editorial.

Chaume, F. (2004). *Cine y traducción.* Madrid: Cátedra.

Chaume, F. (2012). *Audiovisual translation: Dubbing.* London and New York: Routledge.

Chaume, F. (2013). The turn of audiovisual translation. New audiences and new technologies. *Translation Spaces,* 2, 105–123.

Chion, M. (1993). *Cómo se escribe un guión.* Madrid: Cátedra.

Delabastita, D. (1989). Translation and mass-communication: Film and TV translation as evidence of cultural dynamics. *Babel,* 35(4), 193–218.

Deuze, M. (2007). *Media work.* Cambridge: Polity.

Eguíluz, F., Merino, R., Olsen, V., Pajares, E., & Santamaría, J. M. (1994). (Eds.), *Transvases Culturales: Literatura, Cine, Traducción.* Vitoria: Universidad del País Vasco.

Fodor, I. (1976). *Film Dubbing: Phonetic, Semiotic, Esthetic and Psychological Aspects.* Hamburg: Helmut Buske.

Fowler G. A., & Chozick, A. (2007). Cartoon characters get big makeover for overseas fans. *The Wall Street Journal,* available online at: http://www.wsj.com/articles/SB119247837839459642 (Retrieved April 6, 2015).

Fowler, R. (1986). *Linguistic criticism.* London: Oxford University Press.

Gambier, Y. (2003). Introduction. Screen transadaptation: Perception and reception. *The Translator,* 9(2), 171–189.

Gobé, M. (2001). *Emotional branding; the new paradigm for connecting brands to people.* New York: Allworth Press.

Ho, G. (2004). Translating advertisements across heterogeneous cultures. *The Translator: Studies in Intercultural Communication,* 10(2), 221–243.

Mangiron, C., & O'Hagan, M. (2006). Game localisation: Unleashing imagination with "restricted" translation. *Jostrans,* 6, 10–21, available online at: http://www.jostrans.org/issue06/art_ohagan.php (Retrieved April 6, 2015).

Martínez Sierra, J. J. (2008). *Humor y Traducción: Los Simpson cruzan la frontera.* Castellón de la Plana: Universitat Jaume I.

Martínez Tejerina, A. (2012). La interacción de los códigos en doblaje: juegos de palabras y restricciones visuales. *MonTI,* 4, 155–180.

Mason, I. (1989). Speaker meaning and reader meaning: Preserving coherence in screen translating. In R. Kolmel & J. Payne (Eds.), *Babel. The cultural and linguistic barriers between nations* (pp. 13–24). Aberdeen: Aberdeen University Press.

Mateo, M. (2001). Performing musical texts in a target language: the case of Spain. *Across Languages and Cultures,* 2(1), 31–50.

Metz, C. (1974). *Film language: A semiotics of cinema.* Oxford and Chicago: Oxford University Press and University of Chicago Press.

Neves, J. (2005). Audiovisual translation: Subtitling for the deaf and hard-of-hearing. Unpublished PhD Thesis. University of Roehampton, UK, available online at: http://roehampton.openrepository.com/roehampton/bitstream/10142/12580/1/neves%20audiovisual.pdf (Retrieved April 6, 2015).

The Nielsen Company. (2015). The total audience report: Q1 2015, available online at: http://www.nielsen.com/us/en/insights/reports/2015/the-total-audience-report-q1-2015.html (Retrieved July 13, 2015).

Orrego-Carmona, D. (2015). *The reception of (non)professional subtitling.* Unpublished PhD Thesis. Universitat Rovira i Virgili, Spain. April, 2015.

Pedersen, D. (2014). Exploring the concept of transcreation–transcreation as 'more than translation'? *Cultus. The Journal of Intercultural Mediation and Communication, 7,* 57–71.

Pérez-González, L. (2014). *Audiovisual translation: Theories, methods and issues.* London and New York: Routledge.

Ramière, N. (2006). Reaching a foreign audience: Cultural transfers in audiovisual translation. *Jostrans,* 6, 152–166, available online at: http://www.jostrans.org/issue06/art_ramiere.php (Retrieved April 6, 2015).

Ramière, N. (2010). Are you "lost in translation" (when watching a foreign film)? Towards an alternative approach to judging audiovisual translation. *Australian Journal of French Studies,* 47(1), 100–115.

Snell-Hornby, M. (1988). *Translation studies. An interdiscipline.* Amsterdam and Philadelphia: John Benjamins.

Tapscott, D., & Williams, A. D. (2006). *Wikinomics: How mass collaboration changes everything.* New York: Portfolio.

Titford, C. (1982). Subtitling-Constrained translation. *Lebende Sprachen,* 27(3), 113–116.

Yunker, J. (2005). Transcreation gaining momentum, *Global by Design. Adventures in Web Localisation,* available online at: http://www.globalbydesign.com/2005/06/21/transcreation-gaining-momentum/ (Retrieved April 6, 2015).

Zabalbeascoa, P. (1993). *Developing translationsStudies to better account for audiovisual texts and other new forms of text production.* Unpublished PhD Thesis. Universitat de Lleida, Spain.

5 Transformations of *Montalbano* through Languages and Media

Adapting and Subtitling Dialect in *The Terracotta Dog*

Dionysios Kapsaskis and Irene Artegiani

Introduction: Montalbano as Intertext

The literary and media phenomenon of *Il Commissario Montalbano* is a vast and complex one. The success of Andrea Camilleri's novels is global, with 21 titles of the *Montalbano* series published in Italy, of which 16 have now been translated in over 30 languages. TV adaptation by RAI began in 1999, and *Montalbano* was soon extensively discussed on the Internet and other media such as the press, radio, and even comic books. In Italy, the series has become the nation's favorite, while also receiving consistently high critical praise (Buonanno, 2000: 334–35). The TV series has been dubbed or subtitled in 16 countries. In the UK, the TV series was first aired as *Inspector Montalbano* in 2008, and all nine seasons and 26 episodes of the original RAI productions had been broadcast by the end of 2013.

There has been plenty of scholarly interest on various cultural and linguistic aspects of *Montalbano* (Vitale, 2001; Pistelli, 2003; Serkowska, 2006; Vietina, 2010). The present article is concerned with the *transformations* of Montalbano as a character, rather than the static features of each of his incarnations. Its purpose is to identify some of the ways in which the series and its protagonist evolved as they progressed from the novelistic form to the televisual one and from an Italian to an international audience. This investigation will be conducted through the single prism of the translation of Sicilian dialect, which is one of the main characteristics of the stories as a whole and the eponymous character in particular. We will concentrate on one of the first Montalbano novels, *Il cane di terracotta* (Camilleri, 1996), as well as on the script and the English subtitles of the respective TV episode, while the English translation of the novel by Andrea Sartarelli (Camilleri, 2002) will serve mainly as a reference.

The processes of remediation and internationalization to which Montalbano as a cultural product has been subjected can be considered as forms of translation, in the broad sense that first Jakobson (1959/2000) gave the term, which includes intersemiotic transfers in addition to linguistic ones. As Gianfranco Marrone has argued, Montalbano exists beyond literary or TV narratives, in a series of discourses (reviews, interviews, paratexts, and

images), which retrospectively transform his textual or mediatic incarnations, problematizing what appears to be a linear progress from source to
target texts. Drawing on Levi-Strauss's structural analysis of myth, Marrone
notes that in the case of Montalbano there is a myth-like structure that
continuously feeds back on itself and that ultimately "coincides with the
network of translations/betrayals from one version to another, both in time
and in space" (Marrone, 2003: 28).[1] The literary/televisual/media persona
of Montalbano thus appears to be living in the mode of translation, as a
concatenation of translational acts and impacts. "In this sense, *the character
does not live in a single text* or in a generic context with no textual links;
*it rather lives and feeds itself in the intertextual network in which it is con-
stantly being retranslated*" (Marrone, 2003: 28, emphasis in the original).
Foregrounding the intertextuality and the translatability of Montalbano
allows for a comparative investigation of the way in which images, sounds,
texts, and paratexts affect each other, contributing to a complex cultural
product that partly eschews authorial management and control. In a more
general sense, along with broadening the concept of translation to include
non-linguistic transfers and adaptations, such a comparative approach also
applies to other complex literary and media phenomena that are similar to
Montalbano. As this article will suggest, such phenomena invest equally on
local attachments and global flows and spread eagerly across texts, images,
and media, thus transcending traditional analytical categories such as the
'truthfulness' of the narrative, the 'authenticity' of the cultural references, or
the 'essence' of the characters.

Within the broader discussion of the intertextual representations of Montalbano, the interlingual translations of the novels and the TV series are of
special importance. This is not only because linguistic transfer entails negotiations and reinterpretations of meaning, but also because every new translation is inscribed within a new (inter)national framework and adds new levels
of textuality to the already complex intertext. This is particularly true when
it comes to the so-called *sicilianità* of the *Montalbano* novels and TV series;
that is, the marked presence of local cultural, literary, and socio-political references and the systematic foregrounding of the local dialect. The presence
of the *sicilianità* in Camilleri's novels has been highlighted by critics and
scholars alike, and its role as a feature that lends authenticity to the narratives has been pointed out (Pezzotti, 2012: 125–46). Arguably, it constitutes
one of the major reasons for Montalbano's success both within Italy and
internationally. It also forms part of the identity of the main character of the
novels and TV series, crucially through his peculiar use of local dialect, as
we will discuss further down. However, the *sicilianità* and its attendant effect
of authenticity are felt in different ways depending on whether one is reading the novels in the source language or in translation, or indeed whether
one is watching the TV series with or without subtitles or dubbing. It is
precisely the comparative study of the ways in which authenticity is sought
through the translation of *sicilianità* that allows us to explore some of the

characterological transformations of Montalbano. By choosing to examine these transformations through the translation of local dialect, we are dealing not simply with a linguistic phenomenon (albeit a quite challenging one), but with a crucial 'authenticating' feature of the Montalbano intertext. The presence and variations of dialect are suggestive of authorial intentions and narrative agendas, as much as of translation and adaptation strategies. The translation of dialect is important insofar as it affects individual character perceptions too. Thus, the questions that we will be asking in this article include the following: What is the effect of the use of Sicilian dialect in the original Italian novels? How is dialect used as part of *sicilianità* in the TV series, and to what extent does it survive in the subtitles? Finally, how is the unity of Montalbano's character affected by these complex transformations, and how does it emerge specifically in and through the English subtitles?

The storyline of *Il cane di terracotta*, the novel and TV episode on which we shall focus, is among the most emotional ones of the series. Montalbano is shot by a Mafia family while trying to disentangle a mystery that involves historical memory and personal trauma in addition to the more common themes of amorous passion, greediness, and revenge. The book was the second in the series to be published in Italy, in 1996. Like the rest of the Montalbano novels, the book was translated into English by Stephen Sartarelli and published in 2002 as *The Terracotta Dog* (Camilleri, 2002). The TV episode was broadcast on RAI in 2000 and on BBC4 with subtitles for the first time in 2012, with the title *The Mystery of the Terracotta Dog*. For the current article, we use the Acorn Media UK DVD edition of 2012, which does not specify the name of the subtitler.

Sicilian Dialect Through Languages and Media

The Montalbano Book Series and Italiano Bastardo

For the Italian audience, language is one of the most prominent points when discussing the success behind the Montalbano book series, while a foreign reader/viewer is not necessarily aware of its particularity. As translator Sartarelli and a number of scholars have pointed out, most characters speak a mixture of Sicilian dialect and standard Italian (Sartarelli, 2004; De Meo, 2010: 23; Serkowska, 2006: 164–165; McRae, 2011: 235 ff.; Taffarel, 2012). This hybridized language was defined by Camilleri himself in *Il cane di terracotta* as "italiano bastardo" (Camilleri, 1996: 54, but see also Filipponi, 2002). It is a mixture of standard Italian and Sicilian, showing a pattern of everyday communication whereby standard Italian is used in more formal occasions and usually to express ideas and thoughts, while Sicilian is used in less formal contexts, often to convey feelings and emotions (Tomaiuolo, 2009: 6).

Salvo Montalbano's character also speaks different varieties of language "according to his interlocutors in order to put himself on the same plane"

(McRae, 2011: 82). Overall, it is possible to identify four linguistic variations that are—to a greater or lesser extent—evident to the Italian readership and TV audience. First, the "pure" Sicilian dialect is generally used with elderly or lower-class people, out of respect and to ensure mutual understanding. Second, the *italiano bastardo*, a medium-strength dialect is used by the narrator and the inspector in most occasions. Third, standard Italian, in formal situations and with non-Sicilian characters. And fourth the bureaucratic register is what Montalbano speaks when dealing with self-important high-status characters such as politicians or authorities (McRae, 2011: 82). In each of these cases, Montalbano makes use of the relevant linguistic variety in order to understand and be understood properly, to gain trust and obtain information, or occasionally, as in the case of over-bureaucratic Italian, to mock his interlocutor.

From the Novels to the TV Series

Some research has been conducted on the characterological modifications undergone by the hero in the transition from bestselling *giallo* to prime-time television series. These modifications go beyond the formal constraints imposed by the different mediums, and respond to audience expectations, economic imperatives, and other extratextual factors. Marrone has described how Camilleri has created an essentially different character for the TV series: "Montalbano as a television character is visibly much younger and fitter than his literary counterpart, the places where he lives and works are more beautiful and dramatic, and the people around him are stereotypically more Sicilian" (Marrone, 2004: 4). The tensions between the literary and the TV versions of Montalbano point to the hypothesis that there is no stable set of features that can be attributed to the main character; instead, there are translations and interpretations where various forces and tendencies are at play, including the tendency to domesticate or foreignize the original text. These two concepts, borrowed from Lawrence Venuti's work on translation strategies, define the extent to which the traces of the translation process remain visible in the translated text (Venuti, 2008). Domestication involves eradication by the translator of those signs that indicate untranslatability or subjective interpretation, so that the target text tends to read as fluently as if it were originally written in the target language. At the other end of the spectrum, foreignization entails an effort to retain in the target text those linguistic, textual, cultural, or pragmatic elements that point to differences and gaps between source and target languages. If we apply this distinction at the level of TV adaptation, then choosing between these two strategies would mean, among other things, deciding whether to highlight the originally literary character of Montalbano, whether to resist the tendency to follow TV detective series stereotypes about on-screen action, sex appeal of the hero, attractiveness or the settings and the locales, etc. For Venuti, it is ethically preferable to follow a foreignizing attitude in translating (Venuti,

1995/2008). For our purposes, however, the emphasis is not on evaluation but on the identification of the strategy followed. To that effect, we examined whether the use of dialect as a narrative device is evident in the TV adaptation of *Il cane di Terracotta*. As the following analysis suggests, it is suppressed to a considerable degree, indicating an effort to domesticate the audiovisual text, that is, to make it culturally and linguistically easier to process.

Dialectal expressions are reduced, often toned down, and simplified in the dialogue, so as not to sound too alien to an Italian audience. The Italian viewer is not required to make as much effort as in reading the novels but can clearly recognize the Sicilian intonation. Nevertheless, it is evident from the TV series as well that Montalbano adopts different registers of language, from standard Italian to strong dialect. In spite of the elimination of considerable parts of Sicilian dialect, an average Italian audience can clearly understand the difference between the linguistic variety Montalbano uses with his non-Sicilian girlfriend Livia (standard Italian), with the long-time mafia boss Tano (stronger dialect and intonation), and with his boss, the police commissioner (light dialect and intonation).

As in the book series, dialect is often used when conveying emotions. The linguistic changes brought about by the change in medium could imply an intention to boost comprehensibility at the expense of emotional depth, as we can see in the passage of the death of Tano, where the dialectal terms and their translation are highlighted in bold (see Table 5.1).

Table 5.1 Adaptation of dialect in the TV episode

Novel	*Italian TV script*
Tano: **Mi scanto.** Montalbano: **Non t'affruntari**, non ti vergognare a dirlo. **Magari** per questo tu sei un **omo**. Tutti ci **scanteremo** a questo passo.	Tano: **Aio, aio** paura Montalbano: Non ti vergonare a dirlo. Tutti abbiamo paura a questo passo.
Sartarelli's translation	*Literal translation of the script*
- I'm spooked. - **You needn't be ashamed** to say so. It's **one more** thing that makes you a man. We'll all be **scared** when our time comes.	- **I'm ... I'm** scared. - Don't be ashamed to say so. We're all scared at this stage.

The omission of most dialectal elements in the TV version of *Il cane di terracotta* is important, not least because this is an emotional story—the second book of the series, in which Camilleri's effort at building Montalbano's identity is palpable. In addition to emotional depth, dialect in this scene suggests Montalbano's connection at a human level even with the Mafia, which Tano represents, based on belonging in the same linguistic community.

There are, however, further aspects that need to be taken into account here. First, the loss of emotional complexity during linguistic transfer is at least partly compensated for through the acting, the cinematography, and the *mise-en-scène*. In the scene under discussion, emotion is conveyed through close-ups, slow pace, intonation, and pitch, as well as pauses and silence. Second, even though the use of authentic Sicilian dialect is less frequent than in the book, Montalbano still uses the *italiano bastardo* with the appropriate accent to convey intimacy and emotion. In total, without counting the parts that were excluded from the TV adaptation (for instance, the dialogues with his dialect-speaking housemaid, Adelina) we identified 23 instances of dialectal expressions in the novel; in the TV script, seven of these expressions were completely eliminated or strongly attenuated, and 16 were kept, although some were slightly attenuated.

The English Translation of the Novels

There have been substantial analyses of Sartarelli's translations of the novels, especially by Tomaiuolo (2009) and McRae (2011); this section will summarize and contrast their findings with regard to the use of dialect, with a view to establishing a baseline for the analysis of the English subtitled version of the selected episode, further down.

Sartarelli does not deploy the full range of linguistic variation in his translation, yet he produces a fluent text mostly in standard English. Local color is added with occasional Sicilian expressions and slang from the New York-Brooklynese area, historically the home of Italian and Sicilian immigrants (Tomaiuolo, 2009: 12). At times, Sicilian terms are left untranslated, and regional or Italian idioms are rendered literally, when there is no correspondence in English (McRae, 2011). While this strategy reinforces the presence of the foreign element in the English translation, its impact is often to exoticize Sicily and its language, rather than to demand the reader's effort to understand the foreign elements of the novel (McRae, 2011: 218). With reference to Venuti's analysis of translation strategies, Tomaiuolo argues that "Sartarelli chooses to offer his readers a 'transparent' version of Camilleri's problematic mixture of linguistic codes and registers". He explains with examples "Sartarelli's normalization of Camilleri's Sicilian-sounding syntax" and concludes that "Sartarelli's translating method is a mixed one, with the prevalence of a 'domesticating' strategy over a foreignizing one" (Tomaiuolo, 2009: 11–12).

McRae, on the other hand, examines closely Sartarelli's translation and uncovers several cases of compensation for the loss of dialect. For instance, in rendering housekeeper Adelina's dialect, Sartarelli draws from the sociolect used by Italian Americans—especially the less educated linguistic varieties. To use an example from *Il cane di terracotta*, Adelina's heavily dialectal phrase "Vossia non mangiò né aieri a mezzujorno né aieri sira!" (You did not eat either yesterday midday or yesterday evening) has been rendered as "**Signuri**, you **din't** eat **nothin** yesterday for lunch or dinner!" (McRae, 2011: 234). Here, phonetic and sociolectal markers in English compensate for the untranslatable Sicilian dialect. The vocative 'signuri', which does not lexically appear in the source text, simultaneously conveys i) the use of politeness, which is present in the source text form 'vossia', ii) the Italian context in general, and iii) the dialectal element in particular, for those readers who know that the standard form of the word is *signore*. McRae concludes that "despite the difficulties involved in rendering Camilleri's literary language into English, the translated texts offer the reader insight into the linguistic situation in Sicily and an appreciation of Camilleri's code-switching and hybridization" (McRae, 2011: 269).

Indeed the creative side in Sartarelli's translation is expressed through the most dialect-speaking characters such as Adelina and agent Catarella. The translation of Catarella's ungrammatical idiolect is of particular interest; Sartarelli has invented a distinctive 'macaronic' language for him, made of imaginary and broken words, Brooklynese accent, and elements of slapstick comedy (Tomaiuolo, 2009: 16), which manages to convey a good part of the humor of the original. It is also worth mentioning that at the end of each translated book Sartarelli includes a set of notes with descriptions of Sicilian cuisine, habits, festivities, sayings, words, and references to local history and politics. Inevitably, these notes draw attention to the act of translation as linguistic mediation and to the cultural, anthropological, and linguistic differences between those who read the novel in Italian and those who read it in English. In this way, the inclusion of the notes should be acknowledged as part of the creative and foreignizing impulse at play in the English translation.

The English Subtitles

As is well known, translation choices made in the process of subtitling are dictated by not only by linguistic and cultural criteria. Subtitles have to adhere to certain space and time constraints, that is, limitations that have to do with the length of each subtitle line, and with the time that the subtitle may stay visible on screen. Another limitation is the semiotic context in which the subtitle occurs. The semantics, the aesthetics, and the position of each subtitle have to respect the image on-screen, while subtitles must also follow the visual rhythm of the cinematography and the editing. These limitations create a specific set of criteria outside of which it is not possible to evaluate interlingual subtitling strategies (Ivarsson and Carroll, 1998).

In this subsection, we will discuss the translation of Sicilian dialect as we pass from *Il cane di terracotta*, the novel, to the Italian TV script, and from the latter to the English DVD subtitles. As is expected, in the very frequent cases in which dialectal elements failed to make the transfer from the novel to the TV script, these elements were not present in the English subtitles either. In what follows we will concentrate on examples in which dialectal features survived in the TV script, and we will examine how they were rendered in the subtitles, if at all. Comparisons will be made with the English translation of the novel, where appropriate.

Example 1

In this example, strong dialect is present in the novel, but it is not identical with the dialect used in the TV script. In the English subtitles, dialect has been totally eliminated, and the dialogue has been translated using standard English. Only swearing is retained, in a milder form, as we can see in Table 5.2, where dialect and its translation are highlighted in **bold,** and swearing is <u>underlined</u>.

Table 5.2 Strong dialect is slightly modified in the TV script and completely eliminated in the subtitles

Novel	Italian script	English subtitles
«Chi parla?». «**La to' morti**, parla. Ti voglio dire che non te la passerai liscia, <u>cornuto</u> d'un **tragediatore**! A chi credevi di <u>pigliare per fissa</u> con tutto quel **triatro** che hai fatto col tuo amico Tano? E per questo pagherai, **<u>pi aviri circato di pigliàrinni po' culu</u>**».	MONTALBANO: Ma chi è? CALLER: Chi è? **È la tò morte**. **Nun** te la passi liscia **<u>curnuto</u> d'un <u>curnuto</u>**. Ma chi **pinsavi di <u>pigghiare pu' culu</u> co'** tutto sto **triatro** che hai fatto col tuo amico **Tanu**? E pe' questo la pagherai m'hai **caputo**?	- Who is it? - *It's your death, that's who.* *You won't get away with this, you <u>bastard</u>.* *Did you think that little show you and/ your mate Tano put on could fool us?* *You're going to pay for that.*
Sartarelli's translation	*Literal translation of script*	
'Who is this?' '**It's your death**, that's who. You're not gonna wiggle out of this one so easy, you <u>lousy fucking</u> actor. Who'd you think you were **fooling** with that little **song and dance** you put on with your pal Tano? You're gonna pay **for trying <u>to fuck with us</u>**.	MONTALBANO: But who is it? CALLER: Who is it? **It's your death**. You're **not** going to get away with it, **<u>you asshole</u>**. But who **did you think** you <u>**were getting by the ass**</u> with all this **theatre** that you set up with your friend **Tano**? And for this you will pay, did you understand?	

In this scene, Montalbano receives an anonymous phone call by an unidentified member of the Mafia who threatens to kill him. Verbal confrontation and anger are expressed through the use of swearing and dialect. Dialectal elements that have been retained in the script include variations in morphology, for instance "*la tò morte*" instead of standard Italian "*la tua* morte". In one case, lexical variation is present in the script and not in the novel: *sto* (script) as opposed to the more standard *quel* (novel). The opposite tendency is also present: the highly marked *triatro* in the novel has been rendered as the less marked *tiatro* in the script, both of which differ from standard Italian *teatro*. Phonetic variation seems to be more present in the script than in the novel. For instance, the phrase "*A chi credevi di pigliare per fissa?*" (Whom did you believe you could fool?), which contains standard Italian plus the dialectal swearword *fissa*, has been rendered in the TV script as "*Ma chi pinsavi di pigghiare pu' culu*" (Whom did you think you got by the ass?), which is phonetically much more marked: *pinsavi* instead of the standard *pensavi*, *pigghiare* instead of *pigliare*, *culu* instead of *culo*. Overall, in this case, dialect features strongly in both the novel and the script, in line with our argument that it tends to indicate the expression of emotion.

In the English subtitles, swearing is retained for the most part, but dialect has disappeared leaving only some traces of marked language. There is a visible effort in the subtitles to convey roughness of expression and threat, for example in the repetition "It's your death, *that's who*", and in translating "*curnuto*" to "bastard" (see relevant discussion in McRae, 2011: 267). Compared with Sartarelli's translation, however, there is much more intensive use of marked language in the English translation of the novel than in the English subtitles: "gonna", "wiggle out of", "lousy fucking actor".

If we compare the information that each target audience receives from this sequence, it is possible to argue that i) the reader of Sartarelli's translation will sense the seriously threatening and insulting intentions of the caller but will not be aware of the special linguistic connection between him and Montalbano and will not immediately assume that the caller is a Mafioso; ii) the Italian viewer of the TV program will be fully aware of all of the above dimensions, and will probably respond to the exotic style of the language; and iii) the viewer of the TV episode who relies on the English subtitles will not associate the language with the Sicilian dialect and culture and will not necessarily recognize the caller as a Mafioso. This viewer will also have to surmise that this is an emotionally charged scene based on swearing and traces of marked language in the subtitles, and—perhaps above all—based on the intonation and pitch of the telephone conversation.

Example 2

In the following dialogue between Montalbano and his deputy, Mimì Augello, the text of the subtitles has been significantly condensed compared to the script due to time and space constraints. Sicilian dialect in the TV script is left as in the novel, while the English subtitles bear no trace of it. Non-marked English language is used to translate the dialogue, while in most cases the swearing disappears. There is also another element to consider: in this passage, Camilleri uses the technique of intradiegetic explanation of dialect, which has been perfectly transferred to the TV script. In the novel, the Sicilian word *scantato* is followed by its Italian counterpart, *spaventato*, meaning "scared"; in the TV episode, the word *scantato* is followed by the common Italian expression "*ti sei messo paura*", "you got scared".

Table 5.3 Dialect is maintained in the TV script and completely eliminated in the subtitles

Novel	Italian script	English subtitles
"Ma dove sei stato? Dove ti sei andato ad ammucciare? Ma ti pare modo di fare, **buttana d'una buttana?**" [*text not appearing in the script*]	MIMÌ: Salvo, ma dove ti sei andato a ficcare **buttana di una buttana** si può sapere?	Salvo, are you going to tell me where the <u>hell</u> you've been hiding?

Novel	Italian script	English subtitles
"Mimì, **che ti piglia?**" "Come, **che mi piglia!** **Mi sono scantato,** mi sono!" "Ti sei spaventato? E di che?"	MONTALBANO: Eh. **Ma che ti piglia?** MIMÌ: E **che mi piglia, mi sono scantato, Salvù.** MONTALBANO: **Pecchè ti sei messo paura?**	Mimì, what's got into you? - I got scared. - Scared? Of what?

Sartarelli's translation	Literal translation of script
'Where the hell have you been?! Where've you been **hiding**? What happened to everybody else? **What the fuck** is going on here anyway? [*text not appearing in the script*] 'Mimì, **what's got into you?** 'What's got into me? I got **scared**, that's what!' 'Scared? Of what?'	Salvo, where have you been hiding, <u>for fuck's sake</u>, if I may know? - What's got into you? - What got into me, I got scared, Salvo. - Why where you afraid?

This is a moment in the narrative where Mimì expresses fear, so dialect is prominent. Mimì uses the Sicilian variation "*Salvù*" (instead of "Salvo", Montalbano's forename) to invoke friendship beyond the professional context, and perhaps also to express affection, as he feared for Montalbano's life. It is interesting that the dialectal "*Salvù*" has entered the TV script while it was not part of the original book. Augello then uses the Sicilian expression "*Mi sono scantato*", ("I was scared"), which Montalbano explains in standard Italian for the benefit of the Italian viewer. The English reader of either Sartarelli's translation or the DVD subtitles is not aware of these subtle transactions.

Example 3: "Montalbano sono"

The characteristic expression "*Montalbano sono*" ("I am Montalbano") has become a trademark for Montalbano. With this phrase, the inspector announces his identity in a memorable, if slightly comical, exoticizing fashion. At the same time, Montalbano affirms his *sicilianità* through the syntactic inversion between verb and subject, one of the most salient characteristics of the Sicilian dialect. In the English translation of the novels, including *The Terracotta Dog*, the phrase has been consistently rendered as "Montalbano here" (Camilleri, 2002: 121, 157, 265, 272). In the TV episode under examination, it has been twice translated as "It's Montalbano" (00.32.33 and 01.21.10). It is worth noticing that Sartarelli's translation is sensitive to the hierarchical order between proper noun and verb. Insofar as this catch phrase is suggestive of the main character's personality, the priority of the name over the verb may indicate Montalbano's self-confidence in his social interactions. Insofar as the catchphrase is suggestive of his *sicilianità*, it could be hypothesized that Camilleri makes an amicable and humoristic comment on the stereotypical self-confidence of some Sicilian men, which characterizes other male roles too, for example that of Augello. Be it as it may, some of these connotations are indeed conveyed by the translation "Montalbano here". The English phrase is not grammatically incorrect, but its repetition may create an effect of foreignness and could suggest a level of self-assurance that is only expected of a fictional superhero, such as a detective, rather than any realistically described narrative character.

In this sense, the subtitler's choice, "It's Montalbano", which substitutes the impersonal "it's" for the first person singular, seems to serve above all pragmatic purposes of relevance and communication. It does not convey any psychological subtlety; neither does it add to the characterization of the hero. In the case of the TV episode under discussion, it merely serves to inform Montalbano's interlocutor that Montalbano is calling on the phone. As a translation strategy, the prioritization by the subtitler of propositional over expressive meaning seems to indicate a domesticating tendency, whereby fluency and invisibility of subtitles are deemed more important than subtlety and complexity of meaning. This said, it cannot be ignored that TV viewers will be listening to Montalbano's utterance and will also probably be looking at his face while reading the subtitle; they will be able to perceive the vocal stress on the proper noun "Montalbano" and will rely on the subtitle only for information purposes.

Discussion and Conclusion: The "True Essence" of Montalbano?

In an article about the standardization of regionalisms in literary translation, Ritva Leppihalme (2000: 264) found that some of the main functions of regionalisms include creating a sociocultural context, individualizing the characters, and adding humor. The same can be claimed about the use of dialect in the Montalbano series of novels and TV episodes. Camilleri (quoted in McRae, 2011: 73) seems to agree with the use of dialect as an individualization device when he states that "dialect, or dialects to be more precise, are the *true essence* of the characters" (our emphasis). In this article, we have concentrated on the role of dialect in defining the 'true essence' or 'authenticity' of the Montalbano series, with special emphasis on the titular character. However, based on our comparison of the presence and importance of dialect in successive transformations of Montalbano (the books and the TV series), it seems that there is no single 'true essence'. When we examine Montalbano as a network of literary/mediatic translations through the prism of dialect, different characterological profiles appear for the cultural product as a whole and for the main character in particular. If we consider dialect as one of the implicit cues that convey character information by inference (Culpeper, 2001: 172), then our (necessarily partial) analysis points to the following thoughts:

a) Toning down the dialect in the English translation, the TV series, and even more so in the subtitles of *Il cane di terracotta* results in a reduction and simplification of verbally conveyed emotion. If the expression of emotion plays a specific part in managing the detective puzzles (as in the case of the novel under discussion), then downplaying the complexity and intensity of emotions in the translations and/or adaptations could result in gaps in both understanding the storyline and appreciating its density and refinement. By the same token, the different mediatic and linguistic incarnations of the main character may be construed as partially incompatible variations of Montalbano, lacking what Camilleri intended them to have, a single true essence.

b) Another effect of toning down the dialect is the de-emphasizing of the *sicilianità*. More than a natural or architectural background, in Camilleri's novels Sicily constitutes a marked cultural and anthropological context that provides narrative and aesthetic clues to the reader. Avoiding implicit references to it through the use of dialect may result in Sicily becoming an exotic *décor* of the action, during which known stereotypes about food, the Mafia, etc., are being confirmed. Montalbano's identity risks transforming accordingly. He risks being construed as a cosmopolitan detective capable of thinking, speaking, and acting in universally unproblematic ways.

c) The above remarks can only be considered as a contribution to a broader comparative examination of contextual, intertextual, visual, and televisual parameters than we have allowed for here. While we propose that the reduction of dialect affects the characterization of Montalbano in concrete ways, we also suggest that this reduction may be compensated for through other means. For example, in assessing the effect of adaptation and translation choices, the following elements (or implicit cues: Culpeper, 2001) must be taken into account: accent, intonation, and (im)politeness strategies, as well as facial expression, posture, kinesis, clothing, etc. *Mise-en-scène*, cinematography and editing also play an important role in compensating for the loss of emotion and local reference in the processes of translation and adaptation.

Although the discourse of translation evaluation is often articulated in terms of loss and compensation, examining translation networks, such as the poly-semiotic network of Montalbano, cannot be reduced to such simplifications. It is therefore not our purpose to conclude with a judgment—however tentative—regarding the quality of the TV series, the English translation, or the English subtitles. What the example of the versions and translations of *Il cane di terracotta* seems to indicate, however, is that Montalbano's multiple transformations do not contribute to a unique character profile. These transformations do not necessarily point to a linear progression or to a central narrative management of the character that can be attributed to a single authorial source. On the contrary, we witness a series of agents, including the translators, the subtitlers, and those involved in the TV adaptation of the novel, who follow different norms and conventions and have different priorities and commitments. In line with Marrone's semiotic approach, our brief examination of the fate of dialect in one of Camilleri's best-known novels suggests that Montalbano's multiple versions and reworkings can hardly be synthesized into a single identity; if that identity exists, it must be sought for *not* in terms of authenticity or 'true essence' but in terms of translation, intermediality, and intertextuality.

Note

1. Translated from Italian by the authors. All translations from Italian scholarly sources are by the authors.

References

Buonanno, M. (2000). *Ricomposizioni: la fiction italiana, l'Italia nella fiction, anno undicesimo*. Rome: Radiotelevisione Italiana.

Camilleri, A. (1996). *Il cane di terracotta*. Palermo: Sellerio.

Camilleri, A. (2002). *The Terracotta Dog*. Trans. by Andrea Sartarelli. London: Picador.

Culpeper, J. (2001). *Language and characterisation. People in plays and other texts*. Harlow: Longman.

De Meo, M. (2010). Subtitling dialect and culture-bound language. *Testi e linguaggi*, 4, 19–36.

Filipponi, S. (2002). Il laboratorio del contastorie: Intervista ad Andrea Camilleri. *ACME LV*(2), available online at: http://www.vigata.org/rassegna_stampa/2002/Archivio/Int01_Cam_ago2002_Altri.htm (Retrieved August 4, 2014).

Ivarsson, J., & Carroll, M. (1998). *Subtitling*. Simrishamn: TransEdit.

Jakobson, R. (1959/2000). On linguistic aspects of translation. In L. Venuti (Ed.), *The Translation Studies Reader* (pp. 113–118). London and New York: Routledge.

Leppihalme, R. (2000). The two faces of standardization: On the translations of regionalisms in literary dialogue. In C. Maier (Ed.), *Evaluation and Translation* (pp. 247–269). Manchester: St. Jerome.

Marrone, G. (2003). *Montalbano: affermazioni e trasformazioni di un eroe mediatico*. Torino: Rai-ERI.

Marrone, G. (2004). La guerra dei mondi possibili (ancora sul caso Montalbano). (Paper presented in conference "Remake-rework: sociosemiotica delle pratiche di replicabilità.") Urbino, Centro di semiotica, available online at: http://www.vigata.org/bibliografia/la_guerra_dei_mondi.pdf (Retrieved August 4, 2014).

McRae, E. (2011). *Translation of the Sicilianità in the fictional languages of Giovanni Verga and Andrea Camilleri*. Ph.D. Thesis. The University of Auckland, available online at: https://researchspace.auckland.ac.nz/handle/2292/6974 (Retrieved August 4, 2014).

Pezzotti, B. (2012). *The importance of place in contemporary Italian crime fiction: A bloody journey*. Plymouth UK: Fairleigh Dickinson University Press.

Pistelli, M. (2003). *Montalbano sono: sulle tracce del più famoso commissario di polizia italiano*. Firenze: Le Càriti.

Sartarelli, S. (2004). L'alterità linguistica di Camilleri in inglese. In *Il caso Camilleri: letteratura e storia* (pp. 213–219). Palermo: Sellerio.

Serkowska, H. (2006). Sedurre con il giallo. Il caso di Andrea Camilleri. *Cahiers d'études italiennes, 5*, 163–172.

Taffarel, M. (2012). Un'analisi descrittiva della traduzione dei dialoghi dei personaggi di Andrea Camilleri in castigliano. In G. Nadiani & C. Rundle (Eds.), *InTRAlinea Special Issue: The Translation of Dialects in Multimedia II*, available online at: http://www.intralinea.org/specials/article/1843 (Retrieved August 4, 2014).

Tomaiuolo, S. (2009). I am Montalbano/Montalbano Sono: Fluency and cultural difference in translating Andrea Camilleri's fiction. *Journal of Anglo-Italian Studies*, 10, 201–219.

Venuti, L. (1995/2008). *The translator's invisibility: A history of translation*. London and New York: Routledge.

Vietina, A. (2010). *Montalbano, Maigret & Co. Storia del giallo in televisione*. Alessandria: Falsopiano.

Vitale, A. (2001). *Il mondo del commissario Montalbano*. Caltanissetta: Terzo Millennio.

6 Localizing *Sesame Street*

The Cultural Translation of the Muppets

Aaron Calbreath-Frasieur

On 10 November 1969, a new experimental educational show first broadcast in the US. Within its first few minutes, audiences were introduced to three of the many unique Muppet characters that would define and distinguish the show: Big Bird, Bert, and Ernie. For four uninterrupted decades, these three, joined by a host of Muppet friends, have continued to teach American preschoolers about the alphabet and numbers, health and safety, and numerous other topics relevant to the lives of children. They also entertain and educate around the world, joined in many cases by new Muppet characters unique to particular regional contexts. In South Africa, Kami, a young Muppet monster, copes with disease and models healthy behaviors. In Poland, Bayzli, a friendly dragon, participates in holiday traditions. In Indonesia, a rhino teaches children about protecting the environment. In India, a furry blue monster named Googly sings with his friends about counting. The Muppet characters of this vibrant media franchise, sometimes internationally shared, sometimes heavily localized, entertain and teach children all over the world.

Sesame Street is an educational US show for preschool children that has been moving across borders in multiple directions and in a variety of forms for over 40 years. Its producer, Sesame Workshop, is a very profitable non-profit organization whose educational goals are not incompatible with commercial success. As this case study will demonstrate, the show is at the same time a media franchise[1] engaged in international format trade and a platform for socially responsible activity, using trademarked, licensable characters to address educational and social needs worldwide. This case study explores some of the strategies used by Sesame Workshop to effectively and ethically adapt the show for different countries and cultures, placing particular emphasis on how the Muppets—the puppet characters of all of the *Sesame* shows worldwide—are adapted and deployed to facilitate the localization of the show. The adaptations of the Muppet characters work as a useful focus for this study because they are central to the identity of the show, informing the aesthetics and storytelling, as well as being a major reason for the popularity of the show. The characters are often used as points of identification for the child audience, serving to communicate the social and educational messages of the shows. Moreover, the Muppets function as a physical representation of the adaptation of the show for local contexts.

To examine these localized texts, this chapter has three objectives: to set out the essential background of *Sesame Street* including a characterization of its basic format and an overview of its history as an export; to identify localization practices in production and relate them to the common practice of format sales; and finally to give concrete examples of the textual localization, specifically the adaptation of Muppet characters to different cultures and the application of those characters to specific locally relevant socio-political concerns. The essay concludes with some observations about how the practices and history of this unusual educational franchise could be useful for thinking about localization more broadly, including in relation to commercial properties.

Sesame Street's History as an Export

Sesame Street first appeared on US public broadcasting stations in 1969 and has remained on the air ever since, entering its 45th season in 2014. It is produced by the non-profit Sesame Workshop (formerly Children's Television Workshop). The show is structured mostly in a 'magazine format' (multiple distinct features) with a loose wraparound narrative. Each episode is made up of numerous focused segments, including short films, animations, and Muppet segments. One of the original ideas behind the style of the show was to use the aesthetics and logics of television commercials to teach, with an emphasis on literacy and numeracy (alongside social and health curricula). The narrative framework features humans and Muppets living together in a common social space, the neighborhood "Sesame Street".

The potential of *Sesame Street* as an international export was not originally clear. Co-creator Joan Ganz Cooney and the original team thought the show would be "too 'quintessentially American' to resonate anywhere else" (Gikow, 2009: 252). Indeed, in the UK there was initially strong resistance to importing the show (Christmas, 1971), which was rejected by the BBC, both on media culture grounds as being too didactic and as a resistance against Americanization, especially because the show is targeted at the very young. Differences in educational perspectives combined with discomfort around the foreign character or Americanness of the show prevented it from entering the UK market for a number of years. Yet *Sesame Street* was readily accepted and even sought by other countries. As early as 1972, the show was exported to Brazil and soon after to Germany, Mexico, and Canada. The program has now been shown in 140 countries, with localized adaptations in about 30 countries; Sesame Workshop accordingly has adopted the idea of Sesame Street as "the longest street in the world" (Knell, 2008). The three most recent productions are shows for Indonesia, Pakistan, and Afghanistan. The level of adaptation of the show has differed for each country, but from early on there was a move to create national versions.

Localization Practices

Over the years, different co-production models have been used in localizing the international productions of the show, and I turn now to those models, focusing particularly on full co-productions. The co-productions share some significant attributes with the increasingly common practices of format sales. The study of format trade systems is a growing field; the work of Albert Moran provides a helpful starting point on the topic. According to Moran, the television format is "the total package of information and know-how that increases the adaptability of a program in another place and time" (Moran, 2006: 6). Format sales are a commoditized and systematized version of the practices of unlicensed adoption and adaptation that have been going on as long as television has existed. Formats thus function as a kind of international media franchise. The intellectual property "Sesame Street" is owned by Sesame Workshop and licensed out to media producers in other countries. Keane et al. describe formats in franchising and brand terms:

> Franchising models play a role in reshaping and restructuring global activity in two ways. First, many transferred formats embody high levels of internationalized 'intangibles': notions about value creation, branding, marketing and consulting routinely accompany exchanges and contribute to establishing a culture of competition and business ethics. Second, the resulting productions are in most cases recognizably local: they draw on local tastes and values, they partner with local knowledge, and in doing so, they generate mutual benefits and cultural technology transfer. (2007: 81)

In keeping with this characterization, Sesame Workshop manages an international brand with considerable intangible value, including recognition of the Muppet characters. It develops the shows with local partners and goes to great lengths to indigenize the show.

Across time and location, the form of international *Sesame*s is quite varied, with different degrees of indigenization. At first, the show was simply exported—the US show was dubbed (as necessary) and distributed to interested countries. Most countries still use this form, in which the US show or another international version is dubbed. In a partial co-production, such as the so-called *Open Sesame*, minimal local material may be mixed with dubbed clips from other countries. *Open Sesame* is one of the more common international forms of the show.

> In contrast to the full co-production models, *Open Sesame* shows are dubs, initially packaged as either 13 or 27 segment blocks. In the earliest years, a locally produced opening film, often featuring animated versions of *Sesame Street* characters, introduced the series, and was the only local footage used.
>
> (MuppetWiki)

Full co-productions, by contrast, have a local narrative framework and considerable local material, with access to the Workshop's extensive library for additional clips. There are varieties of ways in which such co-productions take shape. Some co-productions are regional rather than national, generally supporting a cultural proximity model (Straubhaar, 1991), according to which audience appeal is increased by linguistic and cultural familiarity. In other words, in cases where local domestic texts (which are deemed the most appealing) are unavailable, audiences prefer texts coming from countries that share the same language and/or are culturally similar. An Iraqi audience, for instance, might prefer to watch *Iftah ya Simsim*, produced in Kuwait, rather than a dubbed episode of the American show. Whether in regional or national context, Sesame Workshop has continued to expand its localization both in terms of an evolution of its localization practices and in terms of the number of localized versions of the show now produced. Today, an American viewer watching an episode of the Indian or South African shows might recognize the style and some of the extra-narrative segments, but the central characters and story would be largely or completely foreign. For instance, Indonesia's *Jalan Sesama* is set in a small village and featured only local Muppets until Elmo was added to the cast in the third season. This form of international production functions in many ways like the widely used system of format sales.

To the extent that the co-productions of *Sesame Street* function as a format, the basic elements of that format are: The Sesame Workshop Model (which is the research-production-research feedback loop used on all *Sesame* shows),[2] the magazine and short-segment style, some visual elements such as the street sign, educational content (with an emphasis on literacy, numeracy, and locally designed curriculum), access to the Sesame Workshop library of clips, a storyline set in a community neighborhood, and Muppet characters. Not all of these elements are included in all co-productions, but most carry across each version of the show.

The system employed by Sesame Workshop differs from that of standard format sales, however, primarily in that an international version of *Sesame* is not just a licensed format; it is a co-production based on exceptionally close collaboration with the licensor. Sesame Workshop in New York has ongoing involvement with all the various *Sesames* worldwide. The Workshop provides a format and expertise (as in format sales), but it also participates in the production of each show. A producer from the Workshop works with local producers for the duration of the production (Kenworthy, personal interview, 2010). Certain materials for each version come from the US. Specifically, Muppets for each show are usually built in New York, based on the planning done with the local teams. The vast Workshop library of short segments is available to all productions, and this library is in turn fed by the international shows, as well as by the American *Sesame*.

For the full co-production, Sesame Workshop requires considerable local input. Representatives from the Workshop meet with educators (both teachers of young children and university academics), media professionals, and sometimes government officials to discuss the curriculum for the season. Research goes into every aspect of the show's design. Curriculum decisions are made by this predominantly local team (ibid). When possible, the Workshop conducts or instigates summative research to gauge the impact and success of the show.

Production on any given co-production is done in-country, with guidance from a producer from the New York office, though almost all other personnel are local (or regional). The degree of direct involvement of personnel from New York has varied from show to show, particularly as each has become more established. Duncan Kenworthy, a producer with the Workshop in the 1970s, says that by the late '70s the producer mostly coordinated the German show *Sesamstrasse* (NDR, 1973–) and France's *1 Rue Sesame* from the New York office, whereas for *Iftah Ya Simsim* (various, 1979–1982), a new production in 1978, he was in Kuwait overseeing production directly (Personal Interview, 2010). As both the system and local productions continued to evolve over time, established shows required less involvement from New York.

A few examples of *Sesame* co-productions will illustrate the variety of incarnations the show has assumed. *Sesamstrasse* (NDR, 1973–), on the air in Germany since 1973, is an example of the varied approach to co-production. It started as a dub of the American show. In 1978 an original German framework was introduced. Throughout the 1980s and 1990s, *Sesamstrasse* has used many segments from the American show, sometimes as much as 50% of a given show's content being comprised of such material. But in more recent years this practice has declined considerably so that now only one or two segments out of the approximately 25 segments that make up the whole show might be made externally.

While the German show is made for a national audience, other shows are made for multiple countries or attempt to address regions and cultural groups within a country in multiple ways. On some co-productions, the local segments might not all be made centrally; for instance, on *Sesame Park* (CBC, 1996–2002, a Canadian co-production) segments were filmed by nine different regional outlets across Canada then fed back to a central group to evaluate and compile the show, making the show "locally relevant" regionally within Canada as well as nationally. *Iftah Ya Simsim*, the first Arabic language version, was filmed in Kuwait but was designed for regional distribution across the Gulf and into other Arabic-speaking countries. Actors, crew, and researchers for the show were drawn from all over the region. In South Africa, the choice of a spoken language was an issue for the show, one the Workshop has recently tried to address (see Chapter 7 in this collection for more on this). Starting in 2007, *Takalani Sesame* (SABC, 2000–) has been produced in nine of South Africa's 11 official languages. In seasons four and five, each episode was filmed five times, each time in a different language (with English and a different set of four other languages in each season). *Takalani Sesame* radio shows are broadcast in 12 languages, using the language appropriate for each region where the show airs (Sesame, 2007). Each of these productions tackled adaptation and localization in different ways in order to most effectively meet the needs of its audience.

As these examples illustrate, *Sesame Street* provides an innovative case in point of textual localization, with the caveat that 'local' here is generally best understood as national or, in some cases, regional (with cultural and linguistic proximity). *Sesame* is an unusual franchise in that each show is dedicated to education and particular social goals. Sesame Workshop endeavors to deliver a localized, culturally sensitive show in each co-producing country. These efforts have not made it immune to charges of cultural imperialism or Americanization. Heather Hendershot argues that:

> *Sesame Street* is imperialistic not simply because the show itself is a widely disseminated American cultural product, but also because the technology of its production, the testing-production circuit, has been so widely disseminated and accepted by many governments as the best—indeed the *only*—model for producing educational television. (1999: 159–60, italics in original)

This perspective suggests a paradox in that the efforts of the Workshop to create a localized product (through local testing and educator involvement) and thus minimize imperialism, may, in fact, create a kind of production imperialism by cementing its (American) model as the best way to produce educational children's media. Hendershot further states:

> Historically, the U.S. government and U.S. foundations have used broadcasting to disseminate U.S. culture worldwide, and the CTW [Children's Television Workshop, now Sesame Workshop] must be understood in this context. The CTW is one of many organizations that has participated in communications imperialism, though it is certainly one of the smaller, less malevolent players. (ibid: 170)

It is reasonable to view *Sesame Street* in this context. As co-productions with the US, the international shows should not be accepted uncritically. When assessing the show, we would be prudent to consider any socio-political ramifications and possible agendas behind the scenes. At the same time, however, it seems clear that Sesame Workshop is indeed a "less malevolent player" and has made some strong efforts to contend with issues of cultural imperialism in its movement across borders.

The boundaries of this chapter do not allow for an in-depth discussion of the cultural imperialism debate. It is noteworthy, however, that Sesame Workshop at the least approaches international production with such concerns in mind. As Charlotte Cole of the Workshop says, "I think the question of cultural imperialism is a good one and one that we're contending with all the time" (in Knowlton and Hawkins, 2006). How effectively the Workshop negotiates issues around Americanization and cultural imperialism is a complicated question that might differ widely based on the particular national context. But the fact that the Workshop is attempting to navigate these issues is significant. As we will see in the following section, which examines the adaptation of the *Sesame* texts and the Muppets specifically, the Workshop approaches localization with a sense of responsibility to the local audience, aiming to cater to local needs and to systematically learn from mistakes and successes.

One of the most significant factors in localization of the show is that the setting of the show is almost always a neighborhood: a locally relevant community setting. Cultural anthropologist Arjun Appadurai (1990) discusses neighborhoods as part of the production of 'locality', a practice in which these shows are clearly engaged. For him, neighborhoods "refer to the actually existing social forms in which locality, as a dimension or value, is variably realized. Neighborhoods, in this usage, are situated communities characterized by their actuality, whether spatial or virtual, and their potential for social reproduction" (ibid: 178–79). It is striking then that *Sesame,* in its attempt to create a local world, consistently does so by creating a neighborhood. Where sitcoms might focus on a living room or a small set of indoor locations, *Sesame* focuses on a street, plaza, or other culturally proximate neighborhood setting to create a reproducible social environment. There are productions that do not follow this pattern (such as Kosovo's *Ulica Sezam,* which does not use the standard wraparound storyline), but the majority do. While these local neighborhoods are an important facet of indigenization, it is the Muppet characters that literally embody the localization of the show.

Textual Localization: Adapting Muppet Characters

The Muppet characters provide a visual and personified point of difference between shows. The characters are usually designed in-country, with the puppets built in America. Big Bird offers an interesting look at the adaptation of the characters, as most countries have an equivalent character. Big Bird is a 2.5 meters tall yellow bird, a full-body puppet, positioned as a six-year-old. He does not know as much as the older characters on the show, so he is always asking questions, always trying to learn more. He operates as a surrogate for the child-viewer. Most countries with a co-production have their own full-body puppet that fills the same role, though in most cases the character is a different species. *Plaza Sesamo* from Mexico and the Netherlands' *Sesamstraat* are the closest, with the parrot Abelardo (originally a crocodile) and blue bird Pino, respectively. For Poland's *Ulitsa Sezamkova,* the character became Bazyli the Dragon. On *GalliGalli Sim Sim* in India, the character Boombah is a vegetarian Lion. In Russia, Zeliboba is a Dvorovoi, a folkloric spirit, and in Germany, Samson is a bear.

Sesame Workshop takes the position that when it is adapting the show, it must be cautious about the cultural ramifications and try to negotiate the terrain ethically. In addition to addressing the co-production system more generally, Charlotte Cole, former Vice President for International Research at the Workshop, relates the issue of cultural sensitivity specifically to the Muppet characters of the show:

> When we first worked internationally, we didn't have Big Bird, for example, in our international programs. The feeling was that Big Bird was an American icon and that just importing Big Bird around the world would be perceived as too much of a cultural intrusion. That certainly was the case in a lot of European countries where we were working, where people wanted to be able to develop their own characters. (...) But it always struck me as interesting, when we went to places like China after years of working internationally and we start to explain the different characters we have all over the world and they're looking at us like 'you're not going to let us have Big Bird. We want Big Bird'.
>
> (Cole in Knowlton and Hawkins, 2006)

In the end, Da Niao, Big Bird's lookalike cousin, was created for China's *Zhima Jie*. The Muppets themselves are perceived as a key facet of the identity and localness of the show. Though some essential elements of the character remain, such as Big Bird's naïve curiosity, the character is usually significantly redesigned (including physically) to suit the local context. For instance, Workshop producer Gregory Gettas says that, "the Israeli version features 'Kippy Ben-Kippod', a prickly-on-the-outside, sweet-on-the-inside hedgehog said to represent the Israeli national character" (1990: 56). Zeliboba, meanwhile, is a courtyard spirit, specific to the Russian context as that type of spirit originates in Slavic folklore.

In other cases, the physical form and nature of the puppets have been adapted to even greater extents. For *Sisimpur* in Bangladesh, the local producers were concerned that the show needed puppets fashioned in the indigenous style rather than Muppet characters; Sesame Workshop preferred that Muppets be used. This preference suggests that the American producers, while intentional about adapting their show, nevertheless acted to protect their brand by setting some limits for the degree of adaptation. A compromise was reached and Bangladeshi puppets appear on the program alongside the Muppets (Knowlton and Hawkins, 2006). For Pakistan's *Simsim Hamara* (no longer in production due to economic problems within the local production company), the Muppet look was largely abandoned for a distinctly Pakistani look in the puppets. The Muppets served as a physical manifestation of the show and visually represented the level of adaptation that had occurred. Even in Pakistan, however, there was some desire to maintain iconic characters, with Elmo having been included among the show's Muppets.

Beyond this physical and character adaptation, the Muppets often serve key functions in the localization of the show's curriculum. In a number of cases, difficult social issues that are important locally are tackled through the Muppet characters. The social issues these shows navigate are critical in Sesame

Workshop's strategy for ethical localization. One such show is *Sesame Tree* (BBC2 NI, 2008–2010), a program that was specifically designed to address socio-political conflict in Northern Ireland. This conflict-resolution project is a co-production of Sesame Workshop, the BBC, and Sixteen South, a commercial Belfast-based production company; it first broadcast on BBC Northern Ireland and later also on CBeebies throughout the UK. The show went into production after almost 10 years of feasibility and other pre-production research and negotiation (Swann, 2012: 98). *Sesame Tree* works toward the goal of providing "3- to-6-year-olds with an educational foundation of open-mindedness, empathy, and appreciation of diversity" (Sesame Workshop, n.d.). As with other *Sesame*s, the goals of the show are embedded in Muppet characters—in this case, Hilda (an Irish hare) and Potto (a monster), who live together in the eponymous tree. Episodes often focus on the main characters learning about negotiating differences through topics like sharing, being part of a diverse community, communication, apologizing, taking turns, and cultural traditions. Similarly, a show in Kosovo and a twin production (two connected shows) made jointly between Israel and Palestine have aimed at fostering understanding between children on opposite sides of grave political conflicts.

The reception and impact of *Sesame Tree* and the other conflict-oriented *Sesame*s have been mixed and debatable. Media scholar Alexandra Swann (2012) argues that *Sesame Tree*, while an important and worthwhile production on many levels, does not engage explicitly enough with the realities of living in a post-conflict society (even as experienced by pre-schoolers) to be truly effective. She recognizes that "the technique used in *Sesame Tree* where children are shown enjoying culturally specific activities could be held up as an example of an effective means of communicating the message of embracing difference" (ibid: 267). However, she argues that not enough of the "culturally specific activities" depicted on the show were specific to Northern Ireland. In this case, it was not Sesame Workshop that shied away from explicit exploration of sectarian differences; rather the BBC required the show to follow its strictly "neutral" approach, a sentiment shared by the local curriculum developers. Responsibility for this decision rested with the local partners rather than the US co-producer (ibid: 102–103). Regardless of the evaluation and actual impact of these conflict-oriented shows, they serve to illustrate ways producers have attempted to mobilize franchise media to engage with national and international issues, as well as how local culture impacts adaptation (in terms of BBC neutrality rules in this case). Moreover, they demonstrate how the Muppet characters themselves have been used to directly address local concerns.

Besides the conflict-oriented shows, there are other striking examples of ways in which Sesame Workshop has made significant efforts to localize its show and to do so in a way that is respectful of cultural concerns. In addition to its long-term practices of involving local personnel and educators in every step of the production process and of localizing settings and characters, Sesame Workshop has taken further steps toward socially responsible international co-production through explicitly aligning its shows with the United Nations' Millennium Development Goals (MDGs). In 2008, then Sesame Workshop CEO Gary Knell described how the MDGs were a significant part of the Workshop's business plan, saying, "We've done a lot of work in these arenas to try to get partners who share these values [so] that we can use the power of television to promote these" (Knell, 2008). The MDGs are: universal education, gender equality, child health, maternal health, combat HIV/AIDS, environmental sustainability, global partnership, end poverty and hunger (United Nations, 2010). By adhering to internationally agreed-upon tenets, the Workshop reduces (to a degree) the danger of Americanizing texts and demonstrates commitment to ethical internationalization.

The strategies and MDGs focus used in the shows vary by country, though some, such as universal education and child health, have been inherent to the show since the beginning. Often the goals are embedded in the Muppet characters. For instance, Egypt's *Alam Simsim,* in explicit alignment with the MDGs statement on gender equality, has made education and career aspiration for girls a major component of the curriculum. This goal is expressed in large part through a Muppet character, Khokha. Khokha is a young female monster, who likes to imagine all the things she can do and be when she grows up. The social goal of the show resides in the Muppet character. Some of these social goals are made very specifically for a given region, as demonstrated above in the Egyptian case or below by different health-related initiatives in African versions of the franchise.

At the 2008 MDG Malaria Summit, the Sesame Workshop CEO joined presidents, prime ministers, and other world leaders to collaborate in the fight against malaria (Roll Back, 2008). A malaria-prevention initiative was launched as *Kilimani Sesame*, a multi-media campaign including television and radio episodes, books, and educational materials. *Kilimani* is produced for Tanzania and Zambia as part of Roll Back Malaria Partnership's 'Global Malaria Action Plan'. It features "Tanzanian children and Muppets from South Africa's *Takalani Sesame*, and show[s] them modelling healthy behaviours" (Sesame Workshop, 2008).

Perhaps the best and most highly publicized example of Sesame Workshop's locally relevant work in the area of health is the Muppet character Kami. Kami was introduced on South Africa's *Takalani Sesame* in 2002. She is a friendly "monster" (similar to Elmo or Grover on the US show) and represents a 5-year old child, but, unlike any other Muppet, she is HIV-positive. Kami's role is very specific to Africa and was designed to meet the needs of the region. Kami directly engages with the MDG of combating HIV/AIDS. She has since appeared in other African productions such as Nigeria's *Sesame Square* and *Kilimani Sesame*. The UNAIDS website describes Kami's role in this way:

> In South Africa, too, where an estimated 5.7 million people live with HIV the inclusion of the character Kami who is HIV-positive aims to counter stigma and discrimination through creating awareness

and addressing fears and misconceptions about HIV. (…) Part of her character's role is to destigmatize those living with HIV, and to open discussion about sensitive issues including coping with illness and bereavement. (UNAIDS.org)

Thus the goal of combating HIV is not only part of the *Takalani Sesame* show, but it is specifically embedded in a Muppet character. Kami's character is designed to sensitively but explicitly address a variety of issues around HIV/AIDS in Africa.

Puppets in many cultures have historically been used to raise questions that would be more problematic for human actors. By embedding the issue of AIDS in a lovable Muppet character, the show is able to address AIDS in a gentle, open, but still serious way. The *Takalani* Muppets are used to address social stigmas, in terms of speaking about AIDS (not keeping it hidden), combating myths about disease transfer, and talking about issues around grief: Kami's mother has died of AIDS, giving her the opportunity to talk about remembering and loving people who are gone. Despite Kami's Africa-only appearances, Sesame Workshop originally got considerable negative feedback regarding her creation from the religious right in the US. However, Kami has received more positive recognition internationally and was named a "champion for children" by UNICEF in 2003.

The Muppet Kami offers a vibrant example of how a franchised format can be effectively and respectfully localized. This is not to say that there is no cultural homogenization in international *Sesame*s. It is clear, however, that the creators are aware of and sensitive to the cultural imperialism debate and have tried to be ethical as the show crosses borders. The international spread of *Sesame Street* has been executed with an awareness of cultural differences and a strong engagement with locals to design and create the shows. The degree of adaptation on the shows has increased over time, and the application to specific social concerns has ramped up over the years, particularly as the Workshop, known in general for its progressive values, aligned itself with the United Nations. The Muppet characters themselves, embodying as they do much of the shows' aesthetics, story, and social agenda, demonstrate the success the Workshop has had in effectively localizing its product.

Observations

The foregoing sampling of the various incarnations of *Sesame Street* around the globe refutes certain assumptions about media franchises. Format trading, like other forms of franchising, is often associated with repetition and homogenization. Media scholar Derek Johnson writes that for some critics, the concept of media franchising "explains the creative bankruptcy and foregone economic determination of contemporary media industries" sometimes extending to include "the masculinized juvenility of those industries as well" (2013: 1). In this view franchises are "monstrously homogenized, self-determining, and childish", and may be seen as a sign of "cultural bankruptcy" and "cultural blight" (ibid: 2). Silvio Waisbord, while arguing himself that formats can be legitimately localized and lead to effectively hybridized media forms, sums up a conventional view:

> On the surface, the global dissemination of formats may suggest not only the global integration of the economy of the industry but also the standardization of content. What better evidence of cultural homogenization than format television? A dozen media companies are able to do business worldwide by selling the same idea, and audiences seem to be watching national variations of the same show. (2004: 360)

The international *Sesame Street*s do not offer the expected repetition and reproduction commonly associated with franchising. Rather, they illustrate in striking ways that formats can be highly indigenized if that is an important goal for the producers of format-based shows. Their international spread is not a matter of merely stamping the *Sesame* logo on locally significant product; rather there is active, planned hybridization of texts: extensive local input is sought, settings and characters are adapted, and international and local socio-cultural goals are implemented. While franchises can be and may in many cases be culturally homogenizing, the Sesame Workshop demonstrates that they can also take quite heterogeneous forms.

To orient franchise media around problems of political conflict, gender equality and disease may be atypical and seem improbable to occur in commercial franchises. The fact that these franchise texts have been made, however, challenges a reductive understanding of what franchises are, offering alternatives to the expected, stereotypic profit- and consumption-based orientation. In the case of *Sesame Street*, though education rather than profit seems to be the driving goal, there is nonetheless a very successful commercial component (through three major avenues: magazine publishing, domestic merchandising in the US, and revenue from international co-productions) (Morrow, 2006: 165–67). Moreover, an engagement with socio-political issues need not be limited to the franchises of a non-profit organization such as Sesame Workshop. Several commercial-yet-educational franchises like Nickelodeon's *Blue's Clues* and *Dora the Explorer* amply demonstrate the potential profitability of properties that include education in their remit.[3] In fact, Swann argues that in children's programming educational elements may actually increase profitability, writing:

> By ensuring that parents are confident their children are continuing to develop socially and cognitively while watching television, producers increase the likelihood that they select a particular programme for their child. Moreover, parents are more likely to buy merchandise associated with the series, if they approve of its content. Although commercial producers have a financial agenda in creating material that is socially responsible, this lessens neither the impact nor the usefulness of the material. (2012: 253)

Though a non-profit organization, Sesame Workshop can largely fund the US show as well as its extensive research through the proceeds of *Sesame Street* merchandise. In many ways, the socio-political agenda of the *Sesame*s is a natural extension of the idea of educational television and media. Making media "educational" is an idea that, though it may put off commercial producers, is not actually antithetical to profit.

Although *Sesame Street* may be atypical, particularly with respect to the amount of research that goes into production, it serves as a dynamic model that can provoke thought about how transnational franchises might effectively adapt to meet local needs and interests, demonstrate a social conscience in their co-productions, and further internationally agreed-upon humanitarian goals. There is a great deal to be learned about localization from Big Bird, Kami, and their Muppet friends.

Notes

1. The term 'media franchise' or simply 'franchise' is used throughout this article to refer to an intellectual property that is shared between producers through contractual agreements. Derek Johnson writes that, "While at the most broad level, we might start by conceiving of franchising as an economic system for exchanging cultural resources across a network of industrial relations, we also have to recognize it as a shifting set of structures, relations, and imaginative frames for organizing and making sense of the industrial exchange and reproduction of culture" (2013: 29).
2. For more on the Sesame Workshop Model see: Hendershot 1999; Lesser, 1974; Morrow, 2006; Palmer and Fisch, 2001. The Model involves a number of steps including preliminary research before production, testing educational effectiveness during production, and impact research after distribution. The Model is often held up as an ideal practice for educational television.
3. In addition to *Sesame Street*, there are a number of other non-profit educational properties that have also been quite financially successful, such as PBS's *Barney the Dinosaur* and the BBC's *Teletubbies*. Education, socio-political engagement and economic viability are not mutually exclusive.

References

Appadurai, A. (1990). *Modernity at large: Cultural dimensions of globalization*. London: University of Minnesota Press.
Christmas, L. (1971). What price Sesame Street? *The Guardian*, 9. June 3.
Gettas, G. (1990). The globalization of *Sesame Street*: A producer's perspective. *Educational Technology Research and Development*, 38(4), 55–63.
Gikow, L. (2009). *Sesame Street: A celebration: 40 years of life on the Street*. New York: Black Dog & Leventhal.
Hendershot, H. (1999). *Sesame Street*: Cognition and communications imperialism. In M. Kinder (Ed.), *Kids' media culture* (pp. 139–76). London: Duke University Press.
Johnson, D. (2013). *Media franchising: Creative license and collaboration in the culture industries*. London: New York University Press.
Keane, M., Fung, A., & Moran, A. (2007). *New television, globalisation, and the East Asian cultural imagination*. Hong Kong: Hong Kong University Press.

Kenworthy, D. (2010). Personal interview. London, June 1, 2010.

Knell, G. (2008). Lecture: Muppet diplomacy (Gary Knell). Los Angeles: USC Annenberg, YouTube, available online at: http://www.youtube.com/watch?v=3xL5-1ClMuE (Retrieved September 12, 2011).

Knowlton, L. G., & Hawkins, L. (Directors). (2006). *The world according to Sesame Street* [Motion Picture]. USA: Participant Productions.

Lesser, G. S. (1974). *Children and television: Lessons from Sesame Street.* New York: Random House.

Moran, A., & Malbon, J. (2006). *Understanding the global tv format.* Bristol: Intellect Ltd.

Morrow, R. W. (2006). *Sesame Street and the reform of children's television.* Baltimore: Johns Hopkins University Press.

MuppetWiki. (n.d.). Open Sesame, available online at: http://muppet.wikia.com/wiki/Open_Sesame (Retrieved February 9, 2012).

Palmer, E. L., & Fisch, S. M. (2001). The beginnings of *Sesame Street* research. In S. M. Fisch, and R. T. Truglio (Eds.), *"G" Is for growing: Thirty years of research on children and Sesame Street* (pp. 3–23). London: Lawrence Erlbaum Associates.

Roll Back Malaria. (2008). 2008 MDG Malaria Summit: World Leaders Unite, available online at: http://www.rollbackmalaria.org/docs/mdg2008SummaryReport.pdf (Retrieved May 10, 2011).

Sesame Workshop. (2007). Takalani Sesame, first tv & radio series to fully & equitably produce programming across official South African languages, available online at: http://www.sesameworkshop.org/newsandevents/pressreleases/multilingual_takalani (Retrieved July 22, 2011).

Sesame Workshop. (2008). Sesame Workshop uses media to tackle malaria. New York, available online at: http://www.sesameworkshop.org/newsandevents/sesameupdates/kilimani_malaria (Retrieved June 16, 2011).

Sesame Workshop. (n.d.). Sesame Tree. New York, available online at: http://www.sesameworkshop.org/what-we-do/our-initiatives/northern-ireland/ (Retrieved July 18, 2013).

Straubhaar, J. (1991). Beyond media imperialism: Asymmetrical interdependence and cultural proximity. *Critical Studies in Mass Communication,* 8(1), 39–59.

Swann, A. (2012). *The politics and economics of preschool children's television: A production and audience research study.* PhD thesis, University of Ulster.

UNAIDS.org. (2009). South African Muppet Kami speaks the language of acceptance, available online at: http://www.unaids.org/en/Resources/PressCentre/Featurestories/2009/December/20091217SAfricaSesamstreet/ (Retrieved December 17, 2011).

United Nations. (2010). Millennium development goals. New York: United Nations, available online at: http://www.un.org/milleniumgoals/ (Retrieved September 20, 2011).

Waisbord, S. (2004). McTV: Understanding the global popularity of television formats. *Television & New Media,* 5(4), 359–383.

7 Television Formats in Africa
Cultural Considerations in Format Localization

Martin Nkosi Ndlela

The television industry has in the last years witnessed a dramatic increase in the number and variety of reality shows, spanning different genres and platforms and manifesting themselves as formatted scripted or non-scripted shows that get adapted for different markets. These formats are global in nature (Esser, 2014) but have to be adapted to local or regional markets, through various processes of localization (Moran, 2009b; Moran and Keane, 2006; Waisbord, 2004). This chapter focuses on the socio-cultural precincts of television formats in sub-Saharan Africa. It examines cultural considerations in transnational adaptations and the challenges of 'transnational localization' of TV formats, drawing on examples from the pan-African versions of shows such as *Big Brother Africa*, *Idols East Africa*, and *Idols West Africa*. What does localization mean in these regional formats? What are the cultural challenges and limitations to localization in regional formats? This chapter employs the cultural economy analysis framework, drawing on the issues of cultural globalization and responses to it, such as the cultural imperialism discourses. It argues that given the fact that television in sub-Saharan Africa is still bound to the nation-state, television programs that cross national boundaries have to contend with two potential barriers, first, the national media cultural policies and second, the audience configurations and cultural preferences that in some cases are profoundly nation-state bound. These two factors have to be taken into consideration before and during format adaptations, as they can determine the success or failure of a television program. Therefore, when television programs travel across borders, they are most likely to encounter cultural barriers from the authorities, be it political or religious leaders, regulatory authorities, censorship boards, broadcasting managers, or other opinion leaders. For one reason or the other, these authorities can pass judgment on the appropriateness of the program for the national audience. Concerns about the preservation of local cultures and identities can stem the tide against television programs. The same applies to the audiences' cultural preferences, which fundamentally determine the viability of that product for that market.

Why Culture Matters in Television Formats

As Moran (2009a) has noted, the practice of television format franchising generates a cultural need to customize the format to suit local audience taste and outlook in a particular territory (Moran, 2009a). The opportunities and limitations for localization of television formats in sub-Saharan Africa are examined here from cultural economy perspectives. The point of departure is the set of central tenets of "cultural industry" as espoused by the Frankfurt School, in particular in the works of Adorno and Horkheimer (1979), who argued that the way in which cultural items were produced was analogous to how other industries manufactured vast quantities of consumer goods. Adorno and Horkheimer's formulations—that just like any manufacturing industry cultural production had become a routine, standardized repetitive operation—can be seen in the flow and production of television formats worldwide. As Negus notes, one of the three main threads of argument in Adorno and Horkheimer's work is that "the concentration of culture production in a capitalist industry results in a standardized commercial commodity" (Negus, 1997: 73). Some of these classical ideas still have relevance in the current discussions of the implications of cultural industries. Questions on the origins and flows of television programs feature predominantly in the discourses on post-colonial television programming in sub-Saharan Africa.

Concerns about the 'problems' of concentration and implications for national cultures were manifested in the debates under the auspices of UNESCO (United Nations Educational, Scientific and Cultural Organization) in the early 1980s. As noted in the UNESCO publication, *The Culture Industries: A Challenge for the Future of Culture*, developments in information and communication technologies have revolutionized the way in which all forms of cultural expression are produced and disseminated (UNESCO, 1982). However these developments led to the marginalization of certain cultures, especially those from less developed countries in sub-Saharan Africa. Fears were also expressed on what was seen as "uncontrolled mass dissemination of messages which are in most cases culturally incompatible with local situations" (UNESCO, 1982: 10), for example by being in conflict with cultural identities. The UNESCO debates also advocated for strategies to counterbalance the effects of the cultural standardization brought about by the media at national and regional levels. Thus, these debates had profound influence on the articulations of cultural policies in many sub-Saharan African countries, manifested in the form of foreign program quotas, inter-regional exchanges, and co-productions.

Arguments about the cultural inappropriateness of certain programs were recently used by opponents of *Big Brother Africa*. Jacobs (2007) notes for example, how religious groups in Zambia unsuccessfully tried to pressure the government to stop the broadcast of *Big Brother Africa* due to its perceived immoral content and 'un-Africanness'. He further notes how the same religious groups had earlier succeeded in stopping the Zambian national broadcaster from broadcasting South African satellite music video channel, Channel O. Channel O, which is based on the MTV concept, has been a target of criticism for airing videos deemed culturally inappropriate, depicting pictures of half-naked women or playing songs with explicit lyrics.

There were similar attempts to stop *Big Brother Africa* in Malawi, Namibia, and Nigeria. Biltereyst argues that "only very few programs or cultural products in Africa have been able to instigate such a cross-national public debate on cultural quality, social and moral values" (2004: 10). *Big Brother Africa* attracted criticism over its representation of moral issues, nudity sequences, and sex scenes. Across sub-Saharan Africa, *Big Brother Africa* became an object of cultural criticism, reminding us of the importance of cultural sensitivity in television programs. *Big Brother Africa*, being the first truly pan-African reality TV program in terms of participation, shows how cultural considerations can potentially threaten the economic viability of a show. There is a perception amongst policy makers and some sections of the audiences that Big Brother reflects Western cultural values. To some critics, especially in the neo-colonialization spectrum, this is yet another manifestation of cultural imperialism.

The controversies and debates on the threat of cultural homogenization and the cultural imperialism thesis persist in the public discourse. Media, perceived as agents of globalization, play an overwhelming role in the process of cultural imperialism. A central tenet of the media imperialism thesis is that media globalization is resulting in global cultural homogenization (Strelitz, 2003). According to Hamelink, "one conclusion still seems unanimously shared: the impressive variety of the world's cultural systems is waning due to a process of cultural synchronization that is without historic precedent" (Hamelink, 1983: 3). The key arguments raised in the cultural imperialism thesis were based mainly on the unequal one-way flow of news and cultural products (television, movies, music, advertisements) from a few countries in the First world, to the rest of the world (Boyd-Barret, 1980; Hamelink, 1983).

However, the cultural imperialism thesis has its own limitations. In his article, "Globalization and Cultural Imperialism Reconsidered", Morley (2006) identifies four limitations of cultural imperialism, namely the complexities of international communication flows, glocalization, cultural protectionism, and active audiences. In his article, "Beyond Media Imperialism: Asymmetrical Interdependence and Cultural proximity", Straubhaar (1991) analyzes some of the controversies surrounding the cultural imperialism thesis, arguing that most of these arguments are overly simplistic. He argues that we should also analyze the development of increasingly independent cultural industries, including the cycles of technological changes that frequently change structural relations (Straubhaar, 1991). Technological developments have facilitated connectivity of cultural industries within Africa thus creating regional market clusters for production and consumption of television products. These clusters are also linked to other structures in different parts of the world. These structural relations promote different patterns of cultural exchange rather than simply 'flows' as premised in the media imperialism thesis. Similarly, Tomlinson (1999) is skeptical of the idea of the emergence of a unified global culture and the fears of global cultural uniformity (Tomlinson, 1999: 105). As noted by Choi, Tomlison's argument is that what has emerged is deterritorialized "globalized culture" rather than a monolithic imagining of "a global culture" (Choi, 2002: 447).

Localization: A Response to Cultural Homogenization

Even though global flows have become more and more complex, some countries are still more dominant than others, suggesting therefore that inequalities in cultural exchanges and fears of cultural homogenization remain. However, some researchers argue that through localization fears of globalization can be allayed. For example, Waisbord (2004) argues that "unlike canned shows that are steeped in specific national cultures, formats are open texts that can be adapted" and hence "cannot be seen simply as transmission belts for Western values" (Waisbord, 2004: 371). Van Keulen and Krijnen (2013) note how successful localizations like *Farmer Wants a Wife* have been "hailed as one of the finest examples of localization and an argument against cultural homogenization", and "localization is used an argument to dismiss the possible globalizing and homogenizing effects of the international TV format trade" (2013: 2). The implications of localiza-tion attract divergent viewpoints at least for localization theories and those steeped in the cultural imperialist thesis. These divergent viewpoints reflect the general complexities of locating television programs between the local and the global.

The concept of glocalization has been used to capture global-local con-nections. Glocalization refers to "the successful global transfer of products to different localities, by making modifications for such variables as culture, language, gender, or ethnicity, rather than selling the standardized" (Morley, 2006: 39). Format trade captures the ethos of glocalization. The format trade involves both the process of globalization and localization—the exporting licenser, still dominated by the Anglo-Saxon world (Esser, 2014) and an importing licensee who is "granted the opportunity to adapt the format to the needs of the domestic TV market and to balance between cost-efficient standardization and cultural *differentiation*" (Altmeppen, Lantzsch, & Will, 2007: 95). The main thrust behind localization is that formats are trans-lated to local versions that presumably suit national culture and identity (van Keulen & Krijnen, 2013). The process involves connecting the content of the program to the norms, values, beliefs, and all other social-cultural elements of an audience (ibid: 2). This is based on the assumption that audi-ences are most likely to be attracted to programming they can easily iden-tify with, or as Morley (2001) argues, people feel at "home" seeing images and situations that correspond to aspects of their identity. By home, Morley refers not simply to a physical place, but also to a virtual and rhetorical space (Morley, 2001: 25). The popularity of television formats seems to reward the efforts of international and domestic companies to deal with the resilience of national cultures (Waisbord, 2004). According to Waisbord, television formats attest to the fact that television remains tied to local and national cultures (2004: 360). Hence, television formats make it possible to adapt successful programs to national cultures, thereby eliminating cultural barriers or overcoming the phenomena of 'cultural discount', as defined by Hoskins and Mirus (1988). Cultural discount theory argues that a cultural product rooted in one culture "will have a diminished appeal elsewhere as viewers find it difficult to identify with the style, values, beliefs, institutions, and behavioral patterns of the material in question" (Hoskins & Mirus, 1988: 500). Hence, in adapting a television format for an African market, one will have to contend with local differences in language, aesthetic tastes, and social and cultural values. What program attributes should be taken into consideration in order to bring together a seemingly diverse audience?

Linguistic Diversity and Pragmatic Choices

One of the central factors to be taken into consideration in format localization is the choice of language to be used, be it the official language(s), the national language, or a minority or majority (national) language, and its linkages to the targeted market audience. Linguistic configurations have an intricate connection to the local particularity. However, sub-Saharan African countries have a complex multilingual context compounded by migration patterns and influences in the pre-colonial and post-colonial era. As Kashoki (2003) argues, the largely arbitrary nature of the manner in which present-day African countries came into being as sovereign nation states is directly responsible for their present highly multi-ethnic, multicultural, and multilingual national character. Some countries like Nigeria and Tanzania have more than 100 languages or dialects; Kenya has 68 languages. At a regional market level, Southern Africa has more than 50 living languages of which 14 are institutional, West Africa has 888 languages of which 61 are institutional, and East Africa has 432 languages of which 60 are institutional (Ethnologue, 2014). The linguistic diversity and complexity in sub-Saharan Africa has arguably been simplified through the adoption and localization of colonial languages like English, French, and Portuguese. These languages are the de facto languages of business, education, and the media. The choice of these languages is mainly for pragmatic reasons, such as the creation and preservation of national unity, and less to do with cultural preservation. This is one of the first contradictions in the relationship between language and culture. Some African English language researchers like Bagwasi (2014: 196) strongly argue that "in situations where English is used in African contexts, African values, perspectives and viewpoints are compromised and distorted while English values, perspectives and viewpoints are adopted and promoted". This is an inevitable situation given the linguistic complexity cited above. In the localization of transnational television formats like *Big Brother Africa, Idols West Africa,* and *Idols East Africa* English is the main language of choice, because of expedience rather than cultural considerations. There have been attempts however to use local languages, especially in South Africa where Afrikaans has been used in *Afrikaans Idols*. Even though this is an affluent market, the program reaches only a small part of the South African market. Attempts have also been made within the Nigerian film industry, where one finds Yoruba and Hausa films targeting huge local populations within Nigeria. These films however, have a completely different distribution system and target market than formatted television programs. Wildman (1995) notes that language is a factor defining the boundaries of media markets. In the case of Africa, languages, especially colonial languages, have a unifying effect by bringing together different national markets.

Geographical and Cultural Proximity

Another factor to be taken into consideration in the localization of television formats has to do with regional configurations in the sub-Saharan Africa. Besides the language, cultures in sub-Saharan Africa, whether at national or regional level, are very diverse and complex. There is a huge diversity of cultures conditioned by both internal and external influences. Colonial forms and their influences also inform today's cultural formation in the nations and regions of sub-Saharan Africa. In the case of Africa, the epicenter of these cultural flows has historically been Western European countries, mainly through exploration, military expeditions, missionary activities, and colonization. With empires reaching most corners of the world, Western European countries brought various modes of societal organization, ideologies, constructs of nationalism and citizenship, and urbanization. Colonization also brought with it transnational organizations working within a particular global structure. Colonization created within Africa new regions of cultural proximity as well as barriers between these regions. A vivid example is the divisions between the Anglophone, Francophone, and Lusophone Africa, linguistically defined after the dominant colonizers, Britain, France, and Portugal. These regions also constitute market areas. Cultural proximity in this case is linguistically defined. It is primarily the understanding of the English language that binds the audiences of pan-African shows like *Big Brother*, rather than those cultural elements that can be easily associated with any particular local, national, or regional culture. This gives credence to Waisbord's assertion that formats are less prone to having specific reference to the local and national, precisely because they are designed to travel well across national boundaries (2004). *Big Brother Africa* resonates with audiences across the region because it is de-nationalized and cannot be associated with the culture and identity of a specific country. Television programs like *Idols South Africa* and *Masterchef South Africa* carry some traits that are uniquely South African. These shows include cultural artifacts that the audiences in South Africa can identify with. They are national in character.

Understanding the Audience

Audience perspectives are also crucial in the understanding of localization attempts in the sub-Saharan context. Audience configurations, their choices, and preferences ultimately determine the success or failure of television formats. McQuail notes that "a media product is a commodity or service offered for sale to a given body of potential consumers, in competition with other media products" (McQuail, 1987: 221). Potential consumers are conceived of as markets for advertising certain products. The developments in media technologies have increased connectivity between nations and regions, spurning geographical boundaries and thereby enabling the segmentation and consolidation of specific pan-African audience markets for certain media products. The contemporary conceptions of the audience in sub-Saharan Africa transcend national boundaries, reaching transnational as well as international audiences. The latter being strongly reflected in the diaspora reach of television formats like the above. Format producers are increasingly targeting a much wider audience across borders and media platforms. Understanding the cultural preferences of the audiences is therefore crucial to understanding the market demands. Straubhaar points to the issues of cultural relevance and proximity in the audience choices among international, regional, and national television programs. He argues that the audience tends to prefer and select local or national cultural content that is proximate and more relevant to them (Straubhaar, 1991). Flows of African produced programs within Africa are stronger between more culturally proximate African countries. However, preference for national culture is not uniform as other factors such as class affect these preferences (Martín-Barbero, 1988). Certain programs are likely to appeal to affluent middle classes across national borders. In the localization of regional formats like *Big Brother Africa* certain cultural artifacts that identify with specific national cultures are not utilized that much, because doing so will jeopardize the program's pan-African orientation. What then unites the preferences of the audiences across different sub-Saharan African nations?

The Intensification of the Culture of Consumption

Contemporary sub-Saharan African societies are awash with global consumer goods with, for example, branded clothing styles, hip-hop music, and sporting goods. Consumption and popular cultural practices bring together audiences across national boundaries. Therefore, cultural texts such as *Big Brother* and *Idols* and their consumption in Africa can be analyzed within Jean Baudrillard's postmodern postulations. He claims that "we have reached a stage in social and economic development in which 'it is no longer possible to separate the economic or productive realm from the realms of ideology or culture, since cultural artefacts, images, representations, even feelings and psychic structures have become part of the world of the economic" (Connor, 1989: 51). Another way in which the world is becoming postmodern is in its increasing globalization (Storey, 2009: 203), and one aspect of these global cultures is associated with the rise of consumerism, a new social and economic order that is also emerging in African countries. Coupled with the growing number of people considered middle class, the new order encourages consumption of goods and services, including cultural products. The consumption referents circulating in the media and other forms of mediation are finding expressions in the consumer behaviors around the world, including the emerging markets in sub-Saharan Africa. Globalization subsequently enables social comparisons. Consumption referents of the new elites find expression in the political economy of television formats and inform the production choices made in format localization. It can be argued therefore that global culture(s) provide opportunities for closing the cultural gaps, thereby reducing cultural differences in regional market territories. Television consumption preferences resonate around symbols and artifacts with which audiences are already familiar.

Celebrities, Stars, and Fan Cultures

Audiences in sub-Saharan Africa are also imbued in the increasingly global celebrity cultures. The *Big Brother Africa* series has capitalized upon the increasing phenomenon of celebrities, stars, and fan culture by drawing participation from local celebrities such as budding musicians, models, and media personalities. *Big Brother Africa 5 (All-Stars)* (2010) and *Big Brother Africa 7 (StarGame)* (2012) were especially focused around stardom and celebrity cultures. From the global music scene, the *Idols* series is part of an increasingly transnational popular culture. It is a mediated popular culture involving issues of identity and negotiation of cultural meanings. It is also located within somewhat homogenized television content around the world marked by the global reach of a homogenized pop-music genre. *Idols* versions around the world share a similar dramaturgy derived from the format producers. *Idols West Africa* (2007) and *Idols East Africa (2008)*, pan-African franchises based on the format co-owned by FremantleMedia and 19 Entertainment, illustrate the rapid global spread of the brand whose primary goal "is to involve a nation (or a region consisting of several different nations) in a quest for a popular music idol to be admired by all" (de Bruin & Zwaan, 2012). Its global spread is akin to how other brands are marketed. Fairchild (2008) notes that 'Idols' are explicitly developed as brands, and are acquired in the same way a corporation might acquire a brand, purchased as contracted labor and gradually fitted into a pre-existing, pre-formatted communications campaign (Fairchild, 2008: 96). These potential (idols) are tested in the marketplace and adapted to fit consumer requirements, in our case the Pan-African regional markets.

Format adaptation and localization take place throughout the process of searching for, making, and marketing the idols. The local participants and viewers get involved within the "format's four distinct stages, each with its own technological and aesthetic form and particular modes of audience address" (Holmes, 2004: 153). As Holmes describes, the first stage involves

a series of auditions for Idol hopefuls; the second stage features a more professional audition. The third stage adds more formal interaction between the
contestants and the viewers. At this stage, the audience has the opportunity
to influence the outcome of the show. As Holmes argues at this stage, the
contestants direct their performances at the viewer rather than the judges.
At the final stage, the participant with the lowest number of viewer votes is
evicted from the competition. Localization happens throughout these four
stages. For example, during the first stage, participants in the audition are
allowed to sing in both English and local languages, and they can choose
from a wide spectrum of music. However, as Ndlela (2012) notes, in the case
of *Idols South Africa* as the stages progress, song selection represents a who-
is-who in the western pop charts, and the choices are biased toward English.
The same applies to *Idols West Africa* and *Idols East Africa*.

Idols East Africa premiered in April 2008 featuring participating countries in Southern and East African countries after a season of *Idols West
Africa* 2007. The contestants were thus drawn from countries with diverse
cultural and linguistic attributes, including participants from predominantly
French and Portuguese speaking countries. What factors then were used to
eliminate cultural distance between these diverse countries? The quest for
stardom and celebrity culture seems to be one of the major uniting factors
in the reduction of cultural distance. The *Idols* show adds a new stratum
of celebrity value to the African audience, providing avenues for exposure.
The show's different stages give opportunities to Idols hopefuls to prove
themselves on the stage in front of the national and transnational audience. A platform is offered for attaining fame, and possibly celebrity status.
Researchers define celebrity as distinctly a capitalist phenomenon coincid-
ing with changes in communication technology that enabled news forms of
social mobility, the democratization of the consumption of cultural goods,
and the production of secular notions of popular culture (Collins, 2008).

The second factor is imbued in the format's genre—pop music as a unifying element. Through colonial and post-colonial encounters, audiences in
these countries have been susceptible to Western cultural products including pop music. The audience exposure, taste, and preferences are inclined
toward Western music. The countries participating in the contests are
culturally and linguistically diverse, and hence no music within the 'music
in Africa' stable could appeal to audiences in all the participating countries.
Music in Africa has many genres and rhythms. Hence, although some of the
themes in *Idols East Africa* and *Idols West Africa* have been adapted to meet
the cultural considerations of the audiences, the shows are characterized by
many renditions of well-known Western beats.

Concluding Remarks

Localization of television formats in transnational settings invokes a number of cultural issues that challenge the very concept of 'local'. Format adaptation in the pan-African version of *Big Brother Africa*, *Idols East Africa*,

and *Idols West Africa* require careful cultural strategies and sensitivities that enhance the format's success and economic viability. These strategies include the choice of language(s) that potentially connect small national markets into larger regional markets, thereby constituting a geo-linguistically defined market. The popularity of pan-African adaptations depend upon the producers' ability and concerted effort to align format adaptations to market requirements, reducing cultural distance within regional market territories. This also involves aspects of de-nationalization, through the elimination of country-specific cultural traits and utilization of generic cultural artifacts. Adaptations should also strive to negotiate the complexities of regional cultural flows, cultural identities, and the policies of cultural protection. The localization of television formats for regional markets allows us to transcend the local versus global, or homogenization versus heterogenization. In these regional versions the formats seek to, on one hand, address the needs of audiences in different and culturally diverse African countries, and on the other hand, avoid the trappings of homogenization. The cultural inputs imbued in the localized versions are illustrative of the inadequacies of the cultural imperialism thesis. The phenomenon of television format adaptation in the sub-Saharan context requires mixed theoretical approaches that take into consideration the local and global dimension of television as well as variations of television's political economy.

References

Adorno, T. W. and Horkheimer, M. (1979). *Dialectic of Enlightenment*. Harpenden, Herts: Verso.
Altmeppen, K.-D., Lantzsch, K., & Will, A. (2007). Flowing networks in the entertainment business: Organizing international tv format trade. *The International Journal of Media Media Management, 9*(3), 94–104.
Bagwasi, M. M. (2014). Englishising African cultures: Revisiting acculturated forms of English in Botswana. *Language, Culture and Curriculum, 27*(2), 196–208.
Biltereyst, D. (2004). Big Brother and its moral guardians. In E. Mathijs & J. Jones (Eds.), *Big Brother international. Formats, critics and publics* (pp. 9–15). London: Wallflower Press.
Boyd-Barret, O. (1980). *The international news agencies*. Beverley Hills: Sage.
Choi, J. (2002). Globalization and culture. *Journal of Communication Inquiry, 26*, 446–450.
Collins, S. (2008). Making the most out of 15 minutes: Reality tv's dispensable celebrity. *Television & New Media, 9*(2), 87–110.
Connor, S. (1989). *Postmodernist culture: An introduction to theories of the contemporary*. Oxford: Blackwell.
de Bruin, J., & Zwaan, K. (2012). Introduction: Adapting idols. In J. de Bruin & K. Zwaan (Eds.), *Adapting idols: Authenticity, identify and performance in a global television format*. Surrey, England: Ashgate.
Esser, A. (2014). European television programming: exemplifying and theorizing glocalization in the media. In R. Robertson (Ed.), *European glocalization in global context* (pp. 82–102). Basingstoke: Palgrave.

Ethnologue. (2014). *Languages of the World*, available online at: https://www.ethnologue.com/ (Retrieved April 15, 2015).

Fairchild, C. (2008). *Pop idols: Mechanisms of consumption and the global circulation of popular music*. Abingdon, Oxon: Ashgate.

Hamelink, C. (1983). *Cultural autonomy in global communications*. New York: Longman.

Holmes, S. (2004). "Reality goes pop!": Reality tv, popular music, and narratives of stardom in pop idol. *Television & New Media, 5*(2), 147–172.

Hoskins, C., & Mirus, R. (1988). Reasons for U.S. dominance of the international trade in television programmes. *Media, Culture & Society, 10*, 499–515.

Jacobs, S. (2007). Big Brother. Africa is watching. *Media, Culture & Society, 29*(6).

Kashoki, M. E. (2003). Language policy formulation in multilingual Southern Africa. *Journal of Multilingual and Multicultural Development, 24*(3), 184–194.

Martín-Barbero, J. (1988). Communication from culture: The crisis of the national and the emergence of the popular. *Media, Culture & Society, 10*(4), 447–465.

McQuail, D. (1987). *Mass communication theory*. London: Sage Publications.

Moran, A. (2009a). Global franchising, local customizing: The cultural economy of tv program formats. *Continuum, 23*(2), 115–125.

Moran, A. (2009b). *TV formats worldwide: Localising global programs*. Bristol, GBR: Intellect Ltd.

Moran, A., & Keane, M. (2006). Cultural power in international tv format markets. *Continuum, 20*(1), 71–86.

Morley, D. (2001). Belongings: Place, space and identity in a mediated world. *European Journal of Cultural Studies, 4*(4), 425–448.

Morley, D. (2006). Globalisation and cultural imperialism reconsidered: Old questions in new guises. In J. Curran & D. Morley (Eds.), *Media and Cultural Theory* (pp. 30–43). New York: Routledge.

Ndlela, M. N. (2012). Global television formats in Africa—Localizing *Idols*. In T. Oren & S. Shahaf (Eds.), *Global television formats. Understanding television across borders*. New York: Routledge.

Negus, K. (1997). The production of culture. In P. du Gay (Ed.), *Production of culture/ cultures of production* (pp. 67–118). London: Sage Publications.

Storey, J. (2009). *Cultural theory and popular culture. An introduction*. London: Pearson.

Straubhaar, J. (1991). Beyond media imperialism: Asymmetrical interdependence and cultural proximity. *Critical Studies in Mass Communication, 8*, 39–59.

Strelitz, L. (2003). Global media and symbolic distancing. *Ecquid Novi: African Journalism Studies, 24*(2), 136–156.

Tomlinson, J. (1999). *Globalization and culture*. Cambridge: Polity Press.

UNESCO. (1982). The Culture industries: A challenge for the future of culture, available online at: http://unesdoc.unesco.org/images/0004/000499/049972eo.pdf (Retrieved April 14, 2015).

van Keulen, J., & Krijnen, T. (2013). The globalization debate and the limitations of the localization of tv formats: A cross-cultural comparative case study. *International Journal of Cultural Studies*.

Waisbord, S. (2004). McTV: Understanding the global popularity of television formats. *Television & New Media, 5*(4), 359–383.

Wildman, S. S. (1995). Trade liberalization and policy for media industries: A theoretical examination of media flows. *Canadian Journal of Communication, 20*, 367–388.

8 Exploring Factors Influencing the Dubbing of TV Series into Spanish

Key Aspects for the Analysis of Dubbed Dialogue

Rocío Baños

Various scholars in Translation Studies have explored the characteristics of dubbed audiovisual programs and dubbed dialogue in a wide range of languages and cultures. Particular attention has lately been paid to the "prefabricated orality" (Chaume, 2012: 82) of audiovisual texts, that is, to the fact that audiovisual dialogue may seem spontaneous and natural, but that such spontaneity is rather false and 'prefabricated'. Scholars working on audiovisual translation (AVT) have investigated how this specific characteristic of film and TV drama materializes in dubbing. In the same way some researchers have compared audiovisual dialogue to spontaneous conversation to find out what sets them apart and to describe how the former is shaped from a linguistic point of view (see Quaglio, 2009; Bednarek, 2010), in AVT the comparison has often been drawn between translated dialogue and spontaneous conversation in the target language (i.e., the language the audiovisual product is translated into). In an attempt to describe dubbed dialogue, some studies have compared it with non-translated dialogue, including in their analysis films and TV series originally created in the target language (e.g., Matamala, 2008; Pavesi, 2009). Such studies have shown that the linguistic patterning of dubbed dialogue is different from that of non-translated texts, as the features that make dialogues sound more natural and spontaneous tend to be less frequent, more stereotyped and conventional in the former (Baños, 2014: 430). It has also been argued that although we might never be able to put the language of dubbed programs at the same level as that of domestic programs, the analysis of the latter can improve our understanding of the nature of audiovisual dialogue in the target language. It can also help our understanding of the strategies that could be resorted to in order to achieve more credible and natural-sounding dialogues (ibid).

When assessing the similarities and divergences between original and dubbed dialogue, it is imperative to ascertain the complex socio-cultural context surrounding the audiovisual products being contrasted. Whereas many of the above-mentioned differences result from translated texts being "constrained by a fully articulated text in another language" (Baker, 1996: 177), in the case of audiovisual texts, further 'constraints' or factors influence both original and dubbed text production. Factors such as the target audience, the channel in which the program is broadcast, or the many agents involved in the drafting and production process leave traces in the language used by translators and scriptwriters and have an impact on the final product. The purpose of this chapter is to reflect on how these factors influence translated audiovisual texts in general, focusing on the selection of orality markers in a situation comedy dubbed from English into Spanish. Orality markers, understood as "features typifying spontaneous spoken register used in prefabricated dialogue to reinforce its orality and to convey a false sense of spontaneity" (Baños, 2014: 408–409), have been chosen as the main object of study given the challenges prefabricated orality poses to scriptwriters and audiovisual translators alike.

Whenever relevant, a comparison will be established between the factors influencing dubbed dialogue and those influencing non-translated dialogue. This will be done in order to show that we are dealing with very complex products and to illustrate that comparisons between translated and non-translated dialogue should not be limited to a mere linguistic analysis. The aim is to contend that the unnaturalness and marked prefabricated nature of dubbed dialogue reported in the literature may respond to specific constraints and not necessarily to the audiovisual translator's incompetence as may sometimes be argued. By doing so, this chapter reflects not only on how audiovisual products travel across borders, but also on how foreign products are influenced by different powers and governed by different conventions, if compared to domestic products, even if they both belong to the same audiovisual genre and co-exist in the same TV context. To this end, the chapter will draw on methodological considerations in line with Descriptive Translation Studies (DTS) and on examples from a previous study based on a comparable and parallel audiovisual corpus of sitcoms broadcast in Spain (Baños, 2009; 2014). Despite being focused on orality markers in Spanish sitcoms, the aim of the chapter is not to provide specific results (for this see Baños, 2014), but to shed light on the factors influencing the translation of dialogues in dubbing, and how these differ from those affecting the production of this type of text in domestic programs.

Theoretical and Methodological Considerations for the Study of Dubbed Products

Despite its relative youth, AVT is now a consolidated field of research in Translation Studies. One of the key concerns in AVT research has been to emphasize what makes it specific and to factor it appropriately into the analysis of AVT as a process and of audiovisual texts as products. With this aim in mind, scholars have often argued for interdisciplinary, systematic and integrative methodological and theoretical approaches to AVT research. In this regard, Chaume posits that the descriptivist paradigm seems rather suited to AVT inasmuch as it offers "a powerful interdisciplinary framework for translation analysis" (2012: 161). In a similar vein, Díaz Cintas conceives DTS as "a heuristic tool that opens up new avenues for study, strengthens the theoretical component and allows the researcher to come up with substantial analyses" (2004: 31). This chapter takes a similar stance, considering that the descriptivist paradigm provides the appropriate tools to investigate translated audiovisual products in depth, while considering their specific nature and the socio-cultural context in which they are embedded, thus pleading for "autochthonous models" (Pérez-González, 2014: 96) for AVT research.

As Chaume (2012: 162–63) illustrates, since the inception of AVT research several models of analysis that draw on DTS principles have emerged. For the purposes of this chapter, it is interesting to identify how these models integrate the analysis of factors influencing the production of dubbed dialogue. Karamitroglou (2000) was one of the first scholars to acknowledge the importance of a wide range of elements influencing AVT. Drawing on the literary polysystem factors highlighted by Even-Zohar (1990: 31–44), Karamitroglou (ibid: 70) argues that the following factors are essential for the study of translation norms (i.e., regular trends and patterns in translators' behavior) in audiovisual translation: human agents, recipients, market, institution, audiovisual mode, and products. He considers that human agents will try to conform to, or deviate from, established conventions and that the final product, being the accumulation of their normative behavior, "will have to be promoted by the market, accepted by the consumers and finally adopted by the institution". As for the audiovisual mode, Karamitroglou posits that it can be identified with a type of "repertoire" (Even-Zohar, 1990: 39), that is, "the aggregate of rules, items and interrelations with which a specific audiovisual text is produced and understood" (Karamitroglou, 2000: 79–80).

Chaume (ibid: 161) suggests a descriptive and semiotic model for the analysis of dubbed texts consisting of an internal and an external level. The latter takes into account historical factors (such as year or period of the source and target texts, the translation mode used, or the existence of previous versions), professional aspects (deadlines, material available, fees, copyright, dubbing conventions), communicative factors (client, audience, communicative context, genre, or broadcaster) and reception factors (for example, synchrony requirements, dubbing performance, or oral discourse). As regards the relevance of these factors in the analysis of AVT, Chaume (ibid) claims they condition the decisions audiovisual translators make throughout the process and can provide the researcher with a starting point to formulate hypotheses and a solid grounding to initiate translation research. As will be shown below, this chapter argues that these factors are also essential to interpreting the results of the analysis and to establish hypotheses for further research into the language of dubbing and what sets it apart from other forms of text production (e.g., spontaneous conversation and non-translated dialogue).

In order to gather information about these factors, researchers should consult extratextual sources (Toury, 1995: 65), which in the case of audiovisual texts could take very different forms. Reports on audiovisual products can provide useful information about audience ratings and broadcasters' programming policies and strategies, whereas online databases such as

eldoblaje.com in Spain can be consulted to find out broadcast dates of translated products, as well as the names of all those involved in the dubbing
process. As will be illustrated below, all these might influence the linguistic
patterning of translated audiovisual texts and thus explain why dubbed dialogue is not as natural or spontaneous-sounding as native dialogues. Once
this information has been gathered, thanks to the vast amount of data available online, it is easy for researchers to contact these part-takers individu-
ally to arrange interviews or send questionnaires via email to gather more
specific information (e.g., use of software, conventions or guidelines, degree
of involvement of agents in the process, etc.) and even ask for additional
textual sources such as drafts or working documents.

Factors Influencing the Production of Dubbed Dialogue in Spanish: The Case of *Friends*

The aim of this section is to reflect on how the factors mentioned by Karamitroglou (2000) and Chaume (2012) might influence the linguistic patterning
of dubbed products, contributing to their standardization and artificiality,
with an emphasis on those linguistic features that make dialogues sound
spontaneous, bringing them closer to natural conversation. When relevant,
a comparison will be drawn with the factors influencing domestic products (i.e., non-translated). This will be achieved drawing on examples from
two TV series (*Siete Vidas* and *Friends*), which are considered comparable
as they belong to the same genre (situation comedies) and bear significant
resemblances to each other regarding genre conventions, theme, broadcasting characteristics, and viewership. *Friends* is a US television sitcom that
tells the story of six friends in their 30s who live in New York. In Spain, the
dubbed episodes were broadcast from 1997 to 2005 by Canal+ and were
rather successful, especially considering that they were broadcast during the
so-called 'second prime-time' in Spain (from 14.30–17.00), achieving above
average ratings if compared to other programs aired in this channel (GECA,
2000–2005). *Siete Vidas*, aired on Telecinco from 1999 to 2006, is a Spanish
television sitcom that is said to have been originally inspired by *Friends*, an
aspect that not only justifies the comparison but also shows how foreign
audiovisual programs can influence the target TV system and its domestic
content. *Siete Vidas* revolves around the lives of a group of friends living in
Madrid and, like *Friends*, it touches on a wide range of topics such as relationships, sex, love, careers, friendship, and homosexuality.

In the analysis of external factors, particular attention will be paid to the
role of the agents involved in the dubbing process, the audience, the restrictions and conventions of the audiovisual mode, the professional aspects of
this market, and the power exerted by relevant institutions, as well as to
how these might differ in the case of domestic programs. A brief summary
of the factors to be taken into consideration for the purposes of this paper,
adapted from Karamitroglou (2000), is provided in Table 8.1.

Table 8.1 Factors influencing the production of original and dubbed dialogue

Type of program	Factors				
	Human agents involved in dubbing/production	Recipients	Audiovisual product	Audiovisual mode (repertoire)	Market & institution
Domestic programs (non-translated)	Human agents involved: - screenwriters - producers - director - actors - image & sound engineers, etc.	Type of target audience	Audience ratings & broadcast strategy	Genre conventions & priorities	Professional aspects (deadlines, fees, material available, etc.)
	Extent to which actors improvise on set	Audience present on set	Prestige & expectations	Specificities of audiovisual texts & audiovisual medium	Quality standards & policies for quality control Policies & conventions governing production
Dubbed programs	Human agents involved: - translator - dialogue writer - linguistic reviser - dubbing director - dubbing actors/voice talents - image & sound engineers	Type of target audience	Audience ratings & broadcast strategy	Genre conventions & priorities	Professional aspects (deadlines, fees, material available, etc.)
	Extent to which dubbing actors improvise		Prestige & expectations	Dubbing synchronies	Quality standards & policies for quality control
				Specificities of dubbed audiovisual texts & audiovisual medium	Policies & conventions governing translation & dubbing (e.g. dubbing conventions & guidelines)

Information about these factors with regards to *Friends* and *Siete Vidas* was gathered through various means: online databases, industry reports on television programs in Spain (GECA, 1998–2005), online questionnaires answered by part-takers (*Friends'* translator Darryl Clark and Natxo López, one of the screenwriters of *Siete Vidas*), and telephone interviews (e.g., with Raquel Segovia, who worked as a linguistic supervisor at Canal+). As will be shown below, these extratextual sources were essential for interpreting the results of the linguistic analysis of the two series.

Agents Involved in the Process

The wealth of agents involved in the production of dubbed episodes has a substantial impact on the final product. Dubbed products have to go through numerous filters, thus increasing the prefabricated nature of the final dialogue. Once the script has been translated, it needs to be synchronized by the dialogue writer (Chaume, 2004: 43) to make sure that it fits with the articulatory and body movements of the screen actors, and once it has been synchronized it will be interpreted by dubbing actors under the supervision of the dubbing director and the linguistic supervisor (if applicable). It should also be noted that dubbing actors have little leeway to improvise (Matamala, 2008: 93; Sánchez Mompeán, 2015: 277) and to leave traces of their own idiosyncrasies. In most cases, dubbing actors' utterances are recorded separately under the supervision of the dubbing director. The absence of the rest of the 'participants' in the conversation in the dubbing booth, together with the synchronization process required, might hinder the introduction of conversational features while recording the Spanish dubbed track. In addition, as there is often only one actor involved, lines tend to be rehearsed and repeated constantly, an approach that allows for more polished and thus less natural utterances.

In comparison, the situation in which dialogue is produced and recorded in domestic productions is very different. Even though scriptwriters are responsible for dialogue writing in original programs, the decisions made by the series director on the set and the actors' ability to improvise allow for the further inclusion of orality markers. Although no reception studies seem to have been carried out regarding the impact of such improvisation on viewers, I contend that many of these features will infuse dialogues with a false—yet natural-sounding—spontaneity and will make the final product more credible in the eyes of the viewers. The linguistic impact of improvisation on Spanish audiovisual texts has been investigated by Ruiz Gurillo (2013a and 2013b), who has compared written scripts (pre-production) with the final interpreted text (post-production) in the case of humoristic monologues in terms of key register features such as planning, immediacy, face to face interaction, dynamism, and audience feedback. Her work shows that monologists add several linguistic and paralinguistic features typical of spontaneous conversation when dramatizing written scripts, turning monologues into dialogues with the audience: vowel extensions, pauses, contact control markers, improvised additions, allusions to the public, etc. (ibid, 2013a: 123–27). Humoristic monologues are no exception, and it is logical to think that similar mechanisms will be used by sitcom actors when interpreting their lines. As can be seen in the example below from *Siete Vidas*, the comparison of pre- and post-production scripts reveals that the changes implemented on the set are substantial and reinforce the presence of orality markers.

Table 8.2 Example of actors' improvisation in domestic productions (*Siete Vidas*)

TV Series: Siete Vidas	Episode: 138 – Resident Evil TC: 08.08
Sole has decided to move from her flat to a residence for the elderly and has left a letter to let her friends know. As soon as Diana, Gonzalo, Aída and Carlota find out, they go to the residence to convince her to go back to her flat. At the residence, Carlota blames Diana for suggesting that Sole should go on a package holiday with people of her own age.	
Pre-production script	*Post-production script*
DIANA: ¡Lo hice por su bien, ahí se conoce a mucha gente! Además, cuando le da el lumbago, ¿quién le lleva al baño?, ¿eh? ¿O quién le ayuda a subirle la compra? De repente todo el mundo sale con la excusa de que tiene una cita. Y de Vero me lo creo, pero de Aída…	DIANA: <u>Oye, oye, oye, que… que yo</u> lo hice por su bien, <u>¿eh?</u> Que ahí se conoce a mucha gente. Además, <u>oye, cua</u>-cuando le da el lumbago, ¿quién <u>la</u> lleva al baño?, ¿eh? ¿O quién <u>le sube</u> la compra? <u>Porque</u> de repente <u>todos salís</u> con la <u>excusita</u> de que tenéis una cita. Y <u>yo</u> de Vero me lo creo, <u>¿eh?</u>, pero de Aída…
AÍDA: Eh, que os cuente siempre mi vida no quiere decir que no pueda tener una doble vida fascinante. Y yo ya hago suficiente aguantándole el rollo en el bar.	AÍDA: <u>Oye, oye, oye,</u> que os cuente siempre mi vida no quiere decir que no pueda tener una doble vida fascinante. <u>Además,</u> yo <u>bastante</u> hago con aguantar<u>la</u> el rollo en el bar <u>todos los días.</u>
Pre-production script (back translation)	*Post-production script (back translation)*
DIANA: I did it for her own good, you meet many people there! Also, when she has a stiff back, who takes her to the toilet, huh? Or who helps her to carry the shopping upstairs? Suddenly, everyone comes up with the excuse of having a date. And I believe it if it comes from Vero, but from Aída…	DIANA: <u>Hey, hey, hey, well… well,</u> I did it for her own good, <u>huh? Cause</u> you meet many people there. Also, <u>listen, when</u>-when she has a stiff back, who takes her to the toilet, huh? Or who <u>takes her shopping</u> upstairs? <u>Cause,</u> suddenly, <u>you all</u> come up with the <u>little</u> excuse of having a date. And I <u>do</u> believe it if it comes from Vero, <u>huh?</u> but from Aída…
AÍDA: Hey, just because I'm always telling you about my life does not mean that I cannot lead another more fascinating life. And I already do enough listening to her stories at the bar.	AÍDA: Hey, <u>hey, hey,</u> just because I'm always telling you about my life does not mean that I cannot lead another more fascinating life. <u>Also,</u> I do <u>quite</u> enough listening to her stories at the bar <u>every day.</u>

The example above shows that actors improvise and use many features that are typical of spontaneous conversation but that were not present in the pre-production script such as syntactic dysfluencies (*cua-cuando*; *que…, que…*). These features are often used in naturally occurring conversation as repair strategies (Biber et al., 1999: 1067), which provide the speaker with more time to plan what is going to be said next. In *Siete Vidas*, the actress might have resorted to these features to achieve a more natural utterance and, possibly, to remember what she was supposed to say. Syntactic dysfluencies are not the only orality markers that have been added in the example above. By using the question tag *¿eh?* (huh?), the actress elicits the hearer's agreement (Biber et al., 1999: 1080), thus reinforcing the conversational nature of the dialogue. Similarly, the discourse marker *oye* (listen/hey), is used not only as a filler but also to involve the hearer in the conversation. Equally noteworthy is the use of intensifiers (paralinguistic features, use of the first person pronoun *yo*, exaggeration through the use of *todo(s)*), suffixes that act as colloquial markers with a down-toning and humoristic purpose (*excusita* > little excuse instead of *excusa* > excuse), and the amendments in the use of personal pronouns undertaken while shooting the series (*le lleva* > *la lleva*).

These changes and additions show that actors' improvisation plays an essential role for making the utterances sound spontaneous. Although this phenomenon could not be considered improvisation as such, we could refer to a kind of controlled improvisation that enables the addition of non-standard features, as well as of linguistic features that are typical of spontaneous colloquial Spanish. Some of these features could indeed be idiosyncratic of a specific character or, more interestingly, of a specific actor. In *Siete Vidas*, for instance, the phonetic articulation of some characters seems to be consistently more relaxed than that of others. These differences do not seem to have a clear correspondence with the sociocultural origin of the character in question. This suggests that they might depend on the actual actors, especially as those who have more experience in theatrical productions (Amparo Baró as Sole, Blanca Portillo as Carlota, and Gonzalo de Castro as Gonzalo) seem to use these phonetic features less frequently (Baños, 2009: 188). Although this phenomenon needs to be further investigated, it indicates that it is essential to consider not only characterization, but also the origin and trajectory of the actors interpreting the characters when analyzing domestic productions.

As discussed above, controlled improvisation and characters' and actors' idiosyncrasies cannot be realized to the same extent in dubbed dialogue, and this could explain some of the differences identified in studies comparing non-translated and dubbed products as regards linguistic standardization. Similarly, the complexities of the dubbing process might somewhat explain the relative absence of non-standard features in dubbed products (see Baños, 2014: 430). In addition, standardization might be explained by historical factors because, as Chaume argues, "dubbing was consolidated at a time when imitating real spoken language was completely unacceptable" (2012: 91). The television channel where a product is broadcast might also have an effect on linguistic standardization. In fact, television channels could be regarded as patrons of audiovisual products.

Patronage

Drawing on Lefevere's (1992: 15) reflections on the concept of patronage,[1] when analyzing orality markers it is also interesting to consider the role played by the powers (persons, institutions) that can "further or hinder the reading, writing, and rewriting" of audiovisual texts. In our case study, in addition to the role played by the dubbing studio, it is worth exploring the influence of the television channel where the series was broadcast. It is worth noting that *Friends* was aired by Canal+ España, which used to prioritize foreign productions in its schedule and implement a quality control scheme on the translation of audiovisual texts. This was done through the linguistic supervisor. Quality control is a term widely used in the translation industry to refer to the procedures implemented to make sure a translation meets specific quality standards. Quality control can thus take many forms in translation. In addition, quality standards may vary considerably depending on a complex matrix of factors, including commercial issues, budget available, type of translation undertaken, client needs, etc. As Chaume (2012) points out, in the translation for dubbing, these can also vary significantly from one culture to another. Nevertheless, he contends that in most contexts dubbing standards tend to consider the following aspects, to a lesser or greater degree: acceptable lip synchrony, coherent translation (i.e., coherence among images, words, and sounds), loyal translation (e.g., equivalent to the original text), acceptable sound quality, credible acting, and credible spontaneous dialogues (ibid: 14–20). Regarding the latter, translators should bear in mind that dubbed dialogues cannot be too spontaneous, and that the language of dubbing is governed by tacit norms that recommend the use of conservative and standardized language (Ávila, 1997: 25). Domestic programs, on the contrary, seem to respond to different quality standards as far as the use of credible dialogues is concerned: original programs aimed at mirroring spontaneous conversations (e.g., dramas) do not seem to be governed by standardization, correctness, and conservatism, or at least not to the same extent as dubbed products are. In addition, quality control does not seem as relevant as in the translation for dubbing (scripts might be reviewed but not as exhaustively), and this might result in less correct but more spontaneous-sounding dialogues.

These differences ought to be taken into consideration when analyzing the dialogue of dubbed and domestic productions. For example, when comparing *Friends* and *Siete Vidas*, the presence of 'mistakes' (i.e., grammatical inconsistencies) and non-standard uses of Spanish (i.e., incorrect use of verbal tenses) in the latter (Baños, 2014: 417) could be due to the observation of different quality standards and/or to the absence of quality control in Telecinco, the channel where this series was aired. In contrast, linguistic mistakes or inconsistencies are practically absent in *Friends*, where the use of non-standard language is limited and often motivated by the situation (e.g., swear words) (ibid: 429). It could thus be hypothesized that the linguistic policies tacitly implemented by Canal+ or by the dubbing studio have an impact on the final product and that these are stricter than those observed in the domestic sitcom.

Divergences can indeed be due to characteristics of the source text (ST). For instance, it is noteworthy that strong swear words that are common expletives in spontaneous conversation (such as *shit* or *fuck*) are practically absent in *Friends* (Romero-Fresco, 2006). According to Quaglio (2009: 77), this is due to the rules imposed by the US television network (NBC) where the series was originally broadcast, meaning that such swear words were generally not allowed in the show. This only emphasizes the importance of patronage in the patterning of translated and non-translated texts and the consideration of the ST as a constraint when it comes to the implementation of features that are natural in domestic products in the target language.

Professional Factors

On the other hand, the urgency with which audiovisual programs are translated might mistakenly result in the inclusion of non-planned and non-standard orality markers, which are not normally considered suitable for these kinds of text, such as grammatical inconsistencies, incorrect verb tenses, or semantic redundancies. Audiovisual translators often have to meet very tight deadlines, and this will probably have an impact on the quality of the final product. Deadlines seem to be getting tighter, especially as some television networks have lately taken on the challenge of broadcasting dubbed episodes shortly after they have been aired in their country of origin—often the United States—to prevent viewers from downloading or viewing the original episodes online. Thus, it is only fair to admit that audiovisual translators and other dubbing professionals often work under pressure. This could be another reason for the lesser quality of a dubbed text, which, in this case, could paradoxically result in dialogues that are more natural.

Despite the urgency required for the translation of some episodes of *Friends* from English into Spanish,[2] no examples of incorrect or non-standard features of language were identified in the episodes analyzed (Baños, 2014). As mentioned above, the controlled way in which lines are recorded in a dubbing studio allows for more polished utterances: if mistakes are introduced while recording, these will most likely be rectified immediately. In the case of domestic programs such as *Siete Vidas* or the original version of *Friends*, as the shooting takes place in a less controlled environment, mistakes might go unnoticed. In addition, the presence of an audience on the set might also deter the director of the original TV series from re-recording scenes to correct them.

Audience Design

Audience design also has an effect on the linguistic choice made by translators. Nevertheless, translators might not receive instructions regarding the target audience (as was the case with the *Friends'* translator) and be left to their own devices to figure out a potential target viewer and decide on the most appropriate linguistic choices. This could be due to a lack of communication with commissioners, who may well deem that this information is not relevant (especially in the case of low-budget programs). Quite often, the reason could simply be that commissioners do not have a clear picture of the make-up of the target audience. In television, this could justify the implementation of different translation strategies and conventions throughout a specific series and result in remarkable divergences between the first and last seasons of long-running productions. Such differences have been documented by scholars such as Ranzato who, after a detailed analysis of the Italian dubbing of gayspeak in the series *Six Feet Under*, concludes that pilot episodes and first seasons in general tend to be more exposed to censorship, "probably because they have yet to build an audience and that audience has to be as large as possible in the first instance" (2014: 382). The case of Italy is particularly interesting because of the widely acknowledged existence of a board of censors controlling the broadcasting of dubbed movies in theaters and cinemas (Chiaro, 2007: 256; Ledvinka, 2010: 28–34). As Chiaro posits, whereas there is no concrete evidence of the existence of a parallel organization for television broadcasting, "it may not be entirely unlikely that television companies require translators to censure programs containing taboo language so that they can then be freely screened during prime time" (2007: 257). Audience design will not only influence the translation of taboo language, but also of cultural references and other linguistic items that help to connect audiovisual characters with the audience, as will be shown below.

Friends was targeted at a young Spanish audience[3] and, as a result, the series features markers that are typical of colloquial conversation between young people. The connection with the young audience is normally established at the lexical level, through the use of colloquial expressions, slang, youth lingo, vocatives, etc. Regarding the latter, "familiarisers" (Biber et al., 1999: 1109) such as *tío* (man) or *colega* (dude, pal), which are typically used in Spanish colloquial conversation, especially among youngsters (Briz, 2003: 146), are particularly common. As shown by Quaglio (2009: 115), these are also frequent in the original version of *Friends* (and even more frequent than in natural conversation) and are often used as "markers of informality" (ibid: 108). Although the use of these linguistic features in the dubbed version is often motivated by the ST, the translator also resorts to these regardless of the presence of orality markers in the ST. This is shown in Table 8.3, where the first instance of *tío* is motivated by the familiarizer 'man' in the ST, but the second instance could be interpreted as an attempt to situate the characters in a specific age group, thus bringing them closer to the target audience. When contrasting the original and the dubbed version, this addition could also be interpreted as an attempt to compensate for the absence of orality markers that have been omitted in the target text, such as hesitations (huh...) or even Chandler's relaxed phonetic articulation. In addition, the use of the vocative *tío* in the second instance helps the translator to comply with the relevant synchronies (i.e., isochrony), an aspect that will be briefly explored below.

Table 8.3 Example of addition of familiarizers in the Spanish dubbing of *Friends*

TV Series: Friends	Episode: 192 – The one where Rachel is late	TC: 06.09
Joey can only take one friend to his latest movie premiere and he finally decides to take Chandler.		
Original Version	Dubbed Version	
JOEY: [...] You always believed in me, man. Even, even when I didn't believe in myself. CHANDLER: I always knew you were gonna make it. I'm so proud of ya. JOEY: Thanks. Huh... that means a lot to me.	JOEY: [...] Siempre has creído en mí, tío, incluso cuando ni yo creía en mí mismo. CHANDLER: Sabía que ibas a conseguirlo. Estoy orgulloso de ti. JOEY: Gracias, tío. Significa mucho para mí.	

Genre Conventions: Sitcom Conventions and Restrictions of the Audiovisual Medium

In addition to the above-mentioned factors, when analyzing dubbed dialogue it is essential to bear in mind that dubbed texts are expected to comply with specific conventions, determined by both the audiovisual medium and the genre to which they belong. *Friends* complies with sitcom genre conventions, which are highly standardized. The fact that laughter is one of the top priorities of sitcom scriptwriters will also have an impact on the selection of linguistic features and, therefore, on the patterning of prefabricated orality. In these programs, the introduction of jokes, many of which will rely on verbal humor, is indeed quite prefabricated as well. This is reflected in the presence of canned laughter, considered by some as a constraint in audiovisual translation (Romero-Fresco, 2006: 142), and in the high amount of gags and jokes whose frequency does not mirror natural conversation. Speakers are not as funny (or at least not as frequently) in real life as many of the characters of *Friends* and *Siete Vidas* are in their fictional worlds. In these cases, the entertaining purpose of these programs will have priority over their naturalness. In *Friends* the humorous effect will often motivate the inclusion of numerous comparisons based on culture-bound terms, phraseological units, and syntactic dysfluencies, such as incomplete utterances or hesitations. Although these features should bring fictional dialogue closer to spontaneous-sounding conversation, this approach could also backfire and result in a dialogue that seems overloaded and thus not natural. In fact, striking the right balance seems to be one of the main challenges faced by both scriptwriters and translators.

Following Chaume (2003: 175), we could also refer to audiovisual texts as a macrogenre. It seems obvious that audiovisual media do not allow for the exact reproduction of a spontaneous conversation, with its numerous false starts, repetitions, hesitations, fillers, etc., as it will hinder viewers' understanding. In dubbing, together with the tacit target norms, which recommend the use of standardized language, the constraints of the audiovisual medium will have a greater impact due to the synchronization process described above. These constraints might result in some orality markers being omitted (especially false starts, hesitations, fillers, etc.), as shown in Table 8.4.

Table 8.4 Example of omission of orality markers in the Spanish dubbing of *Friends*

TV Series: Friends	Episode: 194 – The One Where Rachel Has A Baby II TC: 06.49
Joey is trying to convince Cliff how wonderful Phoebe is. However, his arguments are not very convincing.	
Original Version	Dubbed Version
JOEY: Uh, if I may? <u>Umm-umm</u> look, Cliff, you told me a lot of personal stuff about you, right? And <u>maybe-maybe</u> it would help <u>if-if</u> you knew some personal stuff about her. <u>Uh</u>, she was married to a gay ice dancer. <u>Uh</u>, she gave birth to her brother's triplets. <u>Oh</u>! Oh-Oh! <u>Her-her</u> twin sister used to do porn!	JOEY: Si me permites. Oye, Cliff, me has contado cantidad de cosas personales sobre ti, ¿no? <u>No sé</u>, a lo mejor ayudaría si supieras algunas cosas personales de ella. <u>Eh...</u> estuvo casada con un patinador gay. <u>Eh...</u> dio a luz a los trillizos de su hermano. ¡Oh, oh, <u>su-su</u> hermana gemela hacía porno!

The previous example shows that although some hesitations are maintained in the dubbed version (her-her > *su-su*; uh > *eh*), some are omitted (if-if or Umm-umm, for instance). In some cases, hesitations are substituted by full utterances expressing hesitation. For instance, 'maybe-maybe' has been translated as *no sé* (I don't know). These omissions inevitably result in a loss in pretended spontaneity. However, the translator can also use the flexibility of the audiovisual medium to her own advantage in order to compensate for potential losses or omissions.

Table 8.5 Example of addition of orality markers in the Spanish dubbing of *Friends*

TV Series: Friends	Episode: 194 – The One Where Rachel Has A Baby II TC: 09.02
Rachel is giving birth and Ross is trying his best to support her.	
Original Version	Dubbed Version
Ross: Oh! Oh! She's upside down but she's coming! She's coming!	Ross: ¡Oh! Está al revés, <u>pero-pero</u> ya sale, ya sale.

In the example above, the repetition of the word *pero* (but), which would be considered a type of dysfluency frequently used in spontaneous speech to gain time (Biber et al., 1999: 1055), is used to match the duration of the dubbed dialogue with that of the original dialogue (isochrony). In this case, the agents involved in the dubbing process have taken advantage of dubbing constraints. This shows that audiovisual constraints do not always result in loss, but might also contribute to the pretended spontaneity of dubbed dialogue.

Conclusion

Drawing on the results revealed in a previous study (Baños, 2009; 2014) and on DTS principles, this chapter has explored the nature and some of the pressures of the dubbing process, focusing on their influence on the patterning of dubbed dialogue in Spanish with regards to its prefabricated orality. Given that dubbed texts are often contrasted with non-translated texts, and that comparisons do not always fully consider the socio-cultural context in which both are produced, a comparison has been established with the pressures governing the production of native texts. It is widely acknowledged that dubbed dialogue is more prefabricated, unnatural, and artificial than non-translated dialogue. However, this chapter has attempted to show that the reasons for this can be very varied, and that the translator is not the only one to 'blame' for the presence of unnatural features in the language of dubbing.[4]

The reflections and examples provided throughout this chapter have shown that the context in which dubbing takes place allows for a more polished and less improvised interpretation of dialogues. Although professional factors might promote the inclusion of non-planned and non-standard features, dubbed products may undergo a strict supervision process, exercised by either the television channel or the dubbing studio, and are subjected to less flexible quality standards as far as the naturalness of dialogues is concerned. The discussion has highlighted that dubbed dialogue is governed by specific norms and that these differ from those governing domestic productions, due to a wide range of factors of historical, professional, or even logistic nature. This does not mean that this situation is irreversible, especially given that norms are indeed "unstable, changing entities" (Toury, 1995: 62). Perhaps it is time for a change in conventions and quality standards—to be instigated by audiences, audiovisual translators, and the various part-takers in the dubbing process—to bring dubbed dialogue closer to original dialogue and natural conversation.

The fact that dubbed texts are constrained by a text in the source language, which was produced in a different context and influenced by different agents, inevitably leaves traces in dubbed dialogues. In addition, one must consider the further constraints that operate in dubbed texts, especially concerning their synchronization with the source texts. In this sense, dubbing constraints can result in the omission of existing source text orality markers in the translation, as well as in the addition of new ones. Thus, the translation of dialogues for dubbing in Spanish is influenced by a wealth of factors that are not just related to the presence of a source text or the particular ability of a translator, but also to the specificities of dubbing and audiovisual dialogue, the audiovisual medium, and all the agents and powers involved in the dubbing and broadcasting of audiovisual texts.

Notes

1. Lefevere (1992: 15) defines this concept as "the powers (persons, institutions) that can further or hinder the reading, writing, and rewriting of literature".
2. This was confirmed by the series translator, Darryl Clark, in a communication with the author via e-mail where he acknowledged that, during very busy times, he translated two and even three episodes in a single day.
3. According to GECA, *Friends* was mainly targeted to a young audience, and their viewers normally belonged to the 18–44 year old group (GECA, 2004: 269).
4. Audiovisual translators feel quite strong about this misconception and about the fact that criticisms often disregard that translation decisions might respond to commercial considerations or to the specific nature of dubbing. A case in point was the response they provided to a recent, rather polemic, opinion article on the translation for dubbing into Spanish of the blockbuster film *Avengers: Age of Ultron* (Joss Whedon, 2015), written by the Spanish journalist and bestselling author Juan Gómez Jurado. The column, published in the Spanish newspaper *ABC* on 9th May 2015, entitled "Venganza contra la traducción" (Revenge on the translation) criticizes translators for decisions that might have been taken by other agents, clearly showing a lack of awareness of the dubbing process. The article resulted in an exchange of numerous tweets between professionals working in the dubbing industry (mainly audiovisual translators but also dubbing actors) and the writer. Some audiovisual translators even felt compelled to explain the dubbing process in blog posts (see, for instance, http://jugandoatraducir.com/en-defensa-del-doblaje-y-la-traduccion-audiovisual/, by Rafael López Sánchez).

References

Ávila, A. (1997). *El doblaje*. Madrid: Cátedra.
Baker, M. (1996). Corpus-based Translation Studies: The challenges that lie ahead. In H. Somers (Ed.), *Terminology, LSP and translation: Studies in language engineering in honour of Juan C. Sager* (pp. 175–186). Amsterdam/Philadelphia: John Benjamins.
Baños, R. (2009). *La oralidad prefabricada en la traducción para el doblaje. Estudio descriptivo-contrastivo del español de dos comedias de situación: Siete Vidas y Friends*. PhD thesis. Universidad de Granada.
Baños, R. (2014). Orality markers in Spanish native and dubbed sitcoms: Pretended spontaneity and prefabricated orality. *Meta*, 59(2), 406–435.
Bednarek, M. (2010). *The language of fictional television: Drama and identity*. London: Continuum.

Biber, D., Johansson, S., Leech, G., Conrad, S. & Finegan, E. (1999). *Longman grammar of spoken and written English*. London: Longman.

Briz, A. (2003). La interacción entre jóvenes. Español coloquial, argot y lenguaje juvenil. In E. Echenique & M. Sánchez Méndez (Eds.), *Lexicografía y lexicología en Europa y América* (pp. 141–154). Madrid: Gredos.

Chaume, F. (2003). *Doblatge i subtitulació per a la TV*. Vic: Eumo.

Chaume, F. (2004). Synchronization in dubbing: A translational approach. In P. Orero (Ed.), *Topics in audiovisual translation* (pp. 35–52). Amsterdam/Philadelphia: John Benjamins.

Chaume, F. (2012). *Audiovisual translation: Dubbing*. Manchester: St Jerome.

Chiaro, D. (2007). Not in front of the children? An analysis of sex on screen in Italy. *Linguistica Antverpiensia*, 6, 255–276.

Clark, Darryl. (2005, May 14). Personal communication.

Díaz Cintas, J. (2004). In search of a theoretical framework for the study of audiovisual translation. In P. Orero (Ed.), *Topics inaudiovisual translation* (pp. 21–34). Amsterdam/Philadelphia: John Benjamins.

Even-Zohar, I. (1990). Polysystem theory. *Poetics Today*, 11(1), 9–94.

GECA Consultores. (1998–2005). *Anuario GECA de la televisión en España*. Madrid: GECA Consultores.

Gómez Jurado, J. (2015, May 9). Venganza contra la traducción. *ABC*, available online at: https://twitter.com/juangomezjurado/status/596969961685438464 (Retrieved July 31, 2015).

Karamitroglou, F. (2000). *Towards a methodology for the investigation of norms in audiovisual translation*. Amsterdam: Rodopi.

Ledvinka, F. R. (2010). *What the fuck are you talking about? Traduzione, omissione e censura nel doppiaggio e nel sottotitolaggio in Italia*. Torino: Eris.

Lefevere, A. (1992). *Translation, rewriting and the manipulation of literary frame*. London/New York: Routledge.

López, Natxo. (2007, October 29). Personal communication.

López Sánchez, R. (2015, May 10). *En defensa del doblaje y la traducción audiovisual* [Blog post], available online at: http://jugandoatraducir.com/en-defensa-del-doblaje-y-la-traduccion-audiovisual/ (Retrieved July 31, 2015).

Matamala, A. (2008). La oralidad en la ficción televisiva: análisis de las interjecciones de un corpus de comedias de situación originales y dobladas. In J. Brumme (Ed.), *La oralidad fingida: descripción y traducción* (pp. 81–94). Madrid: Iberoamericana.

Pavesi, M. (2009). Pronouns in film dubbing and the dynamics of audiovisual communication. In R. Valdeón (Ed.), Special issue of *VIAL* (Vigo International Journal of Applied Linguistics), 6, 89–107.

Pérez-González, L. (2014). *Audiovisual translation: Theories, methods and issues*. Abingdon/New York: Routledge.

Quaglio, P. (2009). *Television dialogue. The sitcom Friends vs. natural conversation*. Amsterdam/Philadelphia: John Benjamins.

Ranzato, I. (2014). Gayspeak and gay subjects in audiovisual translation: Strategies in Italian dubbing. *Meta*, 57(2), 369–384.

Romero-Fresco, P. (2006). The Spanish dubbese: A case of (un)idiomatic *Friends*. *The Journal of Specialised Translation*, 6, 134–151.

Ruiz Gurillo, L. (2013a). Narrative strategies in Buenafuente's humorous monologues. In L. Ruiz-Gurillo & M. B. Alvarado-Ortega (Eds.), *Irony and Humor:*

From Pragmatics to Discourse (pp. 107–140). Amsterdam/Philadelphia: John Benjamins.

Ruiz Gurillo, L. (2013b). Eva Hache y El club de la comedia: del guión monológico al registro dialógico. *Revista Onomázein*, 28, 148–161.

Sánchez Mompeán, S. (2015). Dubbing animation into Spanish: Behind the voices of animated characters. *The Journal of Specialised Translation*, 23, 270–291.

Segovia, Raquel. (2007, June 27). Personal communication.

Toury, G. (1995). *Descriptive translation studies and beyond*. Amsterdam/Philadelphia: John Benjamins.

9 Jerome Bruner and the Transcultural Adaptation of 1970s Hollywood Classics in Turkey

Laurence Raw

In a 2011 call for papers, Ian Hunter and Constantine Verevis came up with the term 'BADaptation', something that they believed could be applied to all adaptations in the sense that they constitute a 'betrayal' of the source-text. This was especially apt in connection with exploitation films that consciously place themselves on the margins, often sacrificing notions of fidelity or artistic integrity for the sake of popular audience appeal. Hunter and Verevis use BADaptation to ask questions such as: "Is a film adaptation intrinsically BAD?" "Are all film adaptations BADaptations of some more authentic artifact?" and "What happens when one adapts a 'bad object'?" (2011). While terms such as 'good' and 'bad' are perpetually culture-specific, we also have to realize that the meanings of 'exploitation films' and even 'adaptations' are equally so. What might be marketed as an exploitation flick in one context might be perceived very differently in another. Witness the fortunes of Michael Winner's *The Nightcomers* (1971), a so-called 'prequel' to Henry James' *The Turn of the Screw* starring Marlon Brando, which was promoted in Britain as a classic adaptation spiced up with racy sex-scenes involving Brando and Stephanie Beacham. In the United States the film was marketed as a sex 'n suspenders epic, a forerunner to *Last Tango in Paris* with the emphasis placed on explicit nudity and sado-masochistic sequences (Raw, 2013). In certain contexts, 'adaptation' has no direct linguistic equivalent; the nearest that Turkish can offer is *alışmak* (to get used to); *alıştırmak* (to get accustomed to); or *uyum sağlamak* (to suit a new purpose, as in the phrase "adapting a native cuisine to suit the food resource of a new country"). The task of separating 'good' from 'bad' adaptations becomes even more complicated when the term 'adaptation' is itself contested.

Perhaps we ought to set aside issues of value and look more closely at *how* and *why* new versions of source-texts are conceived and filmed—and thereby understand more about local cinematic traditions and the audience's specific tastes. Through this approach, I believe we can work toward a more nuanced framework for adaptation studies, one that sets aside preconceived notions of "good" and "bad" and concentrates instead on diversity and pluralism. In this article I discuss two Turkish adaptations—*Şeytan* (*The Devil*) (1974) based on William Friedkin's *The Exorcist* (1973); and *Dünyayı Kutaran Adam* (*The Man Who Saved the World*), a version of *Star*

Wars (1977). Both have been dismissed by reviewers as turkeys with their cheapskate settings, ludicrous acting, and incoherent editing. In the United States *Şeytan* has been likened to a Turkish version of Edward D. Wood Jr's immortal *Plan Nine from Outer Space* (1959), described by one blogger as "a shameless rip-off [....] some goofy shit that's best watched with a bunch of drunken friends" (Campos, 2006).

In the Turkish context, both films appeared during the *Yeşilçam* (or Green Pine) era, which flourished from the late 1950s through the early 1980s. A profusion of small studio outfits turned out a seemingly endless stream of comedies, thrillers, and melodramas, with actors playing similar roles from film to film. Cüneyt Arkın, star of *Dünyayı Kutaran Adam*, played the all-action hero overcoming a series of obstacles to emerge triumphant in the final reel. *Yeşilcam* products made no claim to originality; hence, it was futile to judge whether they were good or bad. The chief pleasure of these films lay in repetition: familiar tales from the west transplanted to local con-texts with little concern for copyright. This might be considered plagiarism from a Western perspective; in Turkish terms, this strategy was designed to make audiences—as well as the creative personnel involved in making the film—feel good about themselves, as they proved how capable they were of emulating the major Hollywood studios. This was an important propa-ganda strategy in a country consolidating itself as a secular republic in the wake of Mustafa Kemal Atatürk's reforms during the mid-twentieth century. *Yeşilcam* films were patriotic products and accepted as such by audiences of the time.

To understand the process of adapting texts across cultures, I shall draw on the work of psychologist Jerome Bruner, who argues in *Making Stories* (2003) that individuals and communities structure their existences in terms of narratives designed to make sense of the world around them. Exactly how they are constructed depends very much on individual perceptions and how they relate to the wider community. The narratives we tell ourselves and the narratives we see on the cinema screen are inextricable, helping us to understand the way we live now and what our aspirations might be for the future. *Yeşilçam* versons of Hollywood classics deliberately constructed new narratives for local audiences that had far more to do with issues of collective well-being than value-judgments. They sustained what Nikos Mourkogiannis has termed 'communities of purpose'—groups of like-minded people com-mitted to maintaining a particular set of narratives (2006: 67). The success of *Şeytan* and *Dünyayı Kutaran Adam* at the Turkish box-office bears wit-ness to the transculturality of the source-texts, as they link and undergo adaptation across borders, while avoiding congruence and uniformization. Cultural diversity arises in a new mode as a transcultural blend rather than a juxtaposition of source and target-texts eliciting value-judgments (Welsch, 1994–1995: 37).

Şeytan consciously reconceives the plot of *The Exorcist* as a melodrama rather than a horror film. While Ayten (Meral Taygun) makes every effort to look after her daughter Gül (Canan Perver), the child lacks a father for guidance. Ayten's husband has quit the family home, while her boyfriend Ekrem (Ekrem Gökkaya) treats Gül as an object to be played with rather than loved. Consequently, Gül becomes vulnerable to corruption by a perverted father figure—the Devil. The child is transformed from a shy student into a monster swearing at every opportunity and taking revenge on Ekrem by breaking his neck.

In Brunerian terms, the narrative constructed in *Şeytan* concentrates on the importance of family values, a familiar theme of *Yeşilçam* cinema. In a piece on the actress Türkân Şoray, I showed how her early and middle films—until the mid-1970s—emphasized the importance of the heroine finding the right mate as a source of personal as well as social security. A good marriage ensured the future health of her community in a rural or urban context. Nonetheless, family life could be precarious; in *Ekmekçi Kadın (The Bread Seller Woman)* (1965), Şoray plays Ayşe, a mother abandoned by her husband, and her daughter Leyla who abandons the home to enjoy the high life in İstanbul. The only way to redemption is for Ayşe to find a suitable husband. She fails in her task and is reduced to selling bread on the streets; Leyla receives a jail sentence for vagrancy (Raw, 2011: 263–64). A similar moral scheme underpins the narrative of *Şeytan*: lacking a stable father figure, Gül becomes a monster. Psychologist Tuğrul (Cihan Ünal) believes he has undergone a similar process after having consigned his widowed mother Fatma (Sabahat Işık) to an asylum. Fatma dies there, leaving Tuğrul with only one solution; if he exorcizes Gül of her devil, then perhaps he can redeem himself, even at the cost of his own life. The plot does not set out to be original; rather it tries to provide local audiences with what Bruner terms "a ready and supple means for dealing with the uncertain outcomes of [human] [...] plans and anticipations" (2003: 28) by conventionalizing the common forms of mishap into the melodramatic genre. *Şeytan* reasserts "a kind of conventional wisdom about what can be expected, even (or especially) what can be expected to go wrong and what might be done to measure or cope with the situation" (2003: 31).

Despite its violent subject matter, *Şeytan* contains an underlying patriotic message, as it employs an adaptive strategy that had become commonplace since the creation of the Republic. Many independent publishers issued versions of classic texts that relocated the action in Turkey while paying scant attention to authorial provenance. Sherlock Holmes was the hero of a sequence of *romanlar* (novels) penned by popular writer Kemal Tahir (writing under the pseudonym of F. M. İkinci). His close friend Selâmi Munir Yurdatap produced new versions of *Dracula* inspired by local folk-tales (Raw, 2012: 6–7). Screenwriters undertook similar projects for the cinema: *Drakula İstanbul'da (Dracula in İstanbul)* (1953) acknowledged Ali Rıza Seyfi's novel *Kazıklı Voyvoda (Impaler Voivode)* (1928) as a source-text, rather than Bram Stoker's work. Twenty-one years later, Yılmaz Tümtürk reworked William Peter Blatty's *Exorcist* script according to *Yeşilçam* conventions. At the end, for instance, the exorcist (Agah Hün) recites lines from the Koran rather than the Bible; both Gül and Ayten understand the significance of this strategy, as they are shown entering a mosque, their heads covered with scarves. Gül sees the imam standing in the corner and discovers to her surprise that it is the exorcist brought back to life. The devil has been transformed into her protector, a suitable father figure for her to work toward family security. This ending might seem contrived, but for locals it proved beyond doubt that Turkish writers could match anything the West could produce; this was especially important in a context where Atatürk had instituted a wide-ranging program of language reform, replacing the Ottoman script with Western-style writing and encouraging the definition of new words and phrases in Turkish. The fact that *Şeytan* was a box-office hit vindicated this policy.

Dünyayı Kutaran Adam is a fine example of what Iain Robert Smith describes as cultural hybridization, a means by which cultures adapt and evolve (2008: 3). The plot is straightforward: Earth has been destroyed by a nuclear holocaust, but some survivors try their best to reconstitute it through sheer brainpower. However, their efforts are threatened by a wizard who repeatedly attacks, leaving a trail of destruction in his wake. Finally, the elders of the earth assemble a team of crack warriors to annihilate the wizard, led by Murat (Cüneyt Arkın) and Ali (Aytekin Akkaya). They repel a group of savages, aided by a sage (Hüseyin Peyda) and his daughter (Fusün Uçar). The subsequent action centers on the search for a golden sword containing all humankind's power and a brain that possess all wisdom, passion, and love. The wizard steals both, but Murat recovers them, melts them down and remakes them into golden gloves. Now possessing all the world's passion and knowledge, he kills the wizard and saves the world.

Although Arkın admitted in an interview that the film was designed as a *Star Wars* parody (as cited in Akser, 2013: 90), the action nonetheless reinforces his heroic star *persona*. Beginning his career in the mid-1960s, he was involved in many of *Yeşilçam*'s "male" genres—historical dramas, science fiction, crime, and westerns—that required action scenes with protracted duels using all kinds of weapons. In *Kara Murat Fatih'in Fedaisi (Kara Murat, Fatih's Defender)* (1972), he plays a dual role, accompanied by his regular team of 'fighter men' who were beaten up in one film after another (including *Dünyayı Kutaran Adam*). One Turkish blogger described him as "an institution of epic proportions, an institution known to all", whose *oeuvre* might seem ridiculous, but nonetheless proved "a real inspiration. A man who puts his heart into his films and is clearly having a lot of fun" (Supreme Nothing, 2009). His presence onscreen reinforces the patriotic ideal; no one it seems—not even the aliens—can defeat him. Director Çetin İnanç and Arkın (as screenwriter) consciously reshape the *Star Wars* plot into an action thriller emphasizing the importance of a strong leader. Murat is a direct descendant of Atatürk, sacrificing personal interest in pursuit of public duty and achieving his objectives no matter what the cost (the loss of Ali, for instance).

The main reason for the success of Arkın's film and *Şeytan* lies in what Bruner describes as the "subjunctivization" of reality, making room not only for what is but for what might be or for what might have been, keeping the familiar and the possible cheek by jowl. The symbolic buffer that protects viewers against the terrors of unlimited possibility is the literary or cinematic form in which the adaptation has been conceived—the melodrama or the action thriller. Like Perseus' mirroring shield that protected him from being turned to stone if he looked at Medusa, the form is a mirroring shield permitting audiences to contemplate the possible without being turned to stone (Bruner, 2003: 53).

Since its original release date in 1982, however, *Dünyayı Kutaran Adam* has been regularly derided for the poor quality of its acting, cinematography and settings, as well as for its deliberate plagiarism of music from *Flash Gordon* and *Raiders of the Lost Ark*. One American blogger speculates that the film was probably not shown throughout Turkey, "due to the whole plagiarism thing", and now exists chiefly for viewers to revel in its "mindless glory" (*The Man Who Saves the World*, 2014). Such observations presuppose that *Yeşilçam* recognized the distinction between "original" and "plagiarized" material. As explained earlier, this did not appear to matter in a context where local creative industries were carving out their own identities as genuine competitors to their foreign counterparts. *Dünyayı Kutaran Adam* consciously challenged Western-inspired conceptions of originality and narrative coherence; in place of logic, director İnanç foregrounds repetition and dissonance, punctuated throughout with snatches of Hollywood action-film themes. What we witness on screen bears little relationship to what we hear—snatches of dialogue are followed by music in a classic mash-up structure. Contrary to the blogger's belief, *Dünyayı Kutaran Adam* was widely distributed throughout Turkey on its original release; according to Utku Uluer, editor of the journal *Sinematik Yeşilçam*, it was especially welcome in small local cinemas in the Anatolian countryside that did not have access to American blockbusters due to high distribution costs. Interest in *Yeşilçam* products was renewed in the early 1990s, as small cinema clubs in İstanbul started tracking down the films and showing them to cinephile audiences (as cited in Williams, 2012).

The film creates two narratives, both designed to encourage a feeling of collective security: Audiences could revel in the sight of the clean-cut hero brushing all obstacles aside, as well as celebrate *Yeşilçam*'s achievement in overcoming their own obstacles—chiefly financial—to produce their own version of a Hollywood blockbuster. It didn't matter if *Dünyayı Kutaran Adam* was believable, so long as filmgoers *believed in* it. This is a good example of what Bruner describes as a text satisfying "a local, inner point of view that wants minding. Culture […] is always local, always particular, however universal its applications […] it [the product] cannot be effective when it is seen as incongruous with the local culture" (Bruner, 2003: 50).

So far we have considered how *Şeytan* and *Dünyayı Kutaran Adam* exemplify Bruner's ideas about the construction of narratives in collective terms appealing to local communities. However, he is also preoccupied with the ways in which such narratives contribute to the individual creation of self; we constantly construct and reconstruct ourselves to meet the needs of the situations we encounter, and we do so with the guidance of memories of the past and our hopes for the future. Telling oneself about oneself resembles putting together a narrative about who we are, what has happened, and why we are doing what we are doing. Telling others about oneself involves embracing the conventions that govern a community and accommodating our own self-narratives to that community (Bruner, 2003: 64–66). Cultures develop through the continual interplay between individuals and the communities they inhabit; sometimes individuals make such an impression that they redefine a community's behavioral conventions; more often than not, a community reshapes the construction of self. Bruner concludes that "the nature and shape of selfhood are indeed as much matters of cultural [and community] concern, *res publica*, as of individual concern. Or, to put it another way, selfhood involves a commitment to others as well as being 'true to oneself'" (2003: 69).

The framework proposed here is not dissimilar to that advanced by psychoanalyst D. W. Winnicott, who wrote as long ago as 1971 about the ways in which children construct narratives about themselves through play as a means of adjusting to the outside world. They forge a precarious balance between "the interplay of personal psychic reality and the experience of control of actual events" (1971: 13). The experience of narrative construction not only involves manipulating external phenomena, but accommodates the experience of shared playing (1971: 50). The continual process of give-and-take between individual and shared experiences of play governs every cultural experience: "Playing is inherently exciting and precarious [...] [it] belongs to the interplay in the child's mind of that which is subjective [...] and that which is objectively pursued (actual, or shared reality)" (1971: 52–53). The outcome of this interplay is what Winnicott terms adaptation; that lifelong process of coming to terms with the people and worlds an individual inhabits, and thereby altering one's concept of selfhood.

Şeytan shows what happens if a child is either unwilling or unable to commit herself to others; her father has absconded, while her mother preoccupies herself with her unsuitable boyfriend. The only path to redemption is for the community—personified by Gül's mother Ayten—to reform itself by seeking forgiveness in the mosque, and thereby subjecting oneself to divine protection. Once that has been achieved—and the exorcist transformed—then Gül can learn how to control events for herself. *Dünyayı Kutaran Adam* turns the idea of communities protecting individuals on its head, as it shows Murat protecting the community by exterminating those forces that threaten its future. He adapts himself to the exigencies of the situation and by doing so sets an example to the community to undergo a similar adaptive process. It is this quality that rendered Cüneyt Arkın so popular with local audiences.

The relationship between individuals and their communities underpinned a political initiative that only lasted for a decade and a half but had a profound effect on the future of the Turkish Republic—the creation of the so-called "Village Institutes" (*Köy Enstitüleri*). The brainchild of educational visionary İsmail Hakkı Tonguç, they were planned as a series of commune-like structures designed to promote mass education in rural areas—not just reading and writing but cultural and agricultural training as well. Through education, the people would acquire sufficient confidence to take a greater role in the way their communities (and the state) were run, and thereby make a significant contribution to the advancement of the Republic. One such institute summarized its founding principles as follows:

1 To educate the Turkish villager in accordance with the demands of the Republican regime and to carry him/her to an advanced and superior level in terms of augmenting his/her skills of thinking, feeling, living, and producing;
2 To train quick-minded, mature, and sensitive personnel for villages, who are dedicated to the Republican principles, have superior living habits, are able to discover means of production [...] will not refrain from overcoming obstacles, and are resolved to realize this cause (Gümüşoğlu, 2012: 83–84).

Education was a continual process involving classes in musical appreciation and acquiring the latest agricultural techniques. The Institutes were founded on a belief in whole-person education; if individuals devoted their leisure-time to reading or other cultural pursuits, they would learn how to adapt themselves better to the demands of their waking lives, including looking after their families. Through this kind of training, they would work to change the societies they inhabited through "thinking, feeling, living, and producing".

Much criticized at the time (conservatives opposed their co-educational philosophy, some parents were reluctant to send their daughters away, while right-wingers accused them of being hotbeds of Marxism opposed to Republican principles), the Institutes were forced to close by 1954, to be replaced by teacher training colleges. Nevertheless, their legacy lived on through the experiences of those fortunate enough to graduate. Kemal Kocabaş, who spent his time at the Ortaklar Institute near Afyon paid tribute to "all the directors, teacher[s], master instructors, and students who participated in the Ortaklar (Adabelen) collaborative work, as well as my fear father Kızılçullu student and his friends, who had bricks in the 'Ortaklar Collaboration'" (2012: 137).

The Institutes' basic principles, embodying Bruner's notion of the creation of selfhood through community association, lived on in *Yeşilçam* films such as *Şeytan* and *Dünyayı Kutaran Adam*. Gül learns how to fend for herself once she enters the mosque, where the deity protects her from further corruption. Murat offers an example of altruistic bravery, as he possesses the kind of 'superior living habits' that anyone inhabiting the Institutes would have been proud of. While both films adapt Hollywood classics according to local conventions, they foreground the importance of adaptation, understood as a process of continuous emotional and psychological transformation, enabling individuals to make a significant contribution to the development of their communities.

What can this case study of *Yeşilçam* products tell us about transcultural adaptations? Most importantly we should refrain from comparing source with target-texts, as the outcome remains predictable, telling us more about the preoccupations (prejudices?) of those making the comparisons rather than contributing to our understanding of either text. To dismiss *Şeytan* or *Dünyayı Kutaran Adam* as cinematic turkeys represents an orientalist judgment based on the assumption that Western source-texts are automatically "better" because they have been created in Hollywood on big budgets. We must likewise rethink what "originality" signifies, especially in contexts where creative artists freely borrow from source-texts without acknowledging their authors (or paying copyright dues). This is not necessarily 'reprehensible'— however much we might criticize our students for doing the same thing—in a newly established country trying to create national cultures.

Both *Şeytan* and *Dünyayı Kutaran Adam* are good examples of transcultural, as opposed to inter- or cross-cultural adaptations; neither film acknowledges a debt to its respective source-text, but rather borrows certain elements from it in an attempt to reinforce the idea of adaptation as a process of creating (and recreating) selfhood. This process is *not* the same as assimilation—in which concepts are absorbed in an attempt to reinforce dominant ideals, but rather represents an expansion of our understanding of genre and psychology. By subjunctivizing reality—to invoke Bruner's term— the films encourage us to rethink our understanding of the familiar and the possible. They remind us that cultural difference (what seems possible in one context might not be so in another) is at best a fragile concept, often undone when we analyze a film's conditions of production that may establish certain affinities between ourselves and those so apparently different from us. David MacDougall writes: "A transcultural perspective accommodates cultural shift, movement, and interchange, which more adequately fits the experience many Westerners as well as populations often identified as indigenous, migrant, or diasporic" (1998: 261).

Using Bruner within a transcultural framework reminds us that the idea of border crossing is a complex one, not only involving geographical but psychological borders. He writes about the importance of autonomy and commitment, of individuals reaching out beyond their comfort-zones in the belief that they possess "a will of [their] own, a certain freedom of choice, a degree of possibility" (2003: 78). They have to learn how to relate "to a world of others—to friends and family, to institutions, to the past, to reference groups" (Bruner, 2003: 78). While that process of reaching out might place limits on their autonomy, the community can take advantage of individual experiences to redefine its own narratives. The continual process of border crossing between individuals and communities is what we term progress: "People rebalance their autonomy and their commitment, usually in a way that honors what they were before" (Bruner, 2003: 84). This rebalancing is achieved through our capacity to narrate that "permits us to hark back selectively to our past while shaping ourselves for the possibilities of an imagined future" (Bruner, 2003: 86–87). Both films show this process at work through Gül and Ayten's process of reform once they enter the mosque, while Murat in *Dunyayı Kutaran Adam* transcends the borders of the self to work on behalf of others, and thereby save the world.

For audiences familiar with the history and significance of the Village Institutes—even if they lacked first-hand experience of inhabiting them—both films emphasize the importance of autonomy and commitment as the foundation of a stable society. While *Yeşilçam* products were first and foremost conceived as popular entertainment, attracting maximum box-office receipts for minimum financial outlay, they appealed to their audiences' sense of collective well-being. Ahmet Mekin noted as long ago as 1961 that *Yeşilçam* had been identified with "our street"—the cacophony of the studio "is the cacophony just about every day on our street […] No doubt one day, we will have big studios and a housing complex set up for the artists around it. And in this manner OUR STREET will become history" (as cited in Arslan, 2012: 232–33). Hence, the films could communicate moral messages while still attracting mass audiences. They had no need to emulate the West; by adapting classic Hollywood works, *Yeşilçam* created new texts for itself that dealt in a direct manner with "what was there"—the day-to-day experiences of local audiences. The films showed the enduring significance of adaptation as a means of negotiating border crossings in an attempt to perpetuate the pioneering spirit associated with the Village Institutes, even if the Institutes had been shut down nearly two decades previously.

References

Akser, M. (2013). The man who saved the world. In E. Atakav (Ed.), *Directory of world cinema: Turkey*. Bristol and Chicago: Intellect.

Arslan, S. (2012). *Cinema in Turkey: A new critical history*. Oxford: Oxford University Press.

Bruner, J. (2003). *Making stories: Law, literature, life*. Cambridge, MA: Harvard University Press.

Campos, E. (2006). Turkish *Exorcist* [*Şeytan*]. *Film threat*, available online at: http://web.archive.org/web/20060614174703/http://filmthreat.com/index.php?section=reviews&Id=3028 (Retrieved July 9, 2014).

Gümüsoğlu, F. (2012). Kars Cılavuz Village Institutes. Trans. Melis Şeyhan Çalışlar. *Mindful seed, speaking soil: Institutes of the republic 1940–1954*. II (pp. 70–93). İstanbul: İstanbul Research Institute Publications.

Hunter, I. Q., and Verevis, C. (2011). BADaptations. *Cfpenglish.upenn.edu*, available online at: https://call-for-papers.sas.upenn.edu/node/42910 (Retrieved July 9, 2014).

Kocabaş, K. (2012). Ortaklar Village Institute through witness accounts. Trans. Melis Şeyhan Çalışlar. *Mindful seed, speaking soul: Village institutes of the republic 1940–1954*. II (pp. 118–37). İstanbul: İstanbul Research Institute Publications.

MacDougall, D. (1998). *Transcultural cinema*. Princeton: Princeton University Press. "The man who saves the world" *TV tropes*, available online at: http://tvtropes. org/pmwiki/pmwiki.php/Film/TheManWhoSavesTheWorld (Retrieved July 11, 2014).

Mourkogiannis, N. (2006). *Purpose: The starting-point of great companies*. Basingstoke and New York: Palgrave.

Raw, L. (2003). Horrific Henry James. *Literature/Film Quarterly*, 31(3), 193–9.

Raw, L. (2011). *Exploring Turkish cultures: Essays, interviews and reviews*. Newcastle-upon-Tyne: Cambridge Scholars Publishing.

Raw, L. (2012). Identifying common ground. In L. Raw (Ed.), *Adaptation, Translation and Transformation* (pp. 1–22). London and New York: Bloomsbury Continuum.

Smith, I. R. (2008). "Beam me up, Ömer: Transnational media flow and the cultural politics of the Turkish *Star Trek* remake". *Velvet Light Trap*, 61, 3–13.

"Supreme Nothing". (2009). Cüneyt Arkın: The greatest action star of all time!, *SupremeNothingBlogspot*, available online at: http://supremenothing.blogspot. co.uk/2009/05/cuneyt-arkn-greatest-turkish-action.html (Retrieved July 11, 2014).

Welsch, W. (1994–5). Transculturality: The puzzling form of cultures today. *California Sociologist*, 17–18, 19–39.

Williams, N. (2012). The Turk who saved the world (and other stories). *BBC News Magazine*, available online at: http://www.bbc.co.uk/news/magazine-18851790 (Retrieved July 11, 2014).

Winnicott, D. W. (1971/2005). *Playing and reality*. London and New York: Routledge.

10 Tracing Asian Franchises

Local and Transnational Reception of *Hana Yori Dango*

Rayna Denison

Remakes, co-productions, and the flows of texts between Asia's core media markets have been increasing over the past two decades as a result of market liberalization and changing patterns of media consumption within the region (Yeh and Davis, 2002; Ciecko, 2006; Hu, 2005). In this melee of exchanges, new kinds of transnational 'Asian' production practices are emerging, ones that borrow across borders, continually repeating narratives as well as reframing and revising the products of national cultures from across the region. One set of such exchanges, emerging out of the Japanese manga property *Hana Yori Dango*, created by Yoko Kamio (1992–2003, the title is a pun usually translated as *Boys over Flowers*), has become the basis for a set of re-productions, translations, and cultural exchanges that have achieved consistently high levels of transnational popularity, academic inquiry, and cross-media expansion. Using *Hana Yori Dango* as a case study thereby reveals some of the complex transnational negotiations at work in the production of piecemeal Asian franchising. Moreover, as a sprawling 'intertextual network' (Meehan, 1991), *Hana Yori Dango*'s varied reception has much to reveal about the way long-running transnational franchises can shift meanings. Depending upon their contexts of consumption, the texts of *Hana Yori Dango* have been variously promoted, remembered, or forgotten.

The growing body of academic work on *Hana Yori Dango* demonstrates the difficulty of holistically analyzing such unplanned, temporally dispersed, and linguistically fragmented Asian 'franchises'. While all the texts share copyrighted material as is typical of a franchise (Johnson, 2013), they tend to be produced by discrete national industries and are often held in tension with their predecessors as their producers try to improve upon and compete with the rest of the foregoing transnational intertextual network. In this way, Asian franchising practices may differ from the pre-planned franchise production of Hollywood conglomerates (see, for example: Thompson, 2007 and Johnson, 2012), but they are not dissimilar to the kinds of intertextuality examined around figures like James Bond (Bennett and Woollacott, 1987) or Batman (Brooker, 2012; Meehan, 1991). What is significant, however, is that *Hana Yori Dango*'s continual reproduction has been less centrally controlled than many of its Euro-American counterparts. Instead, *Hana Yori Dango*'s continual reproduction is a result of complex international and inter-industrial processes that have been generated less from the center outwards than from the outside in. As this suggests, the continual chains of *Hana Yori Dango* productions have resulted from licensees seeking content rather than from a centralizing industrial process on the part of the Japanese rights holders. In this way, *Hana Yori Dango*'s many iterations are a product of a set of industrial practices distinct from those seen elsewhere in franchising and adaptation studies and are consequently worthy of further investigation here.

Hana Yori Dango, in circulation for more than 20 years, is also noteworthy for its breadth of adaptation. It has been adapted into numerous media formats, from animation to live action television and film, with many of those texts then translated (more and less legally) and disseminated around Asia and beyond. Given this ongoing remake landscape, it is difficult to identify a core set of texts or even to delimit the whole of the intertextual network. However, *Hana Yori Dango* has gone through a series of production cycles in different national locales that have achieved high levels of transnational exposure. It was first known as *Hana Yori Dango* (as anime, 1996–1997, and a standalone live action film directed by Yasuyuki Kusuda in 1995). A subsequent cycle revolved around a high profile Japanese television *dorama* or "drama" (with two series, one in 2005 and a second in 2008) and a final film with the same cast and crew in 2008, directed by Yasuharu Ishii. It was outside Japan, however, as *Meteor Garden* (*Liúxīng Huāyuán*, Chinese TV System (CTS), 2001) that *Hana Yori Dango* first became a significant hit, as a live action Taiwanese television show. Then, a further South Korean television adaptation, *Kkot Boda Namja* (*Boys before Flowers*, KBS, 2008), once more reproduced *Hana Yori Dango* as a hit television show in the South Korean market. There has even been an unlicensed remake in China that borrows not from *Hana Yori Dango* directly, but from the Taiwanese *Meteor Garden* as its main source material (*Meteor Shower*, *Liúxīng* Yǔ, Hunan TV, 2009). Further to these adaptations, 2013 and 2014 finally saw the intertextual network spread beyond East Asia with a fan-produced, Kickstarter-funded US version called *Boys before Friends* (2013) and a high profile Indian live action television remake called *Kaisi Yeh Yaariaan* (2014), produced locally by MTV. *Hana Yori Dango* has, as these examples suggest, been continually remade, inspiring cycles of production that borrow and build upon one another, making it one of Asia's most sprawling and "transmedia" intertextual networks (Kinder, 1993). As a result, *Hana Yori Dango* has exceeded its Japanese origins, taking on wider transnational connotations, which makes it a good place to start a consideration of Asian franchising practices.

However, rather than making *Hana Yori Dango* easier to analyze, the franchise's transnationality has become so complex, gone through so many iterations, and become so dispersed as to make it simultaneously difficult to trace and open to a wide range of approaches, methods, and theories. Moreover, and unlike its pre-planned counterparts elsewhere in the world

(Thompson, 2007; Verevis, 2006), the piecemeal and sporadic nature of *Hana Yori Dango*'s textual production has created an unpredictability about the cultural paths its texts travel. This is at least in part because *Hana Yori Dango*'s texts are at one and the same time remakes, remediations, adaptations, translations, and examples of franchise-oriented intellectual property exploitation. Following Constantine Verevis' understanding of remakes as multivalent phenomena identifiable through the textual, industrial, and critical structures through which they flow (2006), I argue that *Hana Yori Dango* complicates the idea of the remake through its emphatic transnational intertextuality.

Indeed, undertaking an analysis of all of these elements, perhaps especially those related to *Hana Yori Dango*'s shifting cultural and linguistic landscapes, makes an holistic understanding of this franchise unlikely, if not impossible. Nonetheless, holism is an essential goal in this study because, as Barbara Klinger argues, "the concept promises to press historians' enquiries beyond established frontiers, broadening the scope of their enterprise, and continually refining their historical methods and perspectives" (1997: 111). In this, Klinger's position concurs with those visible in the methods of recent franchise historians like Derek Johnson (2013), Will Brooker (1999 and 2012) and Avi Santo (2010), all of whom have attempted to trace the practices of franchising through attention paid to the discourses that help to explain franchising processes. Utilizing these discursive approaches, one of the things that makes *Hana Yori Dango* so unusual is the range of academics who have studied parts of its intertextual network, often without attempting to make sense of the whole. The scope and methods used by others to analyze *Hana Yori Dango* have, in part, led me to take up this case study, and for this reason I begin with an analysis of pre-existing academic work on the franchise before shifting into a deeper interrogation of one of the hubs of its production. To this end, I use the kinds of reception studies methods seen in Barbara Klinger's and Janet Staiger's work in the analysis that follows (specifically: Klinger, 1994 and Staiger, 2000). As such, and given my own linguistic and cultural specialisms (limited to English and Japanese), this chapter begins with an examination of pre-existing English-language academic scholarship on *Hana Yori Dango* in order to produce an understanding of the franchise that comes as close as possible to encompassing the whole of its intertext while thinking about the ways academics have attempted to make sense of this expanding 'franchise'. I analyze academic research produced out of a wide range of national and linguistic origins, which, taken together, encompasses much, though not all, of *Hana Yori Dango*'s intertextual history.

In doing this work, I am particularly interested in considering what has been overlooked, ignored, or purposefully written out of *Hana Yori Dango*'s history (Staiger, 2000: 163). In this way, I aim to investigate the politics of franchise memory, extending Julian Stringer's (2007) attempts to map and explain the shifting sense of the 'original' and 'copy' in relation to the transnational *Ringu* (1999) franchise of films. To expand on the pre-existing attempts to map the *Hana Yori Dango* franchise, I take the findings of my academic reception study on *Hana Yori Dango* as the starting point for a supplementary investigation of one of the texts that routinely is passed over within the discussions of the franchise. In doing so I hope to enrich and challenge current conceptions about what is at the 'core' of this franchise and to show how unstable the idea of an original can be within wider franchising practices. In this way, I offer an alternative view regarding how franchising might be understood, using *Hana Yori Dango* as a key example of distinctive Asian franchising practices. Such an attempt to trace the emergence of transnational Asian franchising practices and processes has the potential to reveal much about the politics of franchising in Asia and to more fully delineate the distinctive industrial relations empowering transnational hit franchise production within and beyond the Asian region.

From *Hana Yori Dango to Meteor Garden* (and Back Again): Academic Accounts of the *Hana Yori Dango* Franchise

This section, therefore, takes the form of an analysis of pre-existing studies examining the development of academic discourses around *Hana Yori Dango*. I have sought out clusters of opinion forming around particular texts and the methods used to produce readings of those texts. Moreover, this section reflects on what has been left out as a consequence of those analytical choices (Staiger, 2000: 161–64). It is worth noting that the selected academic studies are themselves varied and transnational in origin, which makes it possible for me to consider texts outside of my own linguistic specialisms. The publication of these academic analyses spans the globe from North America and Europe through to Australia and Japan. As a group, they are also diachronic, ranging across publication dates from 2006 to 2012. They also differ in length and come from writers at diverse stages of their academic careers, with published refereed articles and book chapters being included alongside web-published MA and Ph.D. thesis work. I am, therefore, as cognizant of their differences as I am interested in seeking out the threads of discursive commonality ranged across the eight studies analyzed hereafter.

Within this group of texts on *Hana Yori Dango*, the usual bifurcation between textual and contextual studies abides, although it is perhaps surprising to see quite how many academics have responded to the large scale of this franchise by performing textual analyses (for examples, see: Choo, 2008; Le, 2009; Yasumoto, 2011; and Yoshida, 2011). Lan Xuan Le, for example, explains this choice by suggesting that textual analysis has the power to explain the cultural migration undertaken by texts, where ethnographies and reception studies cannot:

> While reception can locate what meanings viewers construct from the
> text and how they deployed those meanings in their everyday cultural

understanding, it can only gesture broadly to the elements of the text that catch and charge the imaginations of its readers. (2009: 12)

Le thereby suggests a reason for the preponderance of textual analyses within work on *Hana Yori Dango*. In this case at least textual analysis is driven by questions of how and what has changed during repeated adaptations, over and above a search for contextually derived meaning. However, ability of textual analysis to account for the "elements of the text that catch and charge the imaginations of readers" across national borders, in different languages, and over time are as potentially limited and problematic as reception studies' own limitations. By analyzing texts from the position of an idealized reader, moreover, it is Le's position as a critic that becomes crucial to the analysis and not the "elements of the text" that might spark reader or viewer imaginations.

Examined with a pragmatic eye, the consistent use of textual analysis might also be explained by the ability of some types of textual analysis to sift through the large numbers of texts examined in many of these studies. In just one example, by Seiko Yasumoto, she:

> includes an analysis of thirty-seven volumes of the original Japanese manga of *Hana Yori Dango*, eighteen episodes of the Japanese TV drama series adaptations, twenty-five episodes of the Korean drama series remake, and twenty-four episodes of the Taiwanese series remake. (2011: 6)

The volume of texts studied by Yasumoto, Hitomi Yoshida (2011), and others has led these scholars toward structural and content analyses that work to quantify and compare the shifting narratives comprised within *Hana Yori Dango*'s repetitions. These methods emphasize quantitative kinds of data analysis over the more qualitative kinds of close comparative textual analysis often favored by those analyzing adaptation and remakes, simply because of the large numbers of texts involved in this transmedia, transnational franchise (see, for example: Johnson, 2012). However, what is notable here are the texts left out of these analyses. For example, both Yasumoto and Yoshida focus on the manga and its live action television remakes, discounting the anime and film variations also produced during the franchise's history. In this way, their textual analyses posit the core medium of the *Hana Yori Dango* franchise as television, with manga considered the "origin" point and the benchmark of textual legitimacy.

Only one of the academic texts examined here, Kukhee Choo's (2008) analysis of the manga and anime series of *Hana Yori Dango* (Toei-Asahi Broadcasting Corporation, 1996–1997, with a film version made in 1997), covers the earliest Japanese production cycle within the franchise. All of the other academic texts focus on the franchise's various iterations in live action television. Perhaps as a result of its many repetitions as live action television series, there is considerable variation in how the *Hana Yori Dango* canon has been drawn up by academics. For example, the "first" television drama adaptation and the most recently successful television show have been the most frequently analyzed. Re-titled *Meteor Garden* (*Liúxīng Huāyuán*, Chinese TV System (CTS), 2001, with a special, *Meteor Rain* in 2001, and a second series, *Meteor Garden II* in 2002), the Taiwanese version of *Hana Yori Dango* is acclaimed as having "started" the franchise proper (Deppman, 2009). By contrast, the more recent 2009 South Korean television adaptation titled *Boys before Flowers* has been deemed the highest profile and most successful of the franchise's texts by academics (Yoshida, 2011: 81). By selecting exceptional texts from within the wider franchise, and by comparing similar kinds of franchise texts, the *Hana Yori Dango* intertext has been continually re-written by academics, becoming a more coherent television-oriented franchise with a defined central medium.

For example, Hsui-Chuang Deppman (2009) links the production of *Meteor Garden* to the wider rise of 'trendy', or 'idol' (Asian star-oriented) dramas, which Koichi Iwabuchi (2002 and 2004) has shown began to circulate to popular acclaim within Asia in the late 1990s. Deppman argues that *Meteor Garden* led to the production of a homegrown idol drama genre on Taiwanese television, used as a tool to resist Chinese cultural influence (2009: 92–93). Iwabuchi also briefly analyzed the franchise early in its life. He adopts an outward looking perspective that agrees with Deppman's position, arguing that in *Meteor Garden*, "The hybrid composition of Japanese and Taiwanese cultural imaginations has brought about a new East Asian youth culture that resists rigid political regulations" (2004: 18). These accounts highlight the porous borders between Asia's media production hubs in order to argue for a resistant use of *Hana Yori Dango* as television. As nationalism and medium specificity creep into these discourses, however, Japan's multiple cycles of *Hana Yori Dango* production become increasingly obscured by academics' desire to discuss the franchise's transnational remakes.

Fang-chih Irene Yang, going further than either Deppman or Iwabuchi, discusses only the Taiwanese version of the franchise, making *Meteor Garden* its most significant textual iteration. Arguing for the right of Taiwanese audiences to watch Korean dramas, including the South Korean remake, *Kkot Boda Namja*, Yang aligns the South Korean television show with its Taiwanese predecessor in a way that obscures its Japanese precursors and the franchise's manga origins (2012). Yang's justifications run as follows: "This paper uses the notion of 'fantasy genre' to analyze *Meteor Garden*, with particular attention to the Korean and the Taiwanese adaptations as they are the most favoured versions for many fans in Taiwan" (2012: 422). No evidence is offered in support of this claim, which neatly works to obfuscate the impact, if any, of the two seasons of Japanese live action drama that interceded between the Taiwanese and South Korean remakes and of the manga and the anime and film from Japan that pre-date its television incarnations. In framing *Meteor Garden* and *Kkot Boda Namja* as the two central texts of the franchise in this way, Deppman's and Yang's readings thereby insert Taiwanese nationalism into the discourse, proclaiming the *Hana Yori Dango* franchise as a product of transnationalism in Taiwanese culture.

Most of the textual analyses are performed for the sake of broader ideological and political discourses. Seiko Yasumoto, for instance, builds her case for a comparative textual analysis of the *Hana Yori Dango* television texts through claims about the franchise's soft power: "I discuss adaptation as a form of soft power by examining *Hana Yori Dango*, a paradigmatic example of media cultural adaptation and exchange" (2011: 1). In this instance, the act of remaking is read as an ideologically charged process that "translates into Japanese soft power and elevates the status of Japan in receptor regions" (2011: 5). Hitomi Yoshida, likewise, compares the three live action television texts to the manga in order to "permit an investigation of the existence or otherwise of a shared East Asian contemporary space informed by a multilayered imaginary of modernity which allows for a plurality of culturally specific experiences" (2011: 79). Borrowing heavily from Koichi Iwabuchi's edited collection *Feeling Asian Modernities* (2004) Yoshida and Yasumoto reframe other scholars' claims for the importance of Taiwanese iterations of *Hana Yori Dango*, seeking instead signs of a shared textual vision of Asian modernity, demonstrating how open and flexible the Japanese source materials are to local inflection.

However, the intertextual network has also been inflected by globalizing discourses, perhaps especially the European fairy tale Cinderella. Yoshida, for example, leans heavily on a Proppian form of textual analysis proclaiming *Hana Yori Dango* to be "a modern variant of the classic Cinderella folk tale" (2011: 83). This has become a common thread in genre-related analyses of *Hana Yori Dango* also seen, for instance, when Choo declares it a "modern day Cinderella" text (2008: 282), and when Deppman refers to protagonist Shan Cai (Tsukushi Makino in the Japanese version) as having a 'Cinderella experience' (2009: 104). The narrative, loosely outlined, sees the heroine's slow progress toward accepting the rich, spoiled, and selfish Tsukasa Domyōji (Japanese)/ Dao ming Si (Taiwanese)/ Gu Jun Pyo (Korean)/ Murong Yunhai (Chinese) as her partner, while he in turn learns to appreciate the value of others as he tries to become someone the female protagonist could love. The narrative, which centers on the relationships between a poor girl and four rich boys, who all attend the same elite school, is thereby made part of a wider transnational, Western-inflected intertext of Cinderella re-tellings. Associating the *Hana Yori Dango* texts with this subgenre enables these scholars to draw links with a wider, emerging pan-Asian field of television production, despite the franchise's roots in another medium. Moreover, reading *Hana Yori Dango* as a set of Cinderella re-tellings ignores other possible comparison points (perhaps most obviously with the *shōjo* genre of manga, the *Beauty and the Beast* fairytale and Jane Austen's *Pride and Prejudice*), helping to simplify and make sense of the variable content of its texts. However, these references to Cinderella may be misleading, referring not to a European 'original' but to an emerging subgenre of Asian television, wherein the idea of a 'Cinderella' story refers more to representations of contemporary Asian class divisions than to a Western fairy tale.

Masako Matsuda and Nozomi Higashi declare that such idol dramas "have projected an image of Japan as idealistically modernized and westernized among Asian countries" (2006: 20), suggesting that academic textual analyses are following where producers and promotion have previously led the way. Matsuda and Higashi's interpretation of *Meteor Garden* also suggests reasons for its popularity, as does Yang, who reads Tsukushi Makino as an audience cipher, easily replaced by 'us', though neither study engages deeply with audience studies methods. This makes Xiaochang Li's (2011) investigation of English-speaking online fandom for *Hana Yori Dango* a rare attempt to solicit audience responses to the franchise, revealing how the franchise is considered a 'gateway drug' text that draws fans into wider Asian television drama fandom. On the other hand, its narratives are often criticized by these English-speaking fans for their reliance on fantasy (100–104). Moreover, the melodrama of Tsukushi Makino's struggles are recounted a major draw by this audience, making her less a cipher than a receptor of audience sympathy and pity (105–106). In these findings, Li's study of fans challenges the perceptions presented by Yang and Matsuda and Higashi's textual analyses, suggesting the need for more, and different, approaches to be taken to this franchise in order to more holistically trace its meanings.

Several studies examined here attempt to mix their methods, using economic and industrial analyses to motivate and justify textual analyses of the *Hana Yori Dango* intertext. Choo, for example, justifies her choice of the manga on economic grounds claiming, "Spanning over eleven years, *Hana Yori Dango* has been the highest-grossing *shōjo* manga series in Japanese history" (2008: 276). Likewise, Yoshida lists the many texts and their successes, building to the declaration that, "The Korean version was a huge success both domestically and throughout Asia with a peak local viewer rating of 35%" (2011: 81). Matsuda and Higashi take this sort of concrete assertion of success a stage further arguing that *Hana Yori Dango*'s franchise longevity has been a product of it getting caught up in a series of recent cultural exchange "booms" that have more readily moved texts across the Asian region (2006: 20). Through these discussions of the industrial clout of *Hana Yori Dango*'s various texts, a sense of the intertext's roles in wider debates about soft power and globalization become apparent.

These are the terms in which Iwabuchi and Seiko Yasumoto (also writing under the name Seiko King, 2012) introduce their appreciations of the franchise. Yasumoto returns to the importance of the transnational exchanges in *Hana Yori Dango* texts in her conclusion, confirming their role in Japan's soft power debate. She writes:

> Commonality can be shared and mutually enjoyed, and audiences create a new culture and world where they communicate through media products such as *Hana Yori Dango* and other forms of remaking towards a new cultural reception. (2011: 12)

The globalization discourse centers on the concept of Japan's soft power, raised first by Iwabuchi but accepted by many others (Yoshida, 2011; Yang, 2012). The reason *Hana Yori Dango* has succeeded in becoming a major transnational Asian franchise, according to these scholars, is its ability to engage with and represent a shared Asian modernity (Iwabuchi, 2002, 2004).

The global focus on Japan's soft power is still organized around analysis of *Hana Yori Dango*'s television texts, obscuring the variety in its modes and mediums of production. Within the academic discourse, the most commonly overlooked texts are *Hana Yori Dango*'s early ones, especially its anime and the first live action film text (Yasuyuki Kusada, 1995) that were created in Japan before the Taiwanese television adaptation. The latter, starring Yuki Uchida, is rarely mentioned and has not been the subject of analysis to date. Likewise, the most recent cycle of live action Japanese drama and film productions (beginning in 2005 and ending in a film in 2008) seems to be of little interest to those charting the franchise's wider Asian success story. The result is a set of debates about the transnational potential of Japanese television formats, which overlooks Japanese media production. These academic analyses thereby reveal the openness of the *Hana Yori Dango* intertext to continual national and transnational reshaping. From claims about this as a significant Taiwanese product to claims for it as symptomatic of a growing shared regional modern identity, *Hana Yori Dango*'s many iterations demonstrate the contradictory ways that the success of an Asian franchise could be conceptualized. At stake in these analyses is a sense of what "Asia" means, and the political capacity of nations to make themselves prominent members within that shared mediascape. Perhaps most notable within these readings has been the erasure of the most recent cycle of Japanese productions and sometimes even the denial of the intertextual network's Japanese origins.

Therefore, that recent cycle of Japanese production, beginning in 2005 and ending with a new blockbuster scale film in 2008 (Howard, 2010), has been selected because of the way that production cycle sits between other successful parts of the franchise. Moreover, given the emphasis placed on television within other academic accounts of the intertext, I want to pull the focus to look at how another medium, film, relates to its televisual surround. The next section therefore focuses on the promotion of *Boys over Flowers: Final* (*Hana Yori Dango Fainaru*, Yasuharu Ishii), analyzing how the Japanese producers of this phase of the franchise made use of the surrounding intertextual network. In this way, I want to question some of the assumptions made in the academic analyses examined herein: first, the extent to which texts rely on their status as franchise texts. Instead of making assumptions or declarations about the relative importance of franchise texts to the *Boys over Flowers: Final* film, I want to see how the producers made sense of the pre-existing network of texts. Second, the importance of Japan as a context of production, often dismissed or sidelined, will be re-centered hereafter, to allow for a reconsideration of *Hana Yori Dango* within its domestic market. Finally, the way industry, rather than academia, makes sense of the franchise is considered in order to see where and how gaps are emerging between the production and reception of *Hana Yori Dango*.

Hana Yori Dango: Final: Franchising, Originality and Repetition in Japan Media Production

Chronology and franchising appear continuously at the margins and interstices of *Hana Yori Dango Fainaru*'s promotional surround. This trend is not new. It goes back at least as far as the launch of the live action drama series on Japanese television in 2005. For example, in a side-bar to their main article introducing the new cast and storyline of *Hana Yori Dango*, Japan's *TV Guide* announced "The Poison's Spread" before offering a comprehensive list of *Hana Yori Dango*-derived texts: from the manga's first appearance in *Margaret Comics* in 1992 to its first live-action film adaptation in 1995, its appearance on TV Asahi as anime, and in an anime film, between 1996 and 1997, before recounting its adaptations in Taiwan, its cessation as a serialized manga in 2004, and its appearance on TBS as a live-action Japanese drama in 2005 (2005: 13). Despite this detailed franchise history, however, the *Hana Yori Dango* intertext is not named as a "franchise" outright.

An article in a special issue of Japan's most well-respected film magazine, *Kinema Junpo*, for example, introduces the idea of franchising by proxy, discussing the 'visualisation' (*eizōka*) of *Hana Yori Dango* and its 'big hit' status over the preceding 13 years (Kumasaka, 2008: 32). Instead of using the term 'franchising', the promotion for *Hana Yori Dango Fainaru* instead divides up the franchise into production elements and versions, marked by the suffixes '-*ka*' or '-*ban*', with the film being a '*gekijōban*' (theatrical version) or a more generalized '*eizōka*' (*Joshi ni Eiga*, 2008: 8; *Nikkei Entertainment!*, 2008; 104–105). These terms suggest franchising, but the intertextual network is made even more complex in the Japanese context by the lack of recognition of the concept of franchising itself.

Local languages, meanings, and local production cultures dominate the discourse around *Hana Yori Dango Fainaru* in Japan. Tae Kumasaka writes that "the story is drawn from the everyday experiences of the core audience = teenagers: the central realism that comes from bullying at school, the existence of cliques among groups of girls". In particular, Kumasaka cites the increasingly close alignment between the Tsukushi Makino character and the actresses embodying her onscreen as an underlying cause of the franchise's continuing success (2008: 33). Through these means, the Japanese versions of *Hana Yori Dango* are promoted above those of their Taiwanese counterparts, allowing a tacit nationalism to creep into the discourse around the intertextual network's overall success, while suggesting that the Japanese iterations of *Hana Yori Dango* give it consistency as a franchise.

A further strengthening of the bonds between the 'original' manga text and the live action Japanese production cycle can also be found in *Hana Yori Dango Fainaru*'s official theatrical brochure. Produced by the distributor Toho, this brochure provides access to direct marketing accounts of the franchise and its history. In it, a three-way conversation among director Yasuhiro Ishii, producer Katsuaki Setoguchi, and screenwriter Mikio Satake is provided covering the film and the rest of the Japanese production cycle, on which all three worked from its commencement in 2005 (Tomaru, 2008: 27–28). For this reason, the account is reflective, spending considerable time recounting their experiences of making *Hana Yori Dango* as both television and film. However, in their promotional account, Yoko Kamio's manga is the only text beyond their production cycle that is mentioned. Of Kamio's input Setoguchi says, "I did talk about things with Ms Kamio (*Kamio-sensei*), but because it's been long-awaited you have to put your back into making something that can be enjoyed as a film" (2008: 27). Setoguchi goes on to suggest the importance of having a consistent team behind the production cycle, using that consistency to strengthen perceptions of the Japanese production cycle as the core of *Hana Yori Dango*, even to the extent of exceeding the authority of the original author.

Within Japan, this is made easier by the high levels of media coverage generated around the recent production cycle's star-driven cast. Mao Inoue (who plays heroine Tsukushi Makino), for example, when asked at a press conference about what excited her about the film, replied simply that:

> I think because it's an original story for *Hanadan* and, then, it's going to be the last *Hanadan* people are able to see. This time Tsukushi and Tsukasa are engaged, and because of the growth of their relationship, I hope people will be looking forward to it.
>
> (*Nihon Eiga Magazine*, 2008: 57)

Her comments are indicative of the kinds of tension generated between stars promoting their work across the Japanese production cycle, while simultaneously attempting to differentiate the film from its closest precursors. Her use of the shortened title "*Hanadan*" makes the popular phenomenology of *Hana Yori Dango* evident, with the nickname speaking to a pre-existing, knowledgeable audience.

"*Hanadan*" also differentiates these recent Japanese texts from their wider intertext, making this production cycle into an identifiable intra-franchise intertext, more special than and different from, those that went before. Inoue's emphasis on originality was also echoed throughout the commentary by the stars. Tsuyoshi Abe, who plays one of Domyōji's close friends, Akira Mimasaka, states, "Because we finished all of the original (*gensaku*) content in *Returns* (series 2), a new story was going to be born, and I was looking forward to it, thinking it would be really enjoyable and wondering what kind of content it would be" (Tomaru, 2008b: 14). The idea of a "*gensaku*", or 'original work', emphasizes the status of the production cycle as an adaption in Abe's comments. Through the legitimizing presence of the star, the creation of an 'original', non-canon, film is made to seem wondrous rather than foreign, with the newness offset by the re-use of the cast and crew from the preceding *Hana Yori Dango* television drama.

The balancing act between old and new also runs through other aspects of the promotional commentary for *Hana Yori Dango Fainaru*. For example, the phrase 'three times' becomes a repeated motif in the coverage (see, for examples: *Hana Yori Dango Fainaru*, 2008). Jun Matsumoto (Tsukasa Domyōji), narrates his surprise at his repeated opportunities to star in *Hana Yori Dango*:

> When *Part 1* [series 1] was over, I said, "wouldn't it be good if we could do a sequel?", and when *Returns* finished too, I said, "I wish I could do it once more". Like this, I am now able to play the same role a third time, and it is because of the audiences who have loved these texts from the start. I first want to thank everyone for that.
>
> (Takaseki, 2008: 7)

Although it quickly became a popular ratings hit (*Nikkei Entertainment!*, 2008: 104), the piecemeal nature of *Hana Yori Dango*'s production is thrown into relief by Matsumoto's comments. The way Matsumoto describes having played Tsukasa Domyōji three times also deepens the connections between the production cycle's texts, creating an equivalency between television's longer narrative arcs and film's more compressed time-space. From its stars to its producers, then, *Hana Yori Dango Fainaru* was an opportunity to revisit and add an original story to a highly successful set of adaptations. Their Japanese productions, and not a sense of a wider franchise, organize the way these promotional discourses are organized. In this way, the Japanese production context becomes a reassertion of the cultural specificity of these texts, which are dependent on Japanese audiences for their success, as Matsumoto proclaims above. From a transnational phenomenon, *Hana Yori Dango* is reframed here in specifically local, national terms.

Conclusions: Franchising Over Flowers, the Commercial Intertextuality of *Hana Yori Dango*

Within all these discourses, academic and industrial, the concept of franchising is largely absent. At best, it haunts the language of versions, iterations, and repetitions. This language of adaptation, remakes, and intertextuality works to obscure the chains of acknowledgment and ownership involved in producing trans-Asian franchise texts. The temporal dispersal of these productions also begets a focus on production cycles over franchising, demonstrated in producers' and academics' seeming memory loss about particular texts. For example, when *Kinema Junpo* covered *Hana Yori Dango Fainaru*'s predecessors, it remembered all the live action versions, but forgot to mention the anime from the 1990s (Kumasaka 2008: 33). Even in Japan, then, the chains of adaptation and franchising are caught up in industrial wrangling and the politics of taste. *Hana Yori Dango* is very difficult to study, therefore, because it is a franchise continually under reconstruction. Because its texts are transnationally and temporally dispersed and because they constantly disappear and reappear in what might be thought of as 'franchising memory', it is a challenging franchise to trace and analyze.

Moreover, as this analysis has shown, the 'core' texts keep shifting, with academics proclaiming the importance of television, while other moments reveal tensions between national production cycles and between media formats like film, television, and manga. As shown herein, manga is often (but not always) viewed as *Hana Yori Dango*'s origin point, anime appears and disappears as a precursor text, and virtually no one remembers the original live action film, favoring instead the many television variations on the *Hana Yori Dango* theme. The study of *Hana Yori Dango Fainaru* was intended to show how disparate the roles of media formats can be even in repetition. In this case, the film offered a new story, moving beyond the canon of the franchise in order to revisit its perceived pleasures and act as a conclusion to the Japanese production cycle. Originality was therefore a key factor in this film's release, but originality based on the intertext's perceived pleasures, and especially those of the *dorama* production cycle, rather than straightforward repetition or specific transnational borrowings. This insistent re-localization of *Hana Yori Dango* as *Hanadan* thereby reveals the competition between production cycles within the wider intertextual network.

As with genres, repetition is held in tension with originality across the franchise's analysis and promotion. In this respect, each of *Hana Yori Dango*'s remakes has been a reaction and response to what Will Brooker has called the 'vast archive' of potential adaptation sources (Brooker, 2012: 53). If nothing else, taking a holistic and historical view of the *Hana Yori Dango* franchise demonstrates the complexity in the structures of borrowing and especially in the politics of transnational borrowing, to be found in transmedia, transnational Asian media franchising practices. By thinking through the academic responses to *Hana Yori Dango* and comparing them with the promotional discourses from a synchronic point in the franchise's history, I have tried to reveal the distinctive ways a franchise operates when viewed through different temporal lenses. Selecting an under-examined moment, *Hana Yori Dango Fainaru*'s promotion, demonstrates the resonating tensions at work in this franchise, including its emphatically local construction, despite academic assertions about its place in a wider transnational intertext. Essentially, what has been ignored so far in academic work around this franchise are moments of, usually Japanese, production that speak more to Japanese audiences than to the wider world. *Hana Yori Dango* is a significant franchise, all the way from the local to the transnational of Asian media franchising, and it is important not to lose sight of its small and large-scale interventions in the region's popular culture. What I have argued for here is simply that we treat Asian franchises holistically, because in doing so we can see how transnational tensions are continually reshaping Asian media and the local cultures that such exchanges and remakes cultures enable. *Hana Yori Dango* is thereby revealed to be simultaneously Japanese and emphatically Asian, reaching across national borders. But these exchanges constantly involve a partial, imperfect understanding and memory of the wider franchise and an abiding sense of intra-intertextual competition.

References

Anon. (2005, October). Poisoned by *Hanadan*? *TV Guide*, 12–13.

Anon. (2008). The tracks of *Hana Yori Dango*. *Joshi ni Eiga* (*Movies for Women*) *Kinema Junpo*, 1510(6), 8.

Anon. (2008). *Hana Yori Dango: Final* filming commences! *Nihon Eiga Magazine*, 200(4), 56–57.

Anon. (2008). *Hana Yori Dango: Final* (Opening June 28): The super-popular production is completed with an original story movie. *Nikkei Entertainment!*, 2008(5), 104–105.

Bennett, T., and Woollacott, J. (1987). *Bond and beyond: The political career of a popular hero*. Basingstoke: Macmillan Education.

Brooker, W. (1999). Batman: One life, many faces. In D. Cartmell & I. Whelehan (Eds.), *Adaptations: From text to screen, screen to text* (pp. 185–198). London: Routledge.

Brooker, W. (2012). *Hunting the Dark Knight*. New York: IB Tauris.

Choo, K. (2008). Girls return home: Portrayal of femininity in popular Japanese girls' manga and anime texts during the 1990s in *Hana yori Dango* and *Fruits Basket*. *Women: A Cultural Review*, 19(3), 275–296.

Ciecko, A. (2006). *Contemporary Asian cinema: Popular culture in a global frame*. Oxford: Berg.

Darling-Wolf, F. (2004). SMAP, sex, and masculinity: Constructing the perfect female fantasy in Japanese popular music. *Popular Music and Society*, 27(3), 357–370.

Deppman, H. C. (2009). Made in Taiwan: An analysis of *Meteor Garden* as an East Asian Idol drama. In Y. Zhu & C. Berry (Eds.), *TV China* (pp. 90–110). Bloomington: University of Indiana Press.

Holm, N. (2011). Ex(or)casing the spirit of Japan: *Ringu*, *The Ring*, and the persistence of Japan. *Journal of Popular Film and Television*, 39(4), 183–192.

Howard, C. (2010). Contemporary blockbusters. In J. Berra (Ed.), *Directory of world cinema: Japan* (pp. 104–108). Chicago: Intellect Books.

Hu, K. (2005). The power of circulation: Digital technologies and the online Chinese fans of Japanese tv drama. *Inter-Asia Cultural Studies*, 6(2), 171–186.

Iwabuchi, K. (2002). *Recentering globalization: Popular culture and Japanese transnationalism*. Durham: Duke University Press.

Iwabuchi, K. (2004). (Ed.), *Feeling Asian modernities: Transnational consumption of Japanese tv dramas*. Hong Kong: Hong Kong University Press.

Johnson, D. (2012). Cinematic destiny: Marvel Studios and the trade stories of industrial convergence. *Cinema Journal*, 52(1), 1–24.

Johnson, D. (2013). *Media franchising: Creative license and collaboration in the media industries*. New York: New York University Press.

King, S. (2012). The remaking of the manga *Hana Yori Dango*. In *Re-Made in Asia: transformation across Asian markets and popular culture*. PhD Thesis, Queensland University of Technology, pp. 111–146, available online at: http://eprints.qut.edu.au/54738/1/Seiko_King_Thesis.pdf (Retrieved August 28, 2013).

Klinger, B. (1994). *Melodrama and meaning: History, culture, and the films of Douglas Sirk*. Bloomington: University of Indiana Press.

Klinger, B. (1997). Film history terminable and interminable. *Screen*, 38(2), 107–128.

Kumasaka, T. (2008). The process of visualising *Hana Yori Dango*. *Joshi ni Eiga (Movies for Women) Kinema Junpo*, 1510(6), 32–33.

Le, L. X. (2009). *Imaginaries of the Asian modern: Text and context at the juncture of nation and region*. MA Thesis, MIT, Comparative Media Studies Programme, available online at: http://cms.mit.edu/research/theses/LanLe2009.pdf (Retrieved August 27, 2013).

Li, X. (2009). *Dis/Locating audience: Transnational media flows and the online circulation of East Asian television drama*. MA Thesis, MIT, Comparative Media Studies Programme, available online at: http://cms.mit.edu/research/theses/Xiaochang Li2009.pdf (Retrieved August 27, 2013).

Matsuda, M., & Higashi, N. (2006). Popular culture transcending national borders and genres in East Asia. *Journal of Environmental Studies, Nagasaki University*, 9(1), 15–22.

Meehan, E. (1991). Holy commodity fetish, Batman!: The political economy of a commercial intertext. In R. Pearson & W. Uricchio (Eds.), *The many lives of The Batman: Critical approaches to a Superhero and his media* (pp. 47–65). New York: Routledge.

Santo, A. (2010). Batman vs. The Green Hornet: The merchandisable tv text and the paradox of licensing in the Classical Network Era. *Cinema Journal*, 49(2), 63–85.

Staiger, J. (1992). *Interpreting audiences: Studies in the historical reception of American cinema*. Princeton: Princeton University Press.

Staiger, J. (2000). *Perverse spectators: The practices of film reception*. New York: New York University Press.

Stringer, J. (2007). The original and the copy: Nakata Hideo's *Ring* (1998). In J. Stringer & A. Phillips (Eds.), *Japanese cinema: Texts and contexts* (pp. 296–307). London: Routledge.

Takaseki, S. (2008). Jun Matsumoto interview: A heart that pursues roles which are able to demonstrate ambitious work. *Nihon Eiga Magazine*, 218(5), 6–9.

Thompson, K. (2007). *The Frodo Franchise: The Lord of the Rings and modern Hollywood*. Berkeley: University of California Press.

Tomaru, Y. (2008). Akira Mimasaka. *Hana Yori Dango Fainaru* (pp. 13–14). Tokyo: Toho.

Tomaru, Y. (2008). Discussion: Yasuharu Ishii, Mikio Satake and Katsuaki Setoguchi. *Hana Yori Dango Fainaru* (pp. 27–28). Tokyo: Toho.

Verevis, C. (2006). *Film remakes*. Edinburgh: Edinburgh University Press.

Yang, F. I. (2012). From Korean Wave to Korean living: *Meteor Garden* and the politics of love in Taiwan. *Korea Observer*, 43(3), 419–445.

Yasumoto, S. (2011). Impact on soft power of cultural mobility: Japan to East Asia. *Mediascape: UCLA's Journal of Cinema and Media Studies*, available online at: http://www.tft.ucla.edu/mediascape/Winter2011_SoftPower.html (Retrieved August 24, 2013).

Yeh, E. Y. and Davis, D. W. (2002). Japan Hongscreen: Pan-Asian cinemas and flexible accumulation. *Historical Journal of Film, Radio and Television,* 22(1), 61–72.

Yoshida, H. (2011). The localisation of the *Hana Yori Dango* text: Plural modernities in East Asia. *New Voices,* 4, 78–99, available online at: http://newvoices. jpf-sydney.org/vol4.html (Retrieved August 28, 2011).

11 Fiction TV Formats in Poland—Why Bother to Adapt?

Sylwia Szostak

The Polish TV market, as it is today, emerged gradually during the 1990s, when Poland's main broadcaster TVP transitioned from a state operator of the socialist period into a public service broadcaster. Additionally, in the 1990s, Poland's main commercial broadcasters Polsat and TVN were established, in 1994 and 1997 respectively. As a result, the dual structure of the Polish TV market emerged into the public and commercial sectors, following the development of Western European television markets. As with most developing television industries, whose broadcasters lack both the experience and the money to produce varied fiction programming, the Polish TV market was heavily dependent on almost exclusively American imports during those years. This reliance on US programming (particularly television series) was, however, a short-lived phenomenon. American shows started losing prominence in the Polish prime-time schedules in the early 2000s, giving way to domestic TV fiction in the most prominent schedule positions on Polish TV screens (Szostak, 2012). This reveals what we already know about developing television markets: They go from heavy importation in their early years to domestic production as they mature (see Buonanno, 1999; Sinclair, 2000).

A closer examination of the TV fiction programming, and fiction series in particular, produced in the years immediately following the creation of Poland's commercial sector reveals that this local revival of domestic scripted series has been supported by fiction format adaptation. By exploring the views and perceptions of Poland's TV executives of fiction formats, this chapter shows how scripted formats from abroad such as Colombian *Betty, La Fea* (1999–2001, RCN TV) and Hungarian *Barátok közt* (*Between Friends*, 1998–, RTL Klub) proved an instrumental resource in laying the grounds for a much-awaited (re)launch of domestic TV fiction in Poland, thus contributing to the healthy state of contemporary domestic production. The perceived positive contribution of formats in the Polish context this chapter demonstrates goes against what has been traditionally argued about formatted programming. Keane and Moran (2009) claim that program formats may undermine the local research and development capacity in some television industries, especially those that are net-importers of formats for local adaptation. They argue that under the impact of the global movement of formats, local creative talent may become too reliant on outside expertise and resources and that this in time may lead to the reduction of local production potential. Contrary to Keane and Moran's assertion that formats may lead to a "run-down of the research and development (R&D) capacity of a particular national television industry under the impact of this global movement of formats" (2009: 203), I want to argue that formats have assumed an important developmental role in the Polish television environment. To demonstrate that formatting does not necessarily kill innovation in the domestic production sector, this chapter presents a snapshot of format activity through several TV fiction genres that have been amenable to licensing. The discussion of the accounts from production personnel, television executives, and creators from the Polish industry about their experiences with format adaptation of different genres reveals various aspects that make formats not only attractive to local producers and other industry members, but more importantly beneficial for the production capacity and local creative talent. To this end, this chapter starts with the discussion of the reasons producers in local markets turn to global formats in the first place, then moves on to discussing four case studies: format adaptation of a daily soap, a telenovela, a sitcom, and a scripted reality series. I have chosen to concentrate on formats of scripted television series because this particular category of entertainment programming was scarce in the pre-1989 era but began to gradually dominate the Polish broadcasting landscape in the 1990s.

Each case study further contributes to my argument for the beneficial impact on the local production capacity by demonstrating the practical value of each format adaptation. By doing so, this chapter contributes to the understanding of the role that formatted programming plays in nascent television markets and as such reveals aspects of the global format business that can be discussed in a broader context that goes beyond Poland. At the same time, this article, through its focus on the use of foreign formats, contributes to the notion of the transnationalization of local European television markets developed by Esser (2007). This chapter does so in the sense that it demonstrates why certain local, particularly nascent, European television markets may turn to transnational television—in this instance transnational formats—to deal with particular weaknesses of their respective production sectors. In order to arrive at more general conclusions about the global format business, I concentrate on one of Poland's commercial broadcasters—TVN, who began operating in 1997. This particular broadcaster and its gradual growth to a healthy production capacity offer a useful window into the exploration of the practical value of format adaptation.

The Lure of Formats

Formats are attractive to broadcasters for a variety of reasons. It has been argued and empirically demonstrated by Esser that formatting reduces programming risk and offers a proven track record of success in other countries

(2013: 148, 150, 151). Another benefit of using formats is that they fuel local and in-house production and contribute to domestic production quotas. In the programming output statistics, formats are usually labeled as indigenous production, and therefore regulatory agencies look at them as domestic. With audiences, too, the adapted format registers as home-grown (Moran, 1998: 145). Waisbord sees this as a loophole in media regulation, which allows foreign ideas to enter local markets and bypass local programming quotas. If local broadcasters produce domestic versions of foreign shows, these versions help satisfy quota requirements, but if they buy canned foreign shows, they do not (2004: 363).

This may be the case elsewhere, but in Poland formatted programming, scripted (such as television series) or non-scripted (such as a variety of reality programming and quiz shows), does not contribute toward domestic production quotas. Poland's Broadcasting Act defines a domestic program as one that was originally produced in the Polish language. The Act reads:

> program originally produced in the Polish language shall mean a program which meets the criteria of "European work" as defined in this Act, which has been produced on the basis of a script written originally in the Polish language and first registered in the Polish language. (Broadcasting Act of December 29, 1992)

As Polish adaptations of foreign formats are not created from scripts written in the Polish language, such adaptations are not recognized as domestic programs from the legal point of view. Bogdan Czaja, Programming Deputy Director at TVN—one of the two largest commercial channels in Poland— describes this situation as unfair from the point of view of the broadcaster:

> I feel very annoyed with the fact that Polish adaptations of international formats do not qualify as local Polish production. In terms of drama, I can see why it is not treated as local production in the legal sense. But when you consider formats such as *Kitchen Nightmares*, you only really buy the idea (…) All the plots, dialogues, are originally created by our people.
>
> (Czaja, 2011)

Because scripted formats do not contribute toward domestic production quotas, Polish broadcasters clearly must see formats as more valuable than just a fast track to local content. It is worth pointing out that adapting a foreign scripted format is not necessarily considered an easier way to generate content either. Izabela Łopuch, former executive producer at TVN comments:

> I do not like when people assume that format adaptation is the easy way out. It really is not. Producing from scratch and format adaptation

are two different production modes, two different approaches to content production. With formats, we can see the original; we can see what worked well and what did not. We have international consultants that work with us. But all that does not mean that format adaptation requires less work. Adapting a format is actually just like producing a program from scratch – the only exception being that you get the script. But even the script has to be tweaked, to a lesser or greater degree.

(Łopuch, 2012)

If we accept that adaptation is nearly as time-consuming and difficult as producing original content, and that formats do not help satisfy domestic production quotas, there must be other reasons Polish free-to-air broadcasters feel it is worth reaching out for fiction formats.

Formats certainly represent a means of obviating risk, bringing with it promise of success demonstrated in other locations, as has been argued by many scholars (Waisbord, 2004; Bazalgette, 2005; Chalaby, 2010). Bogdan Czaja, Deputy Programming Director at TVN, agrees saying, "when you buy a format, you also buy a certain feeling of security. Scripts that have been tried elsewhere, produced in various markets, that proved successful somewhere else might also work for us" (Czaja, 2011). However, the issue of formatted programming as a way of decreasing risk has an additional dimension for broadcasters and producers in developing markets such as Poland. This is the aspect I want to develop in more detail.

Izabela Łopuch reports that TVN usually has some inclination of what genre it is looking for and that decisions are rarely serendipitous. As the main rationale behind decisions to buy particular formats, Łopuch points to "the lack of scripts in the home market that a broadcaster would be interested in" (Łopuch, 2012). Łopuch elaborates that they "always look for a particular genre of a format" and rarely seek 45-minute scripted programs. This observation demonstrates that TVN is able to generate content for their weekly drama locally, and therefore the broadcaster does not have to seek programming ideas abroad when it comes to this specific type of fiction. Considering the license fee costs involved in format adaptation, the potential loss of control of the final product, and the time needed for the adaptation, the broadcaster will not submit to this if it is not deemed necessary. But in several instances in the past the broadcaster has gone through the trouble of searching for a particular format, negotiating and paying adaptation rights and tweaking the format to fit the local context. In the following, I want to examine why in some instances the broadcaster is willing to do so. The remaining parts of this chapter discuss the role of format adaptation in the production of particular fiction genres and illuminate the ways formats can become a key element of television programming, especially pertaining to those genres and types of programming that are alien to a given audiovisual market or those that a particular production sector struggles with. In the case of Poland, in the years immediately following the creation of the commercial sector, one of the genres that Poland's production sector had no prior experience with was the soap opera. The following considers the production of TVN's first soap television series to demonstrate how turning to format adaptation was a more viable strategy than producing a similar program from scratch.

TVN and Its First Soap

The production context for TVN's first soap is worth considering, as it is a story where the acquisition of the format was driven by TVN's lack of experience with this type of programming. *Na Wspólnej* (*On Wspólna Street*, 2003–) is a soap opera based on *Neighbours*, an internationally formatted soap opera owned by FremantleMedia. The format is produced by the company's local branches in Germany as *Unter Uns* (1994–, RTL) (FremantleMedia, 2012), in Hungary as *Barátok közt* (*Between Friends*, 1998–, RTL Klub)—Hungary's first ever daily serial drama—in Italy as *Un Posto al Sole* (1996–, Rai 3) and in Finland as *Salatut Elämät* (1999–, MTV3) (Molka, 2012). Each local variation is shaped on a pre-existing format idea that echoes the Grundy-branded original soap *Neighbours*, a FremantleMedia Australia production for Network Ten. The Polish variation tells a story of a group of people who became friends as children in an orphanage and whose friendship survives over the years. Thanks to the enterprising spirit of one of the characters, they become joint owners of a new apartment building in Warsaw, located at the titular Wspólna Street. The show's storylines concern the domestic and professional lives of the people who live or frequent the Wspólna apartment block.

Dorota Chamczyk, a showrunner for *Na Wspolnej,* joined TVN to work on this particular show. She recalls that when she was asked to participate in that project there was a sense that soaps are an essential genre for every broadcaster. TVN's competitors, Polsat and TVP1, had already been broadcasting their domestic soaps: Polsat had *Samo Życie* (2002–2010) and TVP had its extremely popular domestic soaps: *Klan* (1997–), *M jak Miłość* (2000–) and *Plebania* (2000–2011). There was a strong conviction that TVN should also have a soap as such a program could easily become a foundation for the whole prime-time schedule and could stabilize the audience ratings. Chamczyk recalls, "TVN was convinced it was important and that they had to do it. It was clearly a response to what our competitors were doing at the time" (Chamczyk, 2012). The broadcaster started to weigh the benefits of producing in-house or relying on a foreign format:

> We started to consider the economic paradigm: should we try and produce in-house, from scratch or should we go look for an ally and rely on the international experience of a third party? We chose to go

with the second option. (...) Secondly, *Na Wspólnej* is the first serial
to be broadcast in prime-time, stripped daily five times a week. It was
a big production challenge.

(Twardowska, 2003)

Na Wspólnej since the very beginning was devised to be a key program, one
that could successfully compete with other terrestrial broadcasters' soaps.
Instead of starting slow by broadcasting their soap two or three times a
week as Polsat and TVP1 did, TVN as the first broadcaster in Poland to do
so– wanted to broadcast their soap daily. There are many challenges and
risks involved in the industrial production of a daily series, such as tight
taping schedules, simultaneous script writing and shooting, and coordinat-
ing a team of writers. Dariusz Gąsiorowski, the show's producer, comments
that "when you take that kind of a risk, it's good to refer to a tested model
and this is precisely the value of a format" (Dariusz Gąsiorowski quoted in
Twardowska, 2003). TVN therefore decided to minimize the risk of producing a continuous serial—a narrative formula and production mode completely alien to TVN's production culture—by getting involved in a project
where not only the script would be an idea tested elsewhere but equally the
show's producer would be one with significant production experience. TVN
thus turned to the global player FremantleMedia: the format owner also
became the show's producer.

Chamczyk recalls that "the decision to produce TVN's first soap based
on a foreign format rather than an original script was dictated by the experience that Fremantle was supposed to bring into the project" (Chamczyk,
2012). Chamczyk elaborates:

Fremantle is a brand of a producer that knows how to successfully
produce a soap opera – daily drama. They have been doing it for years
in Germany, the Netherlands and in Hungary – this fact was important
for us considering the state of development of their TV market. The
Hungarian version is the basis for the Polish version.

(Chamczyk, 2012)

FremantleMedia offered the dramaturgical model, the organization of
scriptwriting and the factory-based system of production of a daily soap,
such as the simultaneous shooting and scripting of the production. It put
to work its own skilled human resources and could guarantee production
standards that Polish personnel at that time would not have been able to
meet, because of their lack of experience with this particular genre and the
concomitant industrial mode of production (Kruk, 2012). TVN thus was
able to initiate a process of 'knowledge transfer' (Moran and Malbon, 2006:
22–23) from the global partner to the local Polish production personnel.

From the point of view of TVN, it was also important that Fremantle-
Media had significant experience in producing that type of programming

elsewhere, thus having the required human resources and competencies for adapting the original templates in accordance with the different national contexts of the adapting countries, as well as guiding/managing the local managers and producers. It is worth pointing out here that FremantleMedia had previously helped to introduce this genre to other local markets. The Italian version, *Un Posto al Sole* (*A Place in the Sun*), was the first locally produced daily soap, and was what Buonanno describes as "the achievement of a well-tempered cooperation between local and global" (257, 2009). *Un Posto al Sole* is produced by FremantleMedia Italia SpA and has become Italy's longest-running soap opera (FremantleMedia, 2012). Buonanno observes that the deal between RAI and Grundy did not merely lay the foundation for factory-based mass production, where only a cottage industry had existed previously. Rather, it triggered a small 'cultural revolution', in that it opened the way for the legitimization of the most popular forms of televisual storytelling, namely the continuous serials that had been absent in the practice of Italian television drama production (Buonanno, 2009).

The impact of the collaboration between the local broadcaster and FremantleMedia was certainly less profound in Poland than it was in Italy, as two Polish terrestrial broadcasters had already been producing their domestic soaps before TVN experimented with the genre. But the collaboration with the global player certainly helped TVN to successfully introduce this genre into their own programming output and to learn the industrial demands of dealing with a daily production such as an accelerated production schedule, short production times and quick turnaround. Of importance is also the fact that FremantleMedia had introduced the genre into Hungary, where the local variation produced by Magyar Grundy UFA (a Grundy UFA subsidiary and sister company of FremantleMedia), has been a tremendous success, becoming the most successful Hungarian TV series, achieving viewing figures of over 50 per cent market share in prime time (FremantleMedia, 2012a). The established success of the local variation of the format in Hungary made it possible to believe that a Polish adaptation could be equally successful, considering the similarities between the Hungarian and Polish TV markets, as both have had similar trajectories of development in the post 1989 period. However, the decision to adapt this format and collaborate with FremantleMedia did not only factor in "the technology, the pace of work, the level of risk"—it was also dictated by the economic rationale. Gąsiorowski recalls: "The local Polish producers we talked to were convinced that the money we were willing to allocate to this project was not enough to produce this show" (Gąsiorowski quoted in Twardowska, 2003). FremantleMedia was able to produce more cheaply and of satisfactory quality.

So far, I have considered the reasons some broadcasters whose production capacity is not fully developed adapt a format instead of taking the risks involved in producing a program from scratch based on a local original idea. Such considerations shed light on the practical value formats have for local broadcasters in developing television markets. Now I would like to discuss what can happen to a formatted program once a given production sector develops it and is able to depart from the ideas and knowledge from abroad. The following section thus looks specifically at the contribution format adaptation has had on TVN's production capacity. In this sense, the TVN case study will demonstrate how formatting can in fact strengthen the research and development capacity of local players.

Formatting and Then What?

Despite relying on a format that proved successful elsewhere, the experience was far from being a seamless transfer of the original format into the Polish environment. Difficulties were encountered in transferring the cultural nuances, and it transpired quite early on that the story created for the Hungarian market did not travel well into the Polish local context. Chamczyk recalls:

> Simple translations didn't work, there were many cultural differences that had to be factored in and not just translated. We knew that if we were to continue to copy the Hungarian model, the ratings would sink. We needed to think, okay we know the Polish environment, we know the viewer, we have to write Polish storylines.
>
> (Chamczyk, 2012)

When it transpired that the adaptations of the Hungarian scripts were incongruent with the local Polish context, the scripts based on the Hungarian version were abandoned, after the series achieved one hundred episodes. After that *Na Wspólnej* was produced based on original Polish scripts. Scott Taylor, the show's head-writer, said that

> such a rapid move away from the format happened only in Poland. It was a huge accomplishment for both the broadcaster and the producer, but also for the local writing team, whose input and talent contributed towards the show's success. (nawspolnej.tvn.pl., 2003)

Despite the initial problems with adapting the format, the experience was nevertheless seen as beneficial for the broadcaster. It provided the basis for the show and a training period and allowed them to learn what is necessary for an adaptation to work in Poland. According to the producer, adapting in this instance provided a trial period, which allowed for the development of certain production skills but also taught the broadcaster about the difficulties and disadvantages of adapting scripts (Chamczyk, 2012). In a relatively short time, as the show's producer put it, the creative talents and local producers managed to overcome the difficult initial phase (Chamczyk, 2012). Chamczyk believes that

> We have learned how hard adapting can be. And after our experi-
> ence in adapting formats we now know that sometimes the adaptation
> requires so many profound changes to the scripts that it is no longer
> worth paying for it.

The maturation of a given production sector to a state where it is able to
fulfill its programming needs locally renders formatting redundant. This
move toward sourcing ideas for scripts locally, instead of relying on foreign knowledge, and demonstrates that work on format adaptation can in
fact inspire and train local talent to produce their own material in a more
independent manner. Especially considering the fee involved in buying a
foreign format, once the production capacity of a given nascent broadcaster
develops it becomes a more viable business strategy to produce in-house.

When *Na Wspólnej* premiered in 2003, TVN was the last of Poland's terrestrial broadcasters to include a soap in its programming output. Despite
TVN entering the genre somewhat late and the problems associated with the
format adaptation, the show delivered and managed to secure itself a stable
position within the Polish fictionscape. *Na Wspólnej* did indeed become
TVN's flagship primetime weekday soap opera, becoming the biggest advertising income generator among all series broadcast in Poland between 2004
and 2014 (Wirtualne Media, 2015) and is still being broadcast in 2015
when this chapter was written.

The consideration of the format adaptation of this particular program,
the success of the adapted Polish version I might add, and the subsequent
progression from the foreign scripts demonstrates the practical value of formatting for nascent broadcasters, including risk management, introduction
of new genres, and boosting the production capacity. Such a scenario can
potentially be treated as a one-off case where formats proved beneficial for
the local market. However, empirical evidence suggests otherwise. In order
to validate this positive impact of the practice of format adaptation as an
industry practice, I would like to further discuss different instances where
similar forces were at play. To demonstrate this, I now move on to discussing
three more case studies of format adaptation. The consideration of other
instances will demonstrate an underlying logic that TVN was following in
their decision to adapt a format.

TVN's Experiment with Telenovelas

The commercial broadcaster TVN's first encounter with the genre of the
telenovela was in the late 1990s when the broadcaster was importing South
American programs such as *Esmeralda* (1997, Televisa), *Rosalinda* (1999,
Canal de las Estrellas), *Ricos y famosos* (1997–1998, Canal 9), *La Intrusa*
(2001, Televisa), *Betty, La Fea* and *Por Un Beso* (2000–2001, Televisa). In
the mid-2000s the network abandoned telenovela importation and decided
to produce telenovelas domestically. In order to minimize the risk involved

in producing a new genre, TVN decided to go with a programming idea that had already proven successful in different markets, adapting *Betty, La Fea*—a truly global phenomenon that started life as a Colombian telenovela in 1999. Izabela Łopuch, TVN's executive producer at the time, explains why the broadcaster decided to adapt:

> Whenever you launch a new thing, and for TVN telenovela was a new genre, it is worth relying on an idea that has been tested elsewhere. The first telenovela that we made was *BrzydUla*, based on *Betty, La Fea*—which of course is a massive hit—you probably cannot name another telenovela format more popular than that.
>
> (Łopuch, 2012)

Like with their first daily soap, TVN therefore decided to adapt a telenovela instead of creating an original one because it was a new genre, one the broadcaster had no previous experience with and no experienced, skilled writers for. Łopuch explains:

> Every genre is quite specific. It's not like a person writing for film can all of a sudden sit down and produce a telenovela script in three months. Every genre has a different way of telling a story, character creation, dialogue and so on. It's really a skill, craft that you have to learn. Every genre has its own rules. Telenovela and soap are seemingly similar genres but at the same time are radically different.
>
> (Łopuch, 2012)

Again, in order to minimize the risk involved in producing a new genre, TVN decided to go with a programming idea that had proven successful in different countries. The decision to start with a format paid off. The Polish adaptation was a huge commercial success. Each episode of the Polish adaptation of Colombian *Betty, La Fea*—*BrzydUla* attracted 3 million viewers on average and was considered one of TVN's biggest programming achievements (Zadrożna, 2009). The success of this adaptation encouraged TVN to seek other telenovela formats. After *BrzydUla*, TVN produced two more telenovela adaptations: *Majka* (2010, TVN) based on Venezuelan *Juana, La Virgen* (2002, RCTV) and *Prosto w Serce* (2011, TVN) based on Argentinian *Sos mi Vida* (2006–2007, Canal 13). Yet, the adaptations of those two formats were done differently. In both cases, the changes to the original story were far more profound.

One of the writers for *Majka* recalls their experience with adapting this format:

> The case of *Majka* was an unusual one because it felt like we weren't really adapting a format but rather creating our own show. The starting point was taken from *Juana La Virgen*. (…) But since day one we

were thinking more in terms of what the Polish viewer would be willing to accept, believe and identify with. (…) The episodes were not translated, we didn't even see the original texts. I personally watched *Juana La Virgen* on DVDs but I only managed to finish watching it after the storyline for all 190 episodes of the Polish version were written. The only monitoring we had was from the broadcaster [TVN]. (…) We had no monitoring or supervision from the format owner.

Similarly in the case of *Prosto w Serce*—TVN's third telenovela adaptation, Łopuch confirms 'we only really took the idea from this format—with the format owner's permission' (Łopuch, 2012). These examples of format adaptation demonstrate the varying degrees to which the broadcaster in a local market remains faithful to the source material. Even if the local producers are allowed a greater creative input into the localized version, the end product is still considered a format.

What this means is that TVN relied heavily on the original script in their first telenovela adaptation, which was produced by the format's owner FremantleMedia. Gradually, however, as the broadcaster was improving their telenovela production skill, the reliance on the original was reduced. The two telenovela adaptations after *BrzydUla* were written for the local broadcaster and were also produced by TVN in-house. Unsurprisingly, after three telenovela adaptations, the time came for TVN's original production in 2012: *Julia*. TVN's original telenovela can therefore be considered a crowning achievement after a long period of training, during which the broadcaster managed to train people how to write a telenovela and learned the production mode of this particular genre through initially adapting telenovelas (Łopuch, 2012).

Considering the intricacies involved in the format business, such as the financial cost of format adaptation, the potential interference from the format owner, and the efforts necessary to adapt the scripts to fit the local context, once the broadcaster is ready to depart from format adaptation, it will do so. The experience of TVN with the industrial practice of telenovela production that started as a format adaptation and progressed into original in-house production demonstrates, similarly to the previous case study of the daily soap, the positive impact of formatting on the local production capacity. To further demonstrate that this is an industrial strategy that spans across many genres, not only long-term daily productions, I wish to discuss two more instances, format adaptation of a scripted reality series and of a sitcom.

Scripted Reality and the Sitcom Genre

Moving on from the telenovela, TVN was also the first Polish broadcaster to experiment with a programming type, which is known as docu-crime. Docu-crime is a genre of procedural crime shows that are scripted but are advertised as a reenactment of real-life crimes. This type of programming was also entirely new to the Polish TV landscape as none of the Polish terrestrial broadcasters had ever imported or produced it before. In this instance also, in order to minimize the risk involved in producing a new genre, TVN decided to go with a programming idea that had proven successful in different markets.

W11-Wydział Śledczy—the first Polish docu-crime series—is based on German *K11- Kommissare im Einsatz* (2002–, Sat1). Bogdan Czaja, TVN's Deputy Programming Director, recalls the following reasons the show was introduced to TVN's programming output:

> *W-11* was a case of introducing a new genre. We decided to adapt this format after seeing how well it did in Germany. (…) In the case of *W-11*, we thought that this is the type of show we are able to make, it is something new, it works in Germany, maybe it will work in Poland too.
>
> (Czaja, 2011)

This approach demonstrated by the Polish executive that "what works well elsewhere will also work well in our market" is a common conviction among industry professionals, who often believe that the proven track record in other countries is likely to translate into good ratings in their domestic market (Esser, 2013).

W-11 met the same fate as *Na Wspólnej*. Quite early on it transpired that the scripts included in the format bible were not appropriate for the local Polish context, so very soon the format took on a life of its own, drifting away from the original format material, where the scripts were exclusively written by local creative talent. A year after TVN launched *W-11*, because of its consistently good ratings of 24% of audience share (Wirtualne Media, 2005), the broadcaster began producing another, this time originally scripted, docu-crime show called *Detektywi*. In this instance, the broadcaster also started with an adaptation and after getting familiar with the production mode characteristic of this particular programming type, moved on to domestically producing the same type of show from scratch. TVN, through its experimentation with a format of a genre entirely new to the Polish landscape, introduced variety not only to its own broadcast schedule but also to that of Polsat's—TVN's main commercial competitor—who in 2009, began broadcasting its own docu-crime show, *Malanowski i Partnerzy* (*Malanowski and Partners*, 2009–).

The above three examples show that scripted formats can be seen as a safer way to experiment with genres and types of programming when the broadcaster has no previous experience with the type. Formats thus seem particularly important for broadcasters in developing TV markets, those that wish to broaden their programming offer with new programming types. TVN's experience with adapting international formats also illustrates, however, that as much as formats are attractive in the initial period, they soon become less attractive. In the cases discussed above, the genre enters the

Polish fictionscape as a format, but then the broadcaster eventually moves toward original domestic content. What this tells us about the industrial practice of formatting is that format adaptation can be a transition period that allows the broadcaster to develop knowhow and tools for in-house production. Yet, formats can also help produce genres with which a particular broadcaster struggles. Buying foreign formats can serve as a steady source for programming ideas that help produce the type of programming that cannot be sourced domestically *ab initio*.

The evidence of this is best visible in sitcoms within the Polish TV landscape. The sitcom, despite its long pedigree, is a production mode and a narrative formula of serialized fiction programming that was completely alien to Polish television culture prior to 1989. This type of programming was introduced to the Polish mediascape in the 1990s when Polsat began to rely heavily on this programming type, importing US shows such as *Caroline in the City* (1995–1999, NBC), *Married with Children* (1987–1997, Fox), *Wings* (1990–1997, NBC), *The Nanny* (1993–1999, CBS), *Ned & Stacey* (1995–1997, Fox) and *Pearl* (1996–1997, CBS). Polsat was not the only broadcaster that imported this type of programming. Other broadcasters, too, imported American sitcoms but not to the extent Polsat did. TVP imported *Everybody Loves Raymond* (1996–2005, CBS), TVN sitcoms such as *The Fresh Prince of Bel-Air* (1990–1996, NBC) and *Full House* (1987–1995, ABC). The reliance on American sitcoms declined toward the end of 1990s, as was the case with US programming more generally. Almost immediately, American sitcoms began to be replaced by those of domestic origin. While Poland's three terrestrial networks all have experimented with producing domestic sitcoms, not many of those shows were successful. Chamczyk (2012) observes:

> We have a significant problem in this domain, and despite a high demand for this genre and broadcasters' willingness to produce, there are not any interesting, creative Polish projects. I think this has to do not necessarily with the lack of ideas or creative talent, but more importantly with the craftsmanship of writing for this particular genre.

This statement was supported by producer Łopuch (2012), who said that as there is "no tradition, no skill of writing sitcoms" in Poland, and Polish broadcasters are weak at producing good sitcoms, adaptations/buying formats became a long-term solution to fill a programming gap that the broadcaster has still not been able to fill with original Polish ideas and scripts.

Conclusion

The above has revealed some interesting aspects of production processes and format adaptation. My starting point was that Keane and Moran have argued that formats may undermine the local research and development capacity in some television industries especially those that are net-importers of formats for local adaptation. Hence, formats represent an imminent danger of stagnation and undermine creativity in the innovative environment of local television industries (Keane and Moran, 2009). But the experience of Poland's terrestrial broadcasters paints a less threatening picture. Exploring the views and perceptions of those working as TV executives in Poland reveals that adapting international scripted formats in Poland is an industrial practice of dealing with particular weaknesses that local broadcasters struggle with, rather than merely a fast track to local content or a hit program. The format may also be a readymade template for success that reduces risk involved in program production as Keane puts it, but at the same time formats can contribute to the development of television industries. In Poland, formats helped broadcasters introduce new types of fiction programming and in the process learn how to create their own local programming in new genres. The reliance on adaptation of foreign formats has caused a resurgence of locally produced content, removing the need for importation, expanding the grammar and the vocabulary of Polish television with new genres, and, in the long run, supporting the shift from importation to domestic production. It is therefore difficult to overestimate the significance of format adaptation on the Polish fictionscape, which leads me to believe that format adaptation is particularly important for developing television markets.

At the same time, I would like to note that the fiction format business is undeniably growing with most recent examples of formats such as the Danish-Swedish crime drama series *Broen* (*The Bridge*), or British *Broadchurch* and many others exported and adapted for local markets. I would like to formulate my general position with respect to the future developments of format adaptation in Poland. In my view some formats will become obsolete, those that were chosen and adapted for the reasons described in this chapter, namely those that helped to deal with certain weaknesses of the production sector. The evidence put forward above suggests that with the development of Poland's production sector, some formats will be abandoned, but some will certainly still be produced, particularly those that enable broadcasters to 'bring down costs by taking out the expenses involved with the development of a new show' and those that decrease programming risk (Chalaby, 2015: 5). It has been argued by Chalaby that even though scripted formats are among the most difficult to adapt, as they require fuller cultural translation, and the risk of failure remains considerably higher than in other genres, drama buyers turn to foreign scripts because it remains easier and cheaper to re-create something they can see on tape (2015: 5). But this chapter has shown that foreign formats in the domain of scripted programming, commercial pressures aside, may have other practical value for broadcasters, particularly in nascent television markets.

References

Industry Interviews

Chamczyk, Dorota. (2012). Executive Producer in TV Drama and Feature Film Production Department at TVN, interview with the author, January 2012.

Czaja, Bogdan. (2011). Deputy Programming Director at TVN, interview with the author, December 2011.

Kruk, Agnieszka. (2012). Television Writer, interview with the author, March 2013.

Łopuch, Izabela. (2012). At the time Producer in the TV Drama and Feature Film Production Department at TVN, interview with the author, January 2012.

Molka, Michał. (2012). FremantleMedia, e-mail message to author, February 21, 2012.

Other References

About FremantleMedia. *FremantleMedia*, available online at: accessed January 20, 2012a, http://careers.fremantlemedia.com/UFA/About-FremantleMedia-UFA.html (Retrieved January 2, 2015).

Bazalgette, P. (2005). *Billion Dollar Game: How Three Men Risked It All and Changed the Face of Television.* London: Time Warner.

Buonanno, M. (1999). (Ed.), *Shifting landscapes. Television fiction in Europe.* New Barnet, Herts: University of Luton Press.

Buonanno, M. (2009). A place in the sun: Global seriality and the revival of domestic drama in Italy. In A. Moran (Ed.), *TV formats worldwide: Localising global programs* (pp. 255–271). Bristol: Intellect Ltd.

Broadcasting Act of December 29, 1992, available online at: http://www.krrit. gov.pl/en/for-broadcasters-and-operators/legal-regulations/ (Retrieved January 2, 2015).

Chalaby, J. (2015). Drama without drama: The late rise of scripted tv formats. *Television & new media,* (forthcoming).

Esser, A. (2007). Audiovisual content in Europe. *Journal of Contemporary European Studies*, 15(2), 163–184.

Esser, A. (2013). The format business: Franchising television content. *International Journal of Digital Television*, 4(2), 141–158.

FremantleMedia Italia SpA. *FremantleMedia*, available online at: http://www. fremantlemedia.com/Production/Our_Production_Companies/FremantleMedia_ Italy.aspx (Retrieved January 2, 2015).

Keane, M. (2012). A revolution in television and a great leap forward for innovation? China in the global television format business. In T. Oren and S. Shahaf (Eds.), *Global Television Formats Understanding Television across Borders* (pp. 306–323). London and New York: Routledge, 2012.

Keane, M., & Moran, A. (2009). (Eds.), *Television across Asia: TV industries, programme formats and globalisation.* London: Routledge.

Moran, A. (1998). *Copycat tv. Globalisation, program formats and cultural identity* Luton: University of Luton Press.

Moran, A. (2009). (Ed.), *TV formats worldwide: Localising global programs.* Bristol: Intellect.

Moran, A., & Malbon, J. (2006). *Understanding the global tv format.* Bristol: Intellect Ltd.

Na Wspólnej - rozmowa ze Scottem Taylorem, *nawspolnej.tvn.pl*, available online at: http://nawspolnej.tvn.pl/informacje/na-wspolnej—rozmowa-ze-scottem-taylorem, 17583,1.html (Retrieved January 2, 2015).

Na Wspólnej najbardziej dochodowym reklamowo serialem dekady. Wirtualne Media, 2015, available online at: http://www.wirtualnemedia.pl/artykul/na-wspolnej- najbardziej-dochodowym-reklamowo-serialem-dekady-a-pierwsza-milosc-2014- roku-top-10 (Retrieved May 2, 2015).

Rutkowska, E. Serial "Brzydula" przyciągał do TVN-u 2,5 mln widzów, *Press*, available online at: http://www.press.pl/newsy/telewizja/pokaz/18947,Serial-Brzydula-przyciagal-do-TVN-u-2_5-mln-widzow (Retrieved January 2, 2015).

Sinclair, J. (2000). Geolinguistic region as global space: The case of Latin America. In G. Wang, J. Servaes, & A. Goonasekera (Eds.), *The new communications landscape: Demystifying media globalization* (pp. 19–32). London: Routledge.

Szostak, S. (2012). Poland's return to Europe—Polish terrestrial broadcasters and tv fiction *Journal of European Television History and Culture,* 1(2), available online at: http://journal.euscreen.eu/index.php/view/issue/view/2 (Retrieved January 2, 2015).

Twardowska, A. Na Wspólnej - rozmowa z Dariuszem Gąsiorowskim. *nawspolnej. tvn.pl,* available online at: http://nawspolnej.tvn.pl/informacje/na-wspolnej—rozmowa-z-dariuszem-gasiorowskim,17584,1.html (Retrieved January 2, 2015).

Udana zamiana TVN. Wirtualne Media, 2005, available online at: http://www.wirtualnemedia.pl/artykul/udana-zamiana-tvn (Retrieved May 2, 2015).

Unter Uns. *FremantleMedia*, available online at: http://www.fremantlemedia.com/Production/Our_Brands/unter-uns.aspx (Retrieved January 2, 2015).

Waisbord, S. (2004). McTV. Understanding the global popularity of television formats. *Television & New Media,* 5(4), 359–383.

Zadrożna, E. Za co Polacy pokochali BrzydUlę, *Plotek.pl*, available online at: http://www.plotek.pl/plotek/1,78649,7387377,Za_co_Polacy_pokochali_BrzydUle_.html (Retrieved January 2, 2015).

12 Analyzing Players' Perceptions on the Translation of Video Games

Assessing the Tension between the Local and the Global Concerning Language Use

Alberto Fernández Costales

Introduction

This chapter analyzes users' perception and preferences regarding the translation of video games and their habits and attitudes toward in-game language when interacting with entertainment software and its related online contents (i.e., websites, official videos, etc.). By exploring these two dimensions, this investigation is intended to identify possible tensions between the local and the global in the reception of video games translation by the target audience as regards language use.

The growth of the game industry has been exponential in recent decades, with figures shadowing other forms of entertainment such as cinema or music. The total consumer spend on games in the US reached $22.41 billion in 2014, with 4 out of 5 American households owning a device used to play video games, according to the Entertainment Software Association (ESA, 2015). Technological development has contributed to the evolution of video games, which have turned into complex multimodal products that can be regarded as an artistic expression (Tavinor, 2009). The influence of entertainment software in today's society can hardly be questioned, and the economic and cultural impact of video games clearly deserves scholarly attention (Bernal, 2014; Mangiron and O'Hagan, 2013). However, in spite of the global resonance and visibility of the game industry, the analysis of interactive entertainment from an academic and scientific point of view is still in an initial stage. Many of the research lines in the field have not been sufficiently explored so far, perhaps because video games "are easily and readily denigrated as trivial" (Newman, 2004: 5). Hence, although video games have become a subject of study in some areas of knowledge, such as Education, (Prensky, 2000), Media Studies (Newman, 2004), or Pedagogy (Gee, 2003), further research is particularly welcome in the humanities (Translation Studies and Applied Linguistics).

Research in the area of Translation Studies has focused on the establishment of video game localization as a sub-genre of Audiovisual Translation (Bernal, 2006; O'Hagan, 2006; O'Hagan and Mangiron, 2013), the cultural adaptation of video games (Di Marco, 2007; Edwards, 2011; Mangiron, 2010; O'Hagan, 2009b), the analysis of translation strategies in game localization (Fernández Costales, 2014), and the study of the localization process itself (Bernal, 2014; Chandler, 2005; Chandler and Deming, 2011). Most researchers have addressed the analysis of entertainment software from the point of view of professional translators in order to identify regularities and tendencies in the translation process (Fernández Costales, 2012; Mangiron, 2012). However, to the best of my knowledge, few studies have addressed users' perception and preferences on the translation of multimedia interactive software (O'Hagan, 2009b). This means that the translation of entertainment software, at least so far, has been investigated by considering only one part of the equation, and consumers have often been ignored. This paper is intended to fill this gap by analyzing players' perception on the translation of their favorite products. The main objective here is twofold: on the one hand, the investigation aims to provide new insights into the study of video games translation by including the audience in the research process. On the other hand, the attitudes and habits of users as regards language when playing games will be explored in order to evaluate possible tensions between the global and the local in the translation/localization of games to different markets. The terms 'translation' and 'localization' will be used equally in this chapter to refer to the linguistic and cultural adaptation of video games from a source to a target market taking into account linguistic, cultural, and technical features.

In order to investigate how video games are translated and the possible impact of this process on the target audience, an essential concept has to be considered: within Translation Studies, the classic distinction between 'foreignization' and 'domestication' strategies (Venuti, 1995) has been widely accepted to categorize the way in which video games are translated into the target market. By 'foreignization', we refer to translation strategies intended to keep the 'foreign taste' of the source text when translated to the destination market. Games such as the *Assassins' Creed* saga provide a good example of foreignization strategies. *Assassins' Creed II* and *Assassins' Creed: Brotherhood* are based on several Italian regions and cities, and this is an essential element of the titles' narrative, with an important amount of names, references, historical plots, and cultural components that are kept untranslated in the localized Spanish version. In addition, Italian expressions abound in these titles, and they are not translated into the corresponding target languages in order to preserve the game's atmosphere. In addition, the professional actors recording the spoken dialogues apply a gentle Italian accent in some of the cut-scenes, contributing to create the compelling atmosphere of the game (Fernández Costales, 2012). Opposing this, we find domestication strategies (Venuti, 1995) intended to bring the game closer to the target market by translating all the in-game elements. This is the case of the *Final Fantasy* saga, where domestication is achieved mainly "by the use in the target text of idiomatic and colloquial language, the adaptation of jokes, sayings, and cultural references, and the recreation of new cultural references and plays on words (Mangiron and O'Hagan, 2006). This also applies to Mario Bros video games, where names, worlds and locations, equipment, cultural references, etc., are normally translated or recreated to suit the taste and expectation of users in the target market (Fernández Costales, 2012).

These two options—foreignization and domestication—are translation strategies to be followed by translators when localizing a video game; although they are not incompatible *per se*, it is understood that translators should consistently stick to one of these approaches when translating a particular title. Although the specialized literature in localization may lead us think that "the more local, the better" is appropriate in most media products, in the particular case of video games the current consumption patterns may not be in line with this statement. In the case of Spain, more and more users prefer to see TV shows in the original English version with Spanish subtitles (Orrego, 2015). This might also be applied to the case of video games. Therefore, this paper relies on two research hypotheses:

1 Players prefer games to be translated by keeping the 'look and feel' of the original product and also the cultural references and other elements from the source text so games have a 'foreign' flavor. In other words, foreignization strategies will be preferred over domestication strategies.
2 Many users may code-switch from Spanish into English when playing video games or interacting with their paratext: visiting official websites of the games or watching launch trailers. The concept of 'paratext' (Gray, 2010: 6) is used here to refer to all additional contents of video games available in any format (including websites, advertising, official videos, printed guides, or any other material). As stated by O'Hagan (2005, 2007, and 2009b), video games have become truly multimodal products; this paper relies on the idea that this multimodality also affects all resources and materials related to the game's universe, which need to be taken into account when translating a title or researching users' engagement with a video game.

These two hypotheses are likely to be related to the impact English has today in the globalized world and—in particular—on the field of technology. The pervasiveness of English in multimedia products, together with the ubiquitous access to media through the Internet may result in alterations as regards the language used by players when interacting with entertainment software. Moreover, although many players seem to demand products be localized into their corresponding markets, with emergent tendencies such as fan-subbing—the amateur subtitling of audiovisual products by fans—or romhacking—hacking a game's ROM in order to be able to modify the game, translate it, or customize it—gaining momentum (Díaz-Cintas and Muñoz Sánchez, 2006; O'Hagan, 2009a). The influence of English as the global language—and the improvement in foreign language competence in younger generations of players—can stress the tensions between the local and the global (see Crystal, 1997 and 2001 and Phillipson, 2003). Although many users demand content in their own language (mainly through forums, blogs, or at specialized video games events), more and more players resort to English to interact with video games.

In order to test the research hypotheses, a questionnaire was specifically designed including questions related to the translation of video games, language preferences, and users' habits as regards video game websites, official videos, and advertising. A sample of 94 Spanish players from the Faculty of Education of the University of Oviedo answered the survey, and the results were analyzed using SPSS (Statistical Package for the Social Sciences) v. 21. Descriptive statistics were used to identify tendencies and patterns in gamers' preferences on the localization of video games.

The chapter is structured as follows. First, the theoretical foundations supporting the translation of video games will be presented in relation to the objectives and scope of this investigation. Second, the research methodology will be commented on, together with the most relevant results and their implications for the localization of video games. Finally, the conclusions will be discussed, and the possible research lines to be followed after this investigation will be outlined.

Localizing Media Products for a Global Market

Translating video games entails adapting complex multimedia products from a source into a target locale, which is understood in Translation Studies as those features of the customer's environment that are dependent upon language, country/region, and cultural conventions (Pym, 1999). The world leaders as regards the production of video games are the United States and—to a lesser extent—Japan, and the usual target languages are the so-called FIGS—French, Italian, German, and Spanish (O'Hagan and Mangiron, 2013: 16). Hence, entertainment software is usually adapted from 'the global culture' (i.e., the US culture, which is supported by the world's lingua franca, the economic and technological hegemony, and the dissemination tool provided by Hollywood's film industry) into more 'localized' target audiences, overall defined by language and an assumed cultural proximity.

Within the field of Translation Studies, research has focused on how video games are localized into the target market from a linguistic, cultural, and technical perspective. Research has been devoted to the analysis of the localization industry and the related processes in the translation of video games (Bernal, 2006, 2007, 2011; Chandler, 2005; Chandler and Deming, 2011; Dietz, 2006; Mangiron, 2007), the cultural adaptation of multimedia and entertainment software (O'Hagan, 2009b), and the recognition of video games localization as a new domain within Translation Studies (O'Hagan, 2007; O'Hagan and Mangiron, 2013).

Besides foundational works contributing to the establishment of games localization as an academic field, research has been conducted in areas such as video game taxonomies and genres (Scholand, 2002), romhacking (Muñoz Sánchez, 2008), amateur video game translation (Díaz Montón, 2011), game accessibility (Mangiron, 2011; Mangiron, Orero and O'Hagan, 2014), the translation of humor (Mangiron, 2010), the multidimensional nature of video games (O'Hagan, 2005, 2007, and 2009b), teaching video games localization as part of audiovisual translation courses (Bernal, 2008; Granell, 2011; Vela, 2011), subtitling in game localization (Mangiron, 2012), translation strategies in video games localization (Di Marco, 2007; Fernández Costales, 2012), and the translation of literature and comic based video games (Bernal, 2009; Fernández Costales, 2014).

The evolution of video games into multimodal products and the incorporation of a range of components (subtitles, audio effects, voices, facial expressions, cut-scenes, online gaming, etc.) suggest that this field can benefit from research into related areas such as Audiovisual Translation, where subtitling, dubbing, and audiodescription have already been approached in depth by several scholars (Agost and Chaume, 2001; Díaz-Cintas, 2001, 2003, 2008; Gambier, 2004; Neves, 2005). The multimodality of video games has clearly modified the way players engage with technology, as modern video games "create a polysemiotic and multimodal environment where the player interacts with the game system via different communication channels" (O'Hagan, 2009b: 213). In this sense, the game localizers can also learn from similar scenarios such as web localization, where the evolution of websites also requires Translation Studies to provide suitable solutions for the demands of the new markets (Jiménez Crespo, 2013; Tercedor, 2005).

The translation of video games is supported by well-established theories and models in Translation Studies, which provide a consistent framework to explain the possibilities and alternatives existing in order to localize video games into a target locale. From a theoretical standpoint, functionalism provides solid grounds for explaining how the process of translating a text is highly dependent on the function it needs to produce in the target audience (Nord, 1991, 1997). The application of functionalist approaches to the translation of video games supports the freedom of translators when selecting particular strategies according to the expectations of the target audience (Fernández Costales, 2012; Mangiron, 2010; O'Hagan and Mangiron, 2013: 150). These approaches are: foreignization (i.e., keeping a foreign 'taste' when translating the game), domestication (i.e., translating the game in a way it suits the characteristics and cultural standards of the destination locale), no-translation (i.e., leaving parts of the game in the source language), and transcreation (i.e., creating a new text in the target language). As far as video games are concerned, the more simplistic concepts of 'right' or 'wrong' translations do not apply, and it is commonly accepted that the main objective is preserving the game experience.

In this regard, one of the main decisions to be taken by translators when adapting a video game is whether to choose a foreignizing or a domesticating approach. The concepts of foreignization and domestication (Venuti, 1995) are intended to establish a difference between translations aimed to keep a 'foreign flavor' or those texts adapted to the particular features and standards of the target market. The objective of foreignization strategies is keeping the look and feel of the original game and transferring the atmosphere and the taste of the source into the target locale. On the other hand, domesticating approaches aim to bring the game closer to the target market. These two concepts should be understood as 'umbrella terms', which include a good number of strategies and approaches depending on the effect to be achieved as regards the perception of the game by the final audience. The strategy of substitution, for instance, is normally employed in the translation of names—changing the original for an analogous name in the target language—in order to add a local flavor to the target market (O'Hagan and Mangiron, 2013: 176). In any case, it is widely accepted that preserving the game experience in the target locale seems to be the main objective when localizing entertainment software (Fernández Costales, 2012; Mangiron and O'Hagan, 2006).

Analyzing Users' Perceptions

Research Sample

The research sample is composed of 94 students of the Faculty of Education who were asked to participate in a study in the Principality of Asturias (a region located in northern Spain). The sample is distributed in the following way: 63 of the game players answering the survey were men, 31 were women (Graph 12.1). Unfortunately, the share of women (33%) falls short of the official statistics regarding female players, which reaches 44% according to the latest report published by the Interactive Software Federation of Europe (ISFE, 2012). However, the results show that there are no significant differences in attitude between male and female players toward video games, so this statistical disparity is unproblematic.

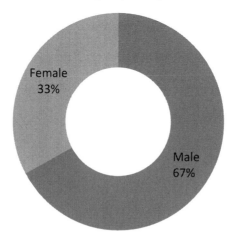

Graph 12.1 Distribution of respondents (by gender).

As for users' ages, Graph 12.2 shows that most participants were between 20 and 30 years old (55%), followed by those between 30 and 40. These figures are in accordance with the statistics of the ISFE, which establishes that most players fall within the ages of 25 and 44 (ISFE, 2012).

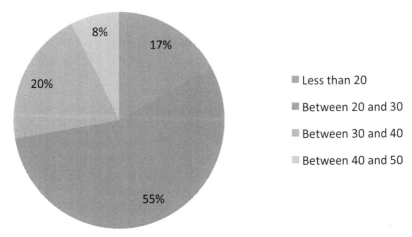

Graph 12.2 Age of the participants of the study.

When asked about their self-perceived level of English (Graph 12.3), most surveyed users reported having an upper-intermediate or advanced level, according to the Common European Framework of Reference for Languages: 76% of interviewees stated they had a level of B2 or higher, with 17% reporting a B1, only 7% answering they had a basic level of English. These figures show that most participants should be able to interact with the video games through the medium of English.

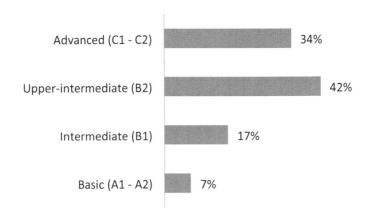

Graph 12.3 Level of English of the participants of the study.

Finally, regarding the frequency of gaming (Graph 12.4), results show there is an even distribution, as 33% of respondents reported they play very frequently (at least 4 times a week), 33% stated they play frequently (2 times a week), and 34% were occasional gamers (1 time a week or less).

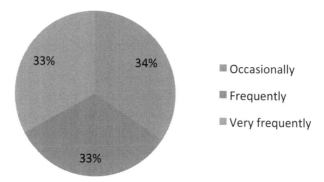

Graph 12.4 Frequency of gaming of the participants of the study.

Research Instrument and Methodology

The research instrument used to analyze users' perceptions was an online questionnaire specifically designed for this investigation and labeled Game Users Translation Survey (GUTSY). A survey was the most effective tool in order to explore users' perceptions and preferences on the translation of video games. To the best of my knowledge, questionnaires are not widely used in Translation Studies to provide empirical data, but using an online questionnaire seemed to be especially suitable in this context, as gamers have a high computer affinity and literacy. The survey included 20 items, which respondents answered by using a Likert scale (1 Fully disagree; 2 Disagree; 3 Agree; 4 Fully agree). An even number of possible answers (4) was intentionally used in order to avoid subjects neglecting to answer the questions directly by selecting the "neutral" or "indefinite" answer to some of the items in the survey.

In addition, the subjects participating in this research had to complete a section intended to provide some basic personal details that were used as the independent variables of the study, namely: gender, age, level of English, and how frequently they played video games.

The survey was structured in two scales. The first (including items 1 to 10) focused on users' perception on the translation of video games, the quality of localization, and the impact translation might have on the game experience; the second scale (items 11 to 20) aimed at exploring gamers' habits regarding video game websites and their language preferences when playing video games.

The reliability of the questionnaire was checked using Alpha Cronbach tests, and the result obtained (.916) shows that the items of the survey clearly have internal consistency and the tool is suitable for research purposes.

The questionnaire was available through surveymonkey (www.survey-monkey.com), and respondents submitted their individual answers anonymously between 1 February and 17 April 2015.

Main Results and Discussion

The results of this study are presented in accordance with the two scales of the questionnaire: first, the most relevant results regarding the items focusing on the translation of video games and its quality will be commented on; second, the most noteworthy facts related to the section addressing video games websites and users' language preferences will be discussed.

The results of the questionnaire (Table 12.1) clearly show that game users fully agree with the idea that good translations of video games imply that players are not aware that the product has been designed for a different locale (Q1). This item has one of the highest means in the survey, with more than 88% of participants stating they 'agree' or 'fully agree'. The means were calculated based on the Likert Scale used in the survey, with 1 being the minimum score and 4 being the maximum.

Table 12.1 Results of the first scale of the survey

	Fully disagree	Disagree	Agree	Fully agree	Mean
Q1. A video game has been properly translated when you do not feel it has been designed in a different language	1.43%	10%	52.85%	35.70%	3.23
Q2. The quality of translation / localization of video games into Spanish is high	8.47%	29.67%	53.29%	8.57%	2.62
Q3. The quality of translation does not have an impact on the game experience	47.14%	31.43%	14.29%	7.14%	1.81
Q4. Playing video games in Spanish improves the game experience	8.57%	31.43%	48.57%	11.43%	2.63
Q5. I like video games to maintain the original cultural references when translated	1.43%	10%	52.86%	35.71%	3.23
Q6. Elements such as names, locations, equipment, etc., should never be translated	5.71%	18.57%	40%	35.71%	3.06
Q7. Humor, jokes and puns cannot be translated	11.43%	28.57%	30%	30%	2.79
Q8. I do not like how games are dubbed into Spanish	14.29%	47.14%	30%	10%	2.39

Second, the participants of the study perceived that the quality of translations into Spanish was quite good (more than 65% of players agree on this). Generally, they rejected the idea that translation is not related to users' game experience when playing in their own language: More than 71% of respondents believed that translation has an impact on the game experience.

As for translation strategies, the questionnaire provides rather interesting results that describe users' preferences and perceptions on how games should be adapted into their own language and culture. Responses to item 5 underlined how gamers prefer that video games keep their original feel when they are translated into Spanish, as 87% report they like the games to maintain the original cultural references. Similarly, players believe that certain elements, such as names or locations, should not be translated from the original (Q6), following a no-translation approach. Finally, most participants think that humor, jokes, or puns cannot be translated from the source text into a different culture (Q7) and they should be left in the original language, as they consider they cannot be replaced with local jokes and puns.

The answers to these three questions (items 6, 7, and 8) show how players clearly prefer games to be localized following a foreignizing approach where the products keep the taste of the original text not adapting certain elements into the target language. Although it is not a surprising fact, this is somewhat contradictory if we take into account that participants consider good translations those in which users do not realize they are playing a foreign video game (Q1). This could be explained based on social desirability bias, a concept used to define the behavior of survey respondents, who not always say what they really think but try to answer a questionnaire according to what they estimate to be most suitable or socially desirable. Game users state they prefer translations to fully localize the games into the corresponding locale but, at the same time, they underline that they enjoy the titles that reflect the source locale as they can probably get easily immersed. Hence, it could be argued that users answered the first question according to what they perceived to be viewed favorably in the context of translation (that a 'good translation' should localize the game by leaving no traces of the source text in the translated version). Also, users regarded translation to be a determining factor in preserving the game experience but—according to the results—it seems that an important amount of players still prefer to resort to English to enjoy the game, as will be shown in the second scale of the survey (Table 12.2). This could also suggest that, although the surveyed players reported having a good opinion of Spanish translations, they might switch into English because the Spanish version is not 'natural', or it somehow provides worse game experiences than the original. A second possible explanation is that English is regarded as the international language that should be commanded by young people and, to a certain extent, there is also a desirability effect here, as most players (and young people in general) like the association with the features linked to the English language (i.e., internationalization, etc.).

The last items of the first scale of the survey confirm respondents are quite satisfied with the quality of dubbing and subtitling of video games into Spanish (items 8 and 9), with slightly higher values in the latter. Finally, most players interviewed in this study (63%) use interlingual subtitles in Spanish when they play video games in English.

The results of the scale of the survey focusing on the translation and localization of video games come to support several theories and ideas commonly accepted in Translation Studies as regards the localization of entertainment products. Translators should focus on keeping the look and feel of the games when transferring the titles to the target language; for translations to be effective, players should not have the feeling that they are playing a game that is different from the original. These conclusions are in line with previous research (Fernández Costales, 2012 and 2014; O'Hagan and Mangiron, 2013: 149–50) supporting the application of well-established theories and schools within Translation Studies (functionalist theories and *skopos* theory). As stated in the first hypothesis of this chapter, players prefer foreignization approaches, as these might contribute to creating the feeling they are actually playing the original game and not a version that has been modified and adapted to their specific locale and, therefore, render a different game experience. However, the fact that respondents consider that some elements cannot be translated from the source to the target text might have some implications that should be analyzed in relation to their language preferences and their attitude toward the translation of video games.

Table 12.2 Results of the second scale of the survey

	Fully disagree	Disagree	Agree	Fully agree	Mean
Q11. I visit the websites of the games I like	11.43%	27.57%	31%	30%	2.80
Q12. I always visit official websites of the video games in my mother tongue	37.14%	44.29%	14.29%	4.29%	1.86
Q13. The official websites of the video games influence me when buying a game	32.86%	38.14%	26.14%	2.86%	2.00
Q14. I like watching the trailers of the games I like in Spanish	22.86%	47.57%	15.72%	13.85%	2.19
Q15. The commercials of the games sound so much better in English	25.71%	24.39%	38.47%	11.43%	2.35
Q16. If a game is not translated into Spanish I do not purchase it	58.57%	28.57%	10%	2.86%	1.57
Q17. All video games should be translated into Spanish	10%	41.43%	24.29%	24.29%	2.63
Q18. Video games should be translated into minority and co-official languages	48.57%	30%	18.57%	2.86%	1.76
Q19. I like playing video games in English	8.57%	21.43%	47.14%	22.86%	2.84
Q20. I like watching films and TV shows in English	7.14%	12.86%	31.43%	48.57%	3.21

The second scale of the survey provides an overall panorama of users' habits when visiting video game websites as well as their language attitudes and preferences when playing games.

It is worth paying attention to the fact that users frequently access these sites in English and do not check the Spanish version (81% of participants agree on this). In the same vein, most players answering the survey reported they preferred watching video game trailers in English (with only 28% using Spanish to enjoy them), and up to 50% thought advertisements sounded much better in English than in their mother tongue.

The results of item 16 render quite revealing information, as only 12% of participants reported they would not buy a game that had not been translated into their mother tongue. Moreover, 51% of the gamers taking part in this study did not consider that all video games should be trans-lated into Spanish. It is worth mentioning that these results have to be nuanced, as users assumed only English as the source language (and all the participants in this study were able to communicate in this language). It is highly likely that the surveyed users would change their minds if asked about games originally developed in Japanese or any language other than English.

The results of item 18 are far more conclusive, as 78% of the participants did not think video games should be adapted into minority or co-official lan-guages. This fact needs to be contextualized in the case of the Principality of Asturias, a region in northern Spain where a regional language is spo-ken (Asturian or Bable) but has not been awarded the status of a co-official language, as in other regions such as Catalonia (Catalan), the Basque Country (Euskera), or Galicia (Galician). Although language attitudes toward Asturian are rather positive, it is estimated that this language is spoken by only 30% of the population, so it is not directly comparable to the situation in the bilingual communities, where there are more favorable attitudes toward the translation of the co-official language and its language use is wider. Although results might be different in other Spanish regions, it is still worth mentioning the fact that the number of users supporting the translation into regional languages for video games is rather low in the case of Asturias. It is worth mentioning that Asturian is less spread among younger generations, and this fact can explain why in many cases players are not concerned about the trans-lation of video games into languages other than Spanish. Also, users' prefer-ence for the 'original' flavor of video games, which could somehow be lost when using the local language when playing sagas such as *Assassins Creed* or *Grand Theft Auto*, where the weight and relevance of the source locale sug-gests no-translation and foreignization strategies are more suitable to allow players to enjoy the title. Nevertheless, the results of item 18 are worrying for the promotion of multilingualism in audiovisual products, a strategy that is in the radar screen of the European Union and has been addressed by a good number of policies and actions of the European Commission (2008).

Item 19 clearly shows how a relevant share of gamers (68%) enjoys play-ing video games in English. Although this figure does not entail that gamers prefer playing in a foreign language than in their mother tongue, it does suggest that the pervasiveness of English nowadays might be altering users' habits and game patterns. In other words, the profile of video game players is not so well defined today and many gamers will prefer interacting with entertainment software through the medium of English. Although this may not apply to other languages (this study only focuses on the case of Spanish speaking users playing games in English), these findings may entail that the gap between English and other languages might be increasing as regards media and this could lead to a divide between the 'English global market' and other locales. In fact, the tendency in Spain is toward an improvement in language proficiency in English in younger generations, which is also supported by the consumption of English language media (mainly TV shows in the original version, but also films and video games).

Finally, the last item of the survey (Q20) was introduced as a control question in order to contrast gamers' language preferences regarding video games with those of other audiovisual products: not surprisingly, 80% of participants stated they liked watching films and TV shows in the original English version with Spanish subtitles. This is a clear tendency in Spain, where, in recent years, more and more users enjoy multimedia products in the original version: Recent research approaching reception studies concludes that language competence is a determining factor as regards the use of subtitles, with consumers with a higher command in the foreign language paying less attention to subtitles (Orrego, 2015).

Arguably, the second scale of the questionnaire suggests that video game websites are an important tool for the promotion of entertainment software, as users visit these sites in order to get information on their favorite games. However, according to the results of the survey, it seems that players do not check game websites in their own language as much as could be expected. This might be related to the language attitudes and preferences observed in the sample of this research: the analysis of results confirms that there is a growing tendency toward the use of English when playing a video game or interacting with its paratext. Analyzing the rationale and motivation of users toward choosing a foreign language to enjoy a video game (e.g., improving their language competence in English, perception that the game experience is better than in the translated version, etc.) falls outside the scope of this paper. Notwithstanding, this research line needs to be further explored, as websites and multimedia products should contribute to foster e-inclusion or the promotion of literacy and cultural diversity instead of monolingual approaches toward the use of technology, according to the European policies in this field (European Commission, 2008).

At this point, and after the analysis of the most relevant results of the questionnaire, it can be stated that the initial hypotheses of this research can be validated, as users prefer foreignization strategies in the translation of video games, and they resort to English to visit websites or watch official videos. This might be a consequence of the influence of global English on users' habits and the possible changes and alterations related to this fact.

Research in Translation Studies underlines the idea that localizing a video game improves the game experience (Bernal, 2014: 14; Mangiron and O'Hagan, 2006; O'Hagan and Mangiron, 2013: 159), a conclusion widely accepted in both academia and the game localization industry. In order to achieve this, either foreignization or domestication strategies are welcome, as no particular approaches have been identified so far to be more effective when translating a game. However, according to the results of the current study, users report that they enjoy playing in English, and they show rather positive attitudes toward the use of this language in video games; in other words, it can be stated that many users prefer playing in the original English version instead of resorting to the translated video game. In addition, they clearly prefer products to have a foreign flavor by keeping many elements in the original and preserving the cultural references of the source text: Hence, foreignization strategies would be preferred by gamers. Also, there are clear divergences between users' perceptions on the translation of humor (which is an unattainable goal, according to the players answering the survey) and the theory in Translation Studies, which states that humor *can* be adapted by means of strategies such as compensation and substitution (see Mangiron, 2010).

This study does not directly refute or contradict previous research in the field, and there are a number of limitations to be taken into account: the sample research is not representative for the whole Spanish context; it only covered the Principality of Asturias and only local students from the Faculty of Education (fairly well-educated young people). Moreover, only the English-Spanish markets are being targeted, the research questionnaire is intended to provide a generic approach to users' perception, and some of the answers might be conditioned by the desirability bias. However, the results of this investigation will hopefully stimulate discussion and much research, as many users—unexpectedly, if we consider the majority of video game translation literature—seem to prefer playing video games in English. The motivation and rationale for preferring the English to the translated video game clearly deserve scholarly attention and should be further investigated. An initial clue has been provided by some of the respondents to the open-ended question included at the end of the survey (where participants could add their comments and remarks regarding the translation of video games). Several players pinpointed the poor quality in the Spanish dubbed versions of some games (providing particular examples, such as the dubbing of Napoleon in *Assassin's Creed Unity*) as a key reason for their choosing the original English version instead of the dubbed one. A second explanation may be found in the prestige of English among the participants of the study: As has been already mentioned, many participants associate speaking English with a particular urban and cosmopolitan lifestyle.

According to the results of the questionnaire, at least for the group surveyed in this study, the positive attitudes of users toward English in video games might not be related to the quality of Spanish translations—which is reasonably high. A possible explanation to support this fact would be that the pervasiveness of English is altering some of the habits and routines of Spanish gamers when interacting with entertainment software. Not surprisingly, the level of English correlates with users' preferences, as players in the study with C1-C2 level have more favorable attitudes toward using English when playing games. These results may lead us to conclude that the panorama in game localization may be changing as a result of the evolution in users' preferences and profiles and the possible alterations in the target audience as regards language habits and attitudes. More users opt to play the games in the original English version (due to their language competence or because they prefer interacting with the original non-translated product), and others prefer games translated under foreignizing approaches (and, of course, other gamers still prefer more 'localized' or domesticating versions). This may suggest that the localization of video games into a specific market is becoming more complex due to the influence of the global on the local.

Conclusions

This paper provides new insights into the field of video games translation by exploring users' perceptions regarding the localization of entertainment software and their language preferences and attitudes when interacting with video games and their associated paratext.

The main conclusion to be drawn from this study is that users underline that translation is a determining factor when improving game experience in the localized versions of the games. Participants also report foreignization strategies are generally preferred as games can be best enjoyed when the look and feel of the source text is maintained. According to the results, users believe that this is the only possible strategy and they are not aware that important components (such as humor or elements like names, places, etc.) can be translated. Second, many players code-switch from their mother tongue into English when visiting websites, watching videos, or even playing games, showing how patterns are changing as regards language uses and attitudes when interacting with technology. This might mean that players consider the game experience is still better in the original English version.

The results of this research stress how the evolution of video games into multimodal forms of art is leading to a dynamic panorama as far as the translation of multimedia products is concerned. Also, the pervasiveness of English and its influence in the dissemination of online contents is promoting a more complicated and diversified interaction between players and video game resources, such as videos or websites. Binary options in translation might not be suitable to fully explain the current panorama, as the profile of players today demands mixed approaches when adapting video games to different markets. In other words, the commonly accepted classic distinction between foreignization and domestication might no longer suffice to address the reality and profile of gamers and the influence the global is having on the local; the lines have become blurred, and more diversity may be required in the selection of translation strategies in order to meet users' demands and preferences.

Users need to be taken into account in Translation Studies and, in fact, emerging trends such as fan-subbing and fan translation have recently drawn scholarly attention (Díaz Cintas and Muñoz Sánchez, 2008; Orrego, 2015). In the field of video game translation, more studies focusing on players' perceptions would be welcome in order to contribute to a more global and comprehensive understanding of the impact on video games and their reception by the audience.

This research does not support an 'enthronement' of users' perceptions so that they have a major influence on the whole translation process or in the development of theoretical models and frameworks, but rather that investigation in Translation Studies include final users so they are not ignored. Prospective research lines might focus on exploring the motivation and rationale for players to code-switch or choose English when playing games and enjoying online contents, analyzing the reception of games translated into co-official languages in bilingual contexts, or designing studies to compare possible differences in the perceptions of video game players and followers of TV shows.

References

Agost, R., & Chaume, F. (2001). (Eds.), *La Traducción en los Medios Audiovisuales*. Castellón de la Plana: Universitat Jaume I.

Bernal, M. (2006). On the translation of video games. *The Journal of Specialized Translation*, 6, 22–36, available online at: http://www.jostrans.org/issue06/art_bernal.php (Retrieved March 17, 2015).

Bernal, M. (2007). Challenges in the translation of video games. *Tradumática*, 5, available online at: http://www.fti.uab.es/tradumatica/revista/num5/articles/02/02art.htm (Retrieved March 17, 2015).

Bernal, M. (2008). Training translators for the video game industry. In J. Díaz-Cintas (Ed.), *The didactics of audiovisual translation* (pp. 141–156). Amsterdam: John Benjamins.

Bernal, M. (2009). Video games and children's books in translation. *The Journal of Specialized Translation*, 11, 234–247, available online at: http://www.jostrans.org/issue06/art_bernal.php (Retrieved March 17, 2015).

Bernal, M. (2011). A brief history of game localization. *Trans*, 15, 11–17, available online at: http://www.trans.uma.es/pdf/Trans_15/11-17.pdf (Retrieved March 17, 2015).

Bernal, M. (2014). *Translation and localisation in video games: Making entertainment software global*. New York: Routledge.

Chandler, H. (2005). *The game localisation handbook*. Massachusetts: Charles River Media.

Chandler, H. M. and Deming, S. O. (2012). *The Game Localization Handbook*, 2nd edition. Sudbury/London: Jones and Bartlett Learning.

Crystal, D. (1997). *English as a global language*. Cambridge: Cambridge University Press.

Crystal, D. (2001). *Language and the Internet*. Cambridge: Cambridge University Press.

Di Marco, F. (2007). Cultural localization: Orientation and disorientation in Japanese video games. *Tradumàtica*, 5, available online at: http://www.fti.uab.es/tradumatica/revista/num5/articles/06/06art.htm (Retrieved March 17, 2015).

Díaz-Cintas, J. (2001). *La Traducción Audiovisual. El subtitulado*. Salamanca: Almar.

Díaz-Cintas, J. (2003). *Teoría y Práctica de la Subtitulación: Inglés/Español*. Barcelona: Ariel.

Díaz-Cintas, J. (2008). *The didactics of audiovisual translation*. Amsterdam: John Benjamins.

Díaz-Cintas, J., & Muñoz Sánchez, P. (2006). Fansubs: Audiovisual translation in an amateur environment. *The Journal of Specialized Translation*, 6, 37–52, available online at: http://www.jostrans.org/issue06/art_diaz_munoz.php (Retrieved March 17, 2015).

Díaz Montón, D. (2011). Amateur videogame translation into Spanish. *Trans*, 15, 69–82, available online at: http://www.trans.uma.es/pdf/Trans_15/69-82.pdf (Retrieved March 17, 2015).

Dietz, F. (2006). Issues in localizing computer games. In K. Dunne (Ed.), *Perspectives on localization* (pp. 122–134). Amsterdam/Philadelphia: John Benjamins.

ESA. (2015). *Essential facts about the computer and video game industry*, available online at: http://theesa.com (Retrieved March 17, 2015).

European Commission. (2008). Council resolution on a European strategy for multilingualism, available online at: http://www.consilium.europa.eu/uedocs/cms_Data/docs/pressdata/en/educ/104230.pdf (Retrieved March 17, 2015).

European Commission. (2012). *Europeans and their languages. Special Eurobarometre*, 386, available online at: http://ec.europa.eu/public_opinion/archives/ebs/ebs_386_en.pdf (Retrieved March 17, 2015).

Fernández Costales, A. (2012). Exploring translation strategies in video games localization. *Monographs in Translation and Interpreting (MonTi)*, 4, 385–408.

Fernández Costales, A. (2014). Video game localization: Adapting superheroes to different cultures. *Quaderns, Revista de Traducció*, 21, 225–239.

Gambier, Y. (2004). La Traduction Audiovisuelle: un Genre en Expansion. *Meta*, 49(1), 1–11.

Gee, J. P. (2003). *What video games have to teach us about learning and literacy*. New York: Palgrave Macmillan.

Granell, X. (2011). Teaching video game localisation in audiovisual translation courses at university. *The Journal of Specialized Translation*, 16, 185–202, available online at: http://www.jostrans.org/issue16/art_granell.php (Retrieved March 17, 2015).

Gray, J. (2010). *Show sold separately: Promos, spoilers and other media paratexts*. New York: New York University Press.

ISFE. (2012). *Video gamers in Europe: Consumer study (Spain)*, available online at: http://www.isfe.eu/ (Retrieved March 17, 2015).

Jiménez Crespo, M. A. (2013). *Translation and web localization*. New York: Routledge.

Mangiron, C. (2007). Video games localisation: Posing new challenges to the translator. *Perspectives—Studies in Translatology*, 14(4), 306–317.

Mangiron, C. (2010). The importance of not being earnest: Translating humor in videogGames. In D. Chiaro (Ed.), *Translation, humor and the media* (pp. 89–107). London/New York: Continuum.

Mangiron, C. (2011). Accesibilidad en los Videojuegos: Estado Actual y Perspectivas Futuras. *Trans,* 15, 53–67.

Mangiron, C. (2012). Subtitling in game localisation: A descriptive study. *Perspectives-Studies in Translatology,* 21(1), 42–56.

Mangiron, C., & O'Hagan, M. (2006). Game localisation: Unleashing imagination with restricted translation. *The Journal of Specialized Translation,* 6, 10–21, available online at: http://www.jostrans.org/issue06/art_ohagan.php (Retrieved March 17, 2015).

Mangiron, C., Orero, P., & O'Hagan, M. (2014). (Eds.), *Fun for all. Translation and accessibility practices in video games.* Bern: Peter Lang.

Muñoz Sánchez, P. (2008). En Torno a la Localización de Videojuegos Clásicos Mediante Técnicas de Romhacking: Particularidades, Calidad y Aspectos Legales. *The Journal of Specialized Translation,* 9, 80–95, available online at: http://www.jostrans.org/issue09/art_munoz_sanchez.php (Retrieved March 17, 2015).

Neves, J. (2005). *Audiovisual translation: Subtitling for the deaf and hard-of-hearing.* PhD thesis. London: Roehampton University.

Newman, J. (2004). *Video games.* New York and London: Routledge.

Nord, C. (1991). Skopos, loyalty and translational conventions. *Target,* 3(1), 91–109.

Nord, C. (1997). *Translating as a purposeful activity. Functionalist approaches explained.* Manchester: St. Jerome.

O'Hagan, M. (2005). Multidimensional translation: A game plan for audiovisual translation in the age of GILT. Plenary presentation at *EU High Level Scientific Conference Series: Multidimensional Translation—MuTra* (Saarbrucken, 2–6 May 2005).

O'Hagan, M. (2007). Video games as a new domain for translation research: from translating text to translating experience. *Tradumática,* 5, available online at: http://www.fti.uab.es/tradumatica/revista/num5/articles/09/09art.htm (Retrieved March 17, 2015).

O'Hagan, M. (2009a). Evolution of user-generated translation: Fansubs, translation hacking and crowdsourcing. *The Journal of Internationalization and Localization,* 1, 94–121.

O'Hagan, M. (2009b). Towards a cross-cultural game design: an explorative study in understanding the player experience of a localized Japanese video game. *The Journal of Specialized Translation,* 11, 211–233, available online at: http://www.jostrans.org/issue11/art_ohagan.pdf (Retrieved March 17, 2015).

O'Hagan, M., & Mangiron, C. (2013). *Game localisation: Translating for the global digital entertainment industry.* Amsterdam: John Benjamins.

Orrego Carmona, D. (2015). *The reception of non-professional subtitling.* PhD thesis (unpublished). Universitat Rovira i Virgili.

Phillipson, R. (2003). *English-Only Europe? Challenging language policy.* London: Routledge.

Pym, A. (1999). Localizing localization in translators' training curricula. *Linguistica Antverpiensia,* 33, 127–137.

Scholand, M. (2002). Localización de Videojuegos. *Tradumática,* 1, available online at: http://www.fti.uab.es/tradumatica/revista/articles/mscholand/art.htm (Retrieved March 17, 2015).

Tavinor, G. (2009). *The art of videogames.* Oxford: Wiley-Blackwell.

Tercedor, M. I. (2005). Aspectos Culturales en la Localización de Productos Multimedia. *Quaderns, Revista de Traducció,* 12, 151–160.

Vela Valido, J. (2011). Academic training of videogame translators in Spain: Challenges and proposals for lecturers and researchers. *Trans*, 15, 89–102, available online at: http://www.trans.uma.es/pdf/Trans_15/89-102.pdf (Retrieved March 17, 2015).

Venuti, L. (1995). *The translator's invisibility.* New York-London: Routledge.

13 Glocalization and Co-Creation
Trends in International Game Production

Miguel Á. Bernal-Merino

Video games have consolidated their place in today's entertainment land-scape establishing interactivity as their unique selling point (USP) where players are invited to embody heroes, influence soundtracks, direct cameras, explore personalities, compete with players around the globe, modify stories, and create playable Mods (player generated levels). In short, although interactive entertainment may utilize content, ideas, and techniques from products such as literature, comics, cinema, music, table games, and TV, games give players decision power over a wide array of elements that changes the gaming experience every time. Surprisingly, although all game companies expect foreign revenues, many still forego internationalization, making localization unnecessarily costly and time-consuming (Bernal-Merino, 2015). Translating and rewriting strategies originated in the realm of literature (Bassnett, 1993; Saussy, 2006), there are examples of localization in children's literature and comics (Lathey, 2006, 2010; Pilcher & Brooks, 2005; Zanettin, 2008). Adaptation and crosspollination amongst the different arts have been common for centuries. For example, the Spanish stage play *Don Juan* became the Italian opera *Don Giovanni* by Austrian composer Mozart 157 years later. Nevertheless, the localization needs of interactive entertainment seem to exceed those of all other media. For this reason, the game industry is refining all previous processes of rewriting, adapting, and localizing and forging a new model. In order for companies to maximize profit and IP value, the international production strategy needs to be glocalized. In other words, it requires a game design and workflow that integrates the contribution of locale-knowledgeable partners in language, culture, and game development so that the reception of the game in foreign lands is not left to chance. This chapter analyzes the new trend that reframes localization within glocalization, a strategy that acknowledges and favors the global market *ab initio*, where co-creation with in-country partners is integrated in international production, offering foreign consumers the true immersive experience that game designers have crafted for their compatriots.

The Multimedia Interactive Entertainment Business

Digital natives have taken to interactive media in high numbers. Fifty-nine % of US citizens (ESA, 2014) and 48.5% of EU citizens (ISFE, 2012) play video games 'regularly', and while solo gaming remains an important part of this recreational experience, multiplayer matches and in-game chat prolong the success of games, enlarging fandoms across countries and languages, which highlights the social aspect of entertainment software. The hyper-connected world of gaming creates rapid bonds amongst distant players; game fandoms become quantum nations, i.e., spontaneous associations of individuals that supersede geopolitical borders and space-time but feel strongly attached to the game lore. Not only that, but gaming has already become a spectator sport, as illustrated by Twitch, a four-year-old live-streaming video platform that broadcasts the best world players competing against each other (Borg, 2015). Forecasts for eSports estimate that revenues will reach $465 million by 2017 (Newzoo, 2015). With serialized DLC (Downloadable Content) for games, F2P (Free to Play) monetization models, mobile gaming, and micro-transactions, the entertainment software industry has made video games accessible, episodic, and immensely profitable worldwide. Surprisingly, for many companies, localization remains a pending subject because they continue to employ approaches used for the translation of text-only static products such as books. On the other side of the spectrum, some companies are leading the way reframing localization within glocalization, a new paradigm that seems very fitting for multimedia interactive entertainment software that places international production and multinational ambition at the center of their global business strategy.

Industry analysts and professionals alike agree that the global market for video games will reach $100 billion by the end of 2017 (Newzoo, 2014) and that, thanks to localization, 30–50% of that revenue is already coming from foreign markets (Chandler & Deming, 2012). The percentage of revenue generated by localization is obviously bigger for non-US developers, as North America remains the biggest market (Newzoo, 2014), with China and Japan as second and third (Table 13.1 see page 204). Although localization plays such an essential role in the global expansion of video games, it is often poorly understood, badly planned for, and creatively untapped, because it is still seen as a mechanistic, post-production task where words are simply swapped between languages in a decontextualized binary matrix. This set of circumstances is even more surprising because business internationalization theories were developed in the 1970s and the idea of glocalization in the 1980s (Robertson, 1992; Hollensen, 2011).

Present research highlights why planning earlier saves time and money, and it enables the translation of playability, guaranteeing that the immersive gaming experience that developers crafted for their compatriots is not broken for foreign players because of bad localization. It is defended that applying a glocalization strategy, understood as the incorporation of creative elements from target countries in product development, can grow game IP (intellectual property) with locale-relevant content that can, in turn, revert back to the other markets, boosting global penetration and brand permanence. Game companies already broke new ground in the entertainment business by embracing the worldwide sim-ship (simultaneous shipment) distribution model in the 1990s (Bernal-Merino, 2015), launching in several countries at the same time in one single global campaign. It meant that they could take advantage of free promotion through media coverage and social networks, as well as combat piracy and grey imports (ibid). It goes without saying that the language services industry has grown as well, and its current global value is estimated at $35,000 billion (Hedge, 2013). It is not only that game goods can travel faster, it is that producers and consumers are communicating more efficiently across borders.

Foreign revenue has never been more in the spotlight. Zynga, a leading online-only US game company that grew under the wing of Facebook, reports that non-US revenue as a percentage of their total was "40% and 41% in 2013 and 2012, respectively" (Zynga, 2014: 50), and that "expansion into international markets is important for [their] growth" (ibid: 16). Similarly, the 2014 report by Activision-Blizzard, the most important developer-publisher in the global game industry, states that half of their revenues come from outside the US and that international sales are a fundamental part of their business strategy for the future (Activision Blizzard, 2013: 4). But selling games in more than one country is only the first step on the long road toward becoming a global brand. In fact, one of the most recurrent topics amongst experts at marketing conferences, such as Brand2Global, is finding and applying the right strategy for brands to expand in the global market, i.e., to grow organically in all their countries of distribution with a confident yet inclusive image by 'bringing in the local' (Goderis, 2014). The tacit admission is that, however international, many companies never had a glocal strategy, that is to say, product design never integrated customer preferences in each locale.

From the mid-1980s, big game companies have practiced partial localization into JFIGS (Japanese, French, Italian, German, Spanish), the languages considered to offer the highest returns. Nowadays, they face not only the stagnation of crowded, established markets but also the constant challenge of agile newcomers working on mobile games. Table 13.1 (below) lists the first 10 countries ranked by the revenue they generate.

Table 13.1 Top ten countries with regards to game revenues (Newzoo, 2104)

	Country	Revenue In US $
1	USA	20,484,628,000
2	China	17,866,677,000
3	Japan	12,219,552,000
4	Germany	3,528,196,000
5	United Kingdom	3,426,259,000
6	Republic of Korea	3,356,202,000
7	France	2,608,818,000
8	Canada	1,717,991,000
9	Italy	1,514,067,000
10	Spain	1,489,366,000

Although 'foreign' does not seem to have a place in the global business concept that has been with us for more than two decades (Hollensen, 2011), this paradigm only cares about basic financial, communication, and transportation structures, for most businesses tend to fall into the fallacy of 'consumer sameness'. This is not uncommon in entertainment industry circles either, and authors on international business and global media marketing (Nichols, 2014; Lieberman and Esgate, 2014; Dekom, 2014) do not even acknowledge translation, let alone localization, internationalization, or glocalization as *conditio sine qua non* features in today's international trade. There seems to be the assumption amongst business heads and marketers that video games are just like footballs, and that foreign markets are simply shops in other places not significantly different to those down the road. It may seem a mere question of process and logistics exacerbated by the legacy from past business environments, but nothing short of a paradigm shift will actually address the complexity being faced and look at it as a business opportunity. The good news is that the Internet provides the information and the physical means to enable this shift. It is down to companies to create the multilingual and multicultural infrastructures that can cater to foreign customers. The challenge for game companies is to entertain in a variety of languages while maintaining IP identity. Glocalization is not only for the market leaders that want to remain at the top, but also for new entrepreneurs that enter the crowded global arena with a less ethnocentric approach and refined understanding of global markets.

Other industries are already implementing a glocal approach in a variety of ways. For example, Nestlé has a tea-flavored *Kit Kat* especially for Asian markets; quiz shows such as *Who Wants to Be a Millionaire* are sold as a TV format (Esser this volume, Nashak, 2013) so that they can be produced in other countries, for example in Brazil. Popular novels are converted into film such as Chordelos' *Les Liaisons Dangereuses* reimagined by Lee as *Untold Scandal* in eighteenth-century Korea.

Glocalization is even more essential now that games are considered a service and not a one-off product by the industry. Developers and publishers need to cooperate to service players wherever they are for as long as the game is profitable (Grindel and Schmitz, 2011). Unfortunately, this remains an aspiration more than a reality for most.

Of course, game designers have always wanted to please their fans, but naturally, they have often had their local community and language in mind when creating games. Traditionally, focus groups have been conducted in one single language: that of the company leading the study. This was the natural beginning of customer engagement initiatives (Downham and Worcester, 1988). Nowadays, thanks to technological improvements in distribution, simultaneous global roll-out and customer demand, companies can reach consumers in many countries. Thus, focus group efforts need to be multilingual, multicultural, and ongoing because the world has changed. Until the mid-1990s, it was common to receive untranslated games and manuals, but digital natives are less forgiving when locked out of their immersive experience due to a lack of, or bad quality, localization. In all fairness, players have a right to complain when this is the case, as having paid around £45 for a new release, they are receiving an incomplete experience. The reason for this lack of preparedness for international distribution can be found in history.

Localization was initially only considered after release, following the logic of the minimum investment equation. It was the natural decision for this new entertainment industry because novels, comics, films, and TV programs did so. National success brings the revenue and confidence that opens the possibility of the international venture. In the late 1990s, localization started to be considered a post-production task of game development (as opposed to somebody else's task), which improved the overall quality of localized products and even originals. Unfortunately, most companies are stuck in that *modus operandi*, and 20 years later, many of the problems that plagued game localization then continue today (Deming, 2014). Such problems may be seen as operational challenges or translation mistakes, which show a failure in high-level strategic thinking. Nadine Martin, senior manager of test operations at Sony Computer Entertainment, showed that 86% of the costs in time and money her department incurred, were down to implementation errors, and only 14% could be attributed to translators' mistakes (2014). Such implementation issues are born out of a badly internationalized process. Her analysis highlighted that even experienced companies still think of games the way they did in the last century, as static products that may or not go global (Bernal-Merino, 2015). From this viewpoint, most localization complications are not the mistakes of managers, programmers, and localizers, but the result of a failure in strategic thinking for the global market. Game company leaders need to have a clear vision to make their products glocal, enabling such vision through the structure of the company. Only this type of approach is likely to clear the road ahead.

A Maturing Global Industry

International trade is obviously nothing new. Cross-continental journeys were already a reality centuries before the Silk Road, more than two thousand years ago, when nomad merchants traded products and ideas among Greece, Egypt, India, and China. These international routes were so very important that they continued to grow and to expand despite the coming and going of kings, emperors, and dynasties (Gupta et al., 2014). Similar relay races where products flow from merchant to merchant, from distributor to retailer, have continued until today. In young markets, most consumers accept the fact that imported products are bound to be costly, unchanged, and untranslated; they enjoy their foreignness, for there tends to be a slight devaluation from domestic products, which may be less developed. The film industry started catering to foreign markets from the 1920s, with a wide variety of options: translation of intertitles, addition of subtitles or side-titles, life narrators, parallel multilingual shooting, and dubbing (Cornu, 2014). The game industry is also trying all possible combinations in order to find the most beneficial ROI formula. However, consumers in older markets, especially the 'millennial' and the 'skipper' generations (MirriAd. com), are more demanding and expect to be catered to with products that acknowledge local preferences (Hollensen, 2011) without losing their brand identity; this is what is meant by being glocal. Creations do not have to favor a particular culture or nationality, they simply need to be creatively consistent within themselves and engage with players by programming in their preferences. The stage prior to glocalization is internationalization, where the characteristics considered more relevant, such as language, are easily modifiable. The following table describes the three basic approaches that companies utilized to distribute internationally.

Table 13.2 Approaches to international distribution

Production is	*Localization options*
Unchanged: There is no planning for international distribution even though profits from foreign markets are expected. The lack of readiness of the management, the code and the teams result in poor localization when plugged at the end.	In these cases, 'forced' localization is the only option. This patchy translation results in an unsatisfactory and incomplete playing experience. Forced localization is time-consuming and prone to a large host of linguistic and playability bugs. Foreign sales will be low.
Internationalized: The game has been functionally internationalized in order to enable the integration of other alphabets, as well as date, time and money formats, keyboard layouts, etc.	Various levels of localization can be achieved with less bugs and better playability. A wide array of localization options is available based on the game experience created. Partial, cheaper localization diminishes playability and full immersion in most cases.
Glocalized: The game design as well as the production process incorporate elements of targeted locales through menus, characters, items, storylines, etc. the ideal option when the game universe does not demand ethnocentricity.	The full spectrum of localization options is open, and games can be co-created for each locale. Foreign players can enjoy the game whichever way they want to, making for a fuller player satisfaction thanks to the playability of localized versions.

Consumers of traditional entertainment are used to unchanged products, for this has been the norm for the longest part of our history. Just like physical goods, myths, stories, and characters have traveled through time and space, and many communities around the world have integrated into their shared background knowledge narratives around Achilles, Mulan, Aladdin, Ashoka, Don Juan, Tarzan, Sherlock Holmes, Cinderella, Pinocchio, Mickey, Asterix, and Smurfette. They are the evidence of the international flow in the entertainment industries. Similar examples from the young game industry are: Pac-Man, Tetris, Zelda, Solid Snake, Super Mario, Master Chief, Grand

Theft Auto, World of Warcraft, Lara Croft, and Angry Birds, to name but a few. The naturalization of these names in different languages evidences not only the entry of foreign images, concepts, and narratives, but also the success of the video games that brought them into each country. Localization is a key factor in that success because, although games are multichannel products that communicate through images, sound, and music, often the written and spoken language carries the greater part of the narrative. This is the reason so few people consume entertainment products that have not been translated at all. The issue is even more imperative in video games because of the customizable nature of digital products that set player expectations. Entertainment software innovated by adding interactivity to the reading, listening, and viewing experience offered by previous media, in other words, games elevate players to the protagonist role, the agents that originate the text, the sounds, and the images onscreen. Story-based video games can only immerse players with high quality localization. This only means that the creation itself sets the rules for translation (Bernal-Merino, 2002) and not that the game world has to be forced into varying ethnocentric versions that diverge from the game world itself. Glocalization integrates localization as part of the creative process, hence co-creation, and not as a disconnected part of postproduction. However, prior to glocalization, there are several localization levels that have traditionally been applied to video games.

Localization Levels

Video game developers and publishers have traditionally established three levels of localization, taking into account the maturity and the expectations for each foreign market. These levels are: No localization, packaging and manual, partial localization (user interface and subtitles), and full localization (voiceover) (Chandler & Deming, 2012: 8–10). The last two levels require some degree of internationalization of the game code. These levels are a simplified version of what happens in reality and tend to artificially separate localization from playability because there is the tacit assumption that content localization is similar to swapping date/time/currency display formats for other locales. This misconception is linked to the delusion of decontextualized literal translation (Bernal-Merino, 2002) that is leading some game localization companies to integrate Machine Translation (MT) in their workflows in an attempt to save money. But just like enthralling stories cannot be written by computers or with simplified 'controlled English' (Cohn et al., 2012), the localization of video games cannot be tackled with automatic processes. Entertainment software requires a high degree of inventiveness, cohesion, and surprise, which is why translators' understanding, penmanship, and creativity are required. While TMIES (the Translation of Multimedia Interactive Entertainment Software) shares some features with the translation of texts for technology, literature, comics, and films, it uniquely features 'playability' (Bernal-Merino, 2015: 40), which sets it apart from other media. From basic player enablement through instructions, to clear UI, avatar creation, and branching storylines, games elicit not only suspension of disbelief and identification, but also immersion and empowerment through agency (Eichner, 2013), i.e., the feeling of true-to-life involvement in the events occurring onscreen. When players talk about their gaming experience they always use the first person, never the third like book readers, filmgoers, or TV watchers; gaming is autobiographical. Unfortunately, the magic of playability may be broken in localized versions because general game development managers neglect internationalization, rush localization, and fail to equip translators with full access to content and tools. The result is that the immersive gaming experience that developers may have created for their compatriots is wrecked by their lack of a glocal strategy for foreign players.

The itemized levels of localization applied to video games can be more clearly understood in Table 13.3. As the game industry matures and more developers enter the market with innovative products for new demographics, localization levels have also diversified introducing middle stages and adding an essential one for companies with global permanence aspirations. The levels go as follows, according to different authors:

Table 13.3 Levels of localization as established by different authors

Chandler & Deming (2012)	McKearney (2007)	Bernal-Merino
No localization	No localization	0- Zero localization
Localization of packaging and manual only	Localization of packaging and manual only	1- (Only some of the assets from level 2 are localized)
		2- **Market enabled** localization (packaging, manual, e-store blurb, website, installation wizard)
Partial localization	Partial localization	3- (Only some of the assets from level 4 are localized)
		4- **Player engagement** (UI, in-game text, subtitles)
		5- (Only some of the assets from level 6 are localized)
Full localization	Full localization	6- **Player immersion** (audio reprocessing, dubbing and lip-synching)
		7- (Only some of the assets from level 8 are localized)
Not typified	Deep (or enhanced) localization	8- **General player customization** (varied options for tailoring avatars, items, cars, etc. from the original designer team)
		9- (Only some of the assets and locales from level 10 are considered)
Not considered	*Not considered*	10- **Glocalization** (Local identity empowerment by varied options for tailoring avatars, items, cars, etc. from designers in each locale, i. e. co-creation)

When localization is forced onto a game that has not been internationalized, i.e., there is no plan for it, and no preparations have been made, problems grow exponentially (Deming, 2014), errors require more time from coding engineers, and games do not reach the localization quality that foreign consumers expect. It is worth noting that when players complain about localization it is not for the fact that the game is in their language, but because of the low production values of the localization. Fortunately, some game developers and publishers are realizing that they can not only avoid the old pitfalls but also harness the potential of localization. The next sections illustrate how with market trends confirm the move toward more localization in all its different levels.

Unstoppable Change

It should be clear by now that localization should go beyond superficial language enablement to immerse players. The old relay race of unlocalized or badly localized products is likely to cost game companies dearly in today's world markets because the skip generation has a wide range of games to choose from and a 24/7 information cycle to pull them away from products that do not communicate with them promptly and genuinely. A good example is the shift toward quality localization of CD Projekt, an unknown Polish game developer/publisher that entered the market with *The Witcher* (2007). The game sold 50 thousand units (vgchartz.com) and was widely criticized for bad translation and poor voiceover acting. A year later it released the "Enhanced Edition" with a completely new English translation and voiceover; it sold an extra 320 thousand units (ibid). Continuing with the increase in quality and languages, *The Witcher 2* (2011) sold a total of 1.74 million copies. Finally, *The Witcher 3* (2015) has sold 2.5 million (ibid) units worldwide in only two months thanks to being localized into 14 languages, seven fully and seven partially localized.

There are no public numbers on players per language, and some companies still struggle to collect and mine their own data, but we can use the existing figures to show meaningful pointers. Steam, a North American digital distribution platform for software, writes on its online survey reports that half of its customers use languages other than English for gaming and buying (Valve, 2014). The Eurobarometer Report on Online Language Preferences (Gallup, 2011) revealed that more than half of Internet users do read and watch free content online in other languages. The surveys by Sargent (2011) and DePalma (2014) conclude that less than 25% of Internet users actually carry out transactions in a foreign language, which suggests that people do not spend money when webpages and products have not been localized. According to Internet World 2014 Stats, 71.4% out of the 2,802 billion netizens favor languages such as Chinese, Spanish, Arabic, Portuguese, Japanese, Russian, German, French, and Korean to browse the net and carry out their business transactions (Internet World Stats, 2014).

But language enablement is only the first step toward customer engagement, product customization, and customer service.

The trend has been clear from the birth of the Internet, only companies that communicate in local languages and understand and address local sensibilities are likely to thrive globally. This was no surprise to the language services industry as the birth of LISA (Localization Industry Standards Association) illustrated. The late 1980s saw the strengthening and global projection of software companies such as Microsoft, Cisco, etc. Michael Anobile, the main driving force behind LISA, recounts that some software firms were already getting 55% of their revenues from the non-English versions of their products (Pfenning, 2012). It was a turning point for software companies because strategists realized that rethinking their production to enable localization opened the road for global market penetration and brand permanence. The '90s were the consolidation of the website and utility software localization industry. Games had by then recuperated from the dip of the late '80s, and companies started to incorporate language enablement into FIGS (French, Italian, German and Spanish) in postproduction. The amount of languages offered at launch has continued to increase, facilitating entry to new markets. Brian Farrel, CEO of THQ, stated at Cloud Gaming USA 2011: "Our games are always on and our players are always connected [...] We have the opportunity to interact with players in new ways that can be reactive to their desires, play habits, and buying habits. The box, ship and done model are transitioning to: observe, measure, and modify" (Aslinger, 2013: 68).

Although Farrel's statement makes perfect sense, the logistics of realizing it globally must not be underestimated. Companies that want to become and remain global have to avoid the fallacy of consumer sameness by analyzing per-country and per-player statistics. Companies in Brazil, Finland, Germany, Korea, Poland, Russia, and Turkey have joined the game industry race, eating away part of the profits of established ones by understanding the local player community and finding new niches (Chronis, 2011). Both the markets and the flux of goods are changing; for example, Korean free-to-play MMOs are popular with Brazilian players thanks to specialized localization companies (Portnow et al., 2013: 76). A better awareness of localization is enabling these young entrepreneurs from all over the world to become contenders in the international arena. In the case of F2P, localization is not an extra but a question of survival due to the small margins.

In other countries, such as India, there was never a slow build-up from playing simple arcade games to complex ones, no shift for PC and console to casual, mobile, and social "everything is happening all at once" (Shaw, 2013: 184). In countries of low income or where interactive entertainment is rather new, mobiles and smartphones are often heralded as the breakthrough platform because F2P allows consumers to experience the game before buying, and micro-transactions spread the expenditure throughout days, weeks, or months (Shaw, 2013: 190). In some countries, such as Spain or Brazil, national creations may replicate elements of US and Japanese games. In others, such as Saudi Arabia and Iran, games combine techno-logical pride with the desire to represent their specific cultural identity and challenge Western stereotypes about them (Šisler, 2013: 257). The global concept describes a marketplace where all countries can compete with their own games "histories, experiences, and culture" (Consalvo, 2013: 120), but although 'global' may give the impression of a single place, markets are closed, legal, and financial spaces, and this is why the 'national' will con-tinue to have specific relevance for media products. The glocal paradigm delivers a content multiplier, for it integrates the preferences and creativity of each locale into a global IP controlled by the owning company. Elements developed for one locale can revert to any other in a positive loop, and global players can discover undreamed-of new content that gravitates around the game-world they love. Such content can be implemented cheaply and seam-lessly once glocalization has been integrated, thanks to the digital, modular nature of entertainment software.

Quantum Nations and the Road to Glocalization

The technology that customers utilize to engage in social activities is the same that companies harness to operate in the global market. This dynamic has reshaped the way fans agglutinate and interact with products and amongst themselves. It is not a question of geographical boundaries being moved; those will remain because of unavoidable issues around politics and sovereignty; it is the opening of fandoms into a much more global, social concept, the 'fansphere', a space made up of quantum nations that supersede geopolitical and geocultural boundaries, time, and space. The approaches to game design, production, and customer services of the last century are too simplistic for the hyper-connected quantum. Promotional campaigns may entice players, but they do not make fans. Social media may generate atten-tion but also viral destruction. Free-to-play models attract users but do not retain players. Partial localization helps players enter a game, but it cannot immerse them fully (unless they are perfectly bilingual). The reason is no less true for being obvious: The global market is not one big shop, but many small ones, with unique players bound together in communities by their love for a game and the language-culture binomium. Foreign players want to partake in the global phenomenon as citizens of these quantum nations but expect to be catered to just like those in the main country of distribu-tion. It has been argued that we are in the era of the 'prosumers' (Dekom, 2014: 160), when customization of design from the bottom up is not a marketing gimmick but a new paradigm for global companies to embrace. It has, of course, been done before with burgers, cars, holiday packages, and even with *Monopoly*, the board game. But today's prosumers expect to influence products and services, so much so that design and production pipelines accommodate consumers' input in order to satisfy them and grow in the market. It is a sobering challenge. Nevertheless, game companies have one ace that allows them to face the test with clear advantage: as software creations, video games are virtual products that can be programmed modularly to allow for as many options and variations as locales may want for any one game. This, in turn, changes glocalization from a survival strategy into an opportunity to grow and thrive. Glocalization integrates the notion of the universal and the local into a strategic production structure for goods that aspire to be globally appealing. Not surprisingly the major companies are starting to take stock. Activision-Blizzard states in its 2013 report that an important element of their strategy is "to develop content that is specifically directed toward local cultures and customs" (Activision-Blizzard, 2013: 4).

The fact that quality localization is wanted is further evidenced by the many player communities around the world that organize themselves and do fan-localization for their peers, translating text, adapting content, and, sometimes, even changing voiceover and graphics. These fan-initiated projects are motivated by the lack of an official translation or the existence of a very disappointing one. Consalvo (2013: 132) writes about the fan-localization project of *Mother 3* (a Japanese game) that only a week after completion got more than 100,000 downloads from the fan website, benefiting Nintendo in the process. Fan-localization is characterized for being quirky but deeply inspired by game lore. The success of these community patches shows the need for quality localization. But the brief shelf life of video games means that only a glocalization strategy can maximize on potential global revenues. A good example is *Travian*, a German RTS (Real Time Strategy) browser game. The localization manager of the company explained how it went from a German-only game in 2004 to adding English fan-localization in 2006 (Herzog, 2014). When the company tried to push fans in other countries to translate the game into their mother tongues, all attempts failed, and they had to outsource to language vendors (ibid). *Travian* has nowadays 41 translated versions, which generate 90% of their revenues; the German version accounts only for 10% and the English one for 12% (ibid). The *Travian* case clearly shows that full localization is a clear benefit for players, a clear sign of the maturing of the game industry.

At the forefront of the industry in localization are companies that focus mainly on online markets. Barnes (2012), senior manager of platform services at Blizzard, received what he called "Carte Blanche" for the localization of *StarCraft II* (2011), a sci-fi Massively Multiplayer Online (MMO) game. The declared goal was to make "the game feel like it was designed for any player that sits down in front of it, regardless of their locale". In a way, it is surprising that this had rarely been the case as illustrated by his astonishment. Barnes was able to localize game assets often considered too expensive or not essential for the functionality of the game. The most illustrative example offered by Barnes was an in-game news broadcast on the TV of the pub where *StarCraft*'s protagonist hangs out between missions. The voiceover, as well as the overlays, the running breaking news at the bottom, and even the handwritten paper where the barman had scribbled on "Don't shoot at screen" were reconsidered artistically for each version, even though they involved considering Unicode, fonts, text, voiceover, graphic assets …, in other words, plenty of time and money (ibid). From this point of view, the 12 language versions of the game were 12 different game builds and not a single build where a few text files had been translated to bridge the language gap. The translation of playability thus is enabled by mindful internationalization, a key step in the maturing of the globalization model, which rationalizes the difficulties experienced up to that point and integrates them into a better-informed localization process. Early planning favors market entry and worldwide penetration, as well as the reduction of gray imports and pirate distribution, i.e., it maximizes success. Such deep (McKearney, 2007) or enhanced localization marked for Blizzard a confident push into the international arena, and it meant that they maintained the world leadership in that game genre.

StarCraft's achievement would be the equivalent of films translating and reprocessing all onscreen text when the creation itself does not require ethnocentricity. Even remarkably accomplished CGI productions such as *Up* (Disney/Pixar, 2009) only managed a few such translations in a silent scene when Carl, the protagonist, mournfully reads the photo album that his wife started when she was only a girl and finished right before dying. They translated, redesigned and rerendered all the plot-essential English sentences into French and German but not Portuguese, Italian, or Japanese. The English-French-German versions are: "My adventure book", "Stuff I'm going to do", "Thanks for the adventure—now go have a new one! Love, Ellie" to "*Mon livre d'aventure*", "*Trucs a faire*", "*Merci pour cette belle aventure— Il est temps pour toi d'en vivre une nouvelle! Je t'aime, Ellie*"; "*Mein Abenteuerbuch*", "*Was ich erleben will*", "*Danke für das Abenteuer—Los, such Dir ein Neues! In Liebe, Ellie*". Although laudable—this attention to foreign markets in the film industry is rare. Disney/Pixar's strategy lacks the consistency of their latest musical films, not only because they left many languages with said text in English, but also because they applied different localization practices, such as when the last of the above sentences is voiced-over in German but not in English or French.

In contrast to Disney/Pixar's example, Bungie's strategy to localize their latest game, *Destiny*, shows the ground breaking localization potential of interactive entertainment. The game developers wanted to avoid the US-centric feel in their game, the most anticipated sci-fi shooter MMO of 2014. The game cost $275 million to develop and market and generated $800 million worldwide on the very first day of release (Griffiths, 2014). It is set 700 years in the future during a war between humans and alien factions. The full localization strategy headed by Slattery, the manager, involved common best practices as described in the Whitepaper by the IGDA Localization SIG (Honeywood et al., 2012). But more interestingly they mixed various languages in all textures wrapping the 3D graphic models, fleshing out the game lore around that all human nations had realized space exploration projects, alone or in coalition (Slattery, 2014). This also allowed for multi-lingual signage in general to be used as a decorative element that gives depth to the game world. What this means is that players of all versions do actu-ally see a *mélange* of languages, including English, French, Italian, German, Spanish, Brazilian, Japanese, and Latin, a believable conception of the future as many people may imagine it (ibid).

In my opinion, it was only a matter of time before the interactive enter-tainment software industry explored fully the glocalization option. Fong (2013) explained in his session during the GDC Localization Summit how his Chinese company, Yodo1, partnered with Defiant Development, an Australian casual game studio, to 'conquer' the Chinese market by co-creating with them Chinese-based avatars, characters, items, and locations for Defiant's game *Ski Safari*. After glocalization and co-creation took place, the game went from 35,000 to 70 million Chinese players. Morgan Jaffit, CEO of the Australian company said: "Working with Yodo1 enabled us to open up the Chinese mobile gaming market and re-tool *Ski Safari* to earn more revenue in China than we ever thought possible" (Fong, 2013). Of course, we must also remember that, although quality game content is essential for the success of any game in any country, creators and businesses are unavoidably constrained by national identities and government poli-cies (Steemer, this volume), such as pride in traditions and protectionism in China (Wheeler, 2013), or targeted censorship in Germany where all Nazi references are banned (Remo, 2009). Game companies that aspire to remain global cannot do so without a well-formulated glocalization strat-egy because only this will give them the flexibility to adapt better to all the challenges they are sure to find abroad.

The Case for Game Glocalization in Short

To sum up, there are six main reasons that put into focus the benefits of G.L.O.C.A.L., a glocalization strategy that embraces co-creation for game companies with global ambition:

a Growth readiness: Once a game has been glocalized, it is prepared to receive new content from any co-creator partner for those locales where player communities are specially engaged and avid, or because the num-ber of followers has dropped in a worrying manner.
b Legal compliance: Legal and economic frameworks cannot be avoided, and each country can create unique regulations, so preparing for them early-on in development will reduce future legal obstacles.
c Outsmart copycats: Companies with the creative zest and the right busi-ness planning can easily emulate the most popular characteristics of any game and make them into a similar one that satiates the urges of local

fans. After a small period of time, players may become fans of the imitation, which will likely evolve its own uniqueness.

 d Charm skippers: Today's digital natives are very unlikely to spend money on any game that is not in their language from start to finish because there is an abundance of games in their mother tongue.

 e Acclaimed IP: a game requires a team of talented individuals and a confident vision to become great, but creativity can be quickly exhausted; this is where glocalization offers new possibilities. The interaction of game creators within a team is extended to the localization experts that can not only render the text into the chosen, sim-ship languages, but also contribute creatively to the game content, characters, and features. In other words, co-creation and shared-authorship are assimilated into the development process from the design. Glocalization is a centralized strategy to systematically source talent from the localization teams living where the product is going to be consumed.

 f Label permanence: the longevity of IPs strengthens player loyalty, label, and brand permanence in the country because the brand becomes organically associated with quality products that cater to local customers.

Similar to the way entertainment licensors have become full-fledged, always-on creative collaborators with developers to generate more profitability (Morris, 2013), collaborating with localizers is the final integration that articulates global input and income. This is the first time in the entertainment industry that companies can address all their global clients directly and simultaneously without surrendering control to any intermediaries. The maturing game industry is starting to put into practice internationalization and glocalization theories embracing shared-authorship with considerable improvements in playability and immersion; the articulation of localization within a glocalization strategy seems to apply also to other audiovisual productions (Nashak, 2013; Esser, Chaume, Calbreath-Frasieur in this volume). This trend has been growing steadily for the past two decades, and all evidence suggests that it will continue to expand. The future belongs to companies that understand glocalization and co-creation and prepare for them from product design by partnering with experts in each locale, not only because foreign clients are as worthy as local ones, but also because they are more numerous.

References

Activision-Blizzard. (2013). Annual report, available online at: http://investor.activision.com/common/download/download.cfm?companyid=ACTI&fileid=746096&filekey=2205B72D-1007-4DCB-A5F1-2D121D8EC95C&filename=Activision_Blizzard_2013_AR.1.pdf (Retrieved November 9, 2014).

Aslinger, B. (2013). Redefining the Console for the Global, Networked Era. In N.B. Huntemann and B. Aslinger (Eds.), *Gaming Globally. Production, Play and Place* (pp. 59–74). New York: Palgrave Macmillan.

Barnes, W. (2012). StarCraft II—Carte Blanche localization, available online at: www.gdcvault.com/play/1015645/StarCraft-II-Carte-Blanche (Retrieved December 7, 2014).

Bassnett, S. (1993). *Comparative Literature: A Critical Introduction*. Oxford: Blackwell Publishers.

Bernal-Merino, M. Á. (2002). *La traducción audiovisual*. Alicante: Publicaciones Universidad de Alicante.

Bernal-Merino, M. Á. (2015). *Translation and localisation in video games. Making entertainment software global*. New York/Oxon: Routledge.

Borg, O. J. (2015). Gaming—The rise of the cyber athletes, available online at: www.bbc.co.uk/programmes/b04xn5p9 (Retrieved April 10, 2015).

Chandler, H. M. and Deming, S. O. (2012). *The Game Localization Handbook,* 2nd edition. Sudbury/London: Jones and Bartlett Learning.

Chronis, G. T. (2011). Joymax set for a breakout, DFC intelligence, available online at: www.dfcint.com/dossier/?qav1b=joymax-set-for-a-breakout (Retrieved February 7, 2015).

Consalvo, M. (2013). Unintended Travel: ROM Hackers and Fan Translations of Japanese Video Games. In N.B. Huntemann and B. Aslinger (Eds.), *Gaming Globally. Production, Play and Place* (pp. 119–129). New York: Palgrave Macmillan.

Cornu, J. F. (2014). *Le doublage et le sous-titrage: Histoire et esthétique*. Rennes: PU Rennes.

Dekom, P. (2014). *Next. Reinventing media, marketing and entertainment*. Marston Gate: HekaRose Publishing.

Deming, S. (2014). How developers complicate the localization process. Presented at the Game Localization Round Table, October 29, 2014, Vancouver.

DePalma, D. (2014). Can't read, won't buy: The conflict between a strong brand and local language, presented at Brand2Global, Common Sense Advisory.

Downham, J., & Worcester, R. M. (1988). *Consumer market research handbook*. London: McGraw-Hill.

Dredge, S. (2013). Angry Birds helped Rovio double its revenues to £129m in 2012. *The Guardian*, available online at: www.theguardian.com/technology/appsblog/2013/apr/03/angry-birds-rovio-financials-2012 (Retrieved January 2015).

Eichner, S. (2013). *Agency and media reception: Experiencing video games, film, and television*. Potsdam: Springer VS.

Esselink, Bert. (2000). *A Practical Guide to Localization*. Amsterdam/Philadelphia: John Benjamins Publishing Company.

Fong, H. (2013). The Western games that conquered China, presentation delivered at the GDC Localization Summit, available online at: www.gdcvault.com/play/1017999/The-Western-Games-That-Conquered (Retrieved January 18, 2015).

Gallup Organization. (2011). User language preferences online. *Flash Eurobarometer n. 313*. Directorate-General, European Commission, available online at: http://ec.europa.eu/public_opinion/flash/fl_313_en.pdf (Retrieved November 9, 2014).

Goderis, T. (2014). Co-Creating with consumers in Asian markets. Delivered at Brand2Global on October 2, 2014 in London.

Griffiths, S. (2014). World's most expensive video game goes on sale. *Mail Online*. www.dailymail.co.uk/sciencetech/article-2749053/Worlds-expensive-video-game-goes-sale-Destiny-cost-310-MILLION-develop.html#ixzz3Pq2pIwTB (Retrieved January 25, 2015).

Grindel, B., & C. Schmitz. (2011). Settlers online: Moving a traditional European boxed game to a worldwide Free to Play MMO experience. GDC Online, available online at: www.gdcvault.com/play/1015051/Settlers-Online-Moving-a-Traditional (Retrieved December 5, 2014).

Gupta, A. K., Pande, G., and Wang, H. (2014). *Silk Road rediscovered: How Indian and Chinese companies are becoming globally stronger by winning in each other's markets.* San Francisco: Wiley.

Hegde, V. (2013). The language services market slows down in 2013, but grows nevertheless. Common sense advisory blogs, available online at: www.common senseadvisory.com/Default.aspx?Aid=5516&Contenttype=ArticleDetAD&moduleId=390&tabID=63 (Retrieved March 22, 2015).

Herzog, R. (2014). Localisation at Travian Games. Presented at the Game Localization Round Table, Localization World International Conference. Dublin, 4th June.

Hollensen, S. (2011). *Global marketing: A decision-oriented approach.* Harlow: Financial Times Prentice Hall.

Honeywood, R. et al. (2012). IGDA localization SIG (Special Interest Group).

Internet World Stats. (2014). Internet world users by language, available online at: www.internetworldstats.com/stats7.htm (Retrieved November 9, 2014).

Kerr, A. (2013). Space Wars: The Politics of Games Production in Europe. In N.B. Huntemann and B. Aslinger (Eds.), *Gaming Globally. Production, Play and Place* (pp. 215–232). New York: Palgrave Macmillan.

Lathey, G. (2006). (Ed.), *The translation of children's literature: A reader.* Clevedon, UK: Multilingual Matters Ltd.

Lathey, G. (2010). *The role of translators in children's literature: Invisible storytellers.* London: Routledge.

Lieberman, A. and Esgate, P. (2014). *The Definitive Guide to Entertainment Marketing. Bringing the Moguls, the Media, and the Magic to the World.* Upper Saddle River: Financial Times/Pearson.

Ma, W., Wang, F., & Wong, G. (2014). PlayStation game: Xbox, censors. *The Wall Street Journal.* Accessed December 15, 2014.

Martin, N. (2014). The Future of Localization Testing. Localization Summit, GDC, available online at: www.gdcvault.com/play/1020537/The-Future-of-Localization (Retrieved December 6, 2014).

McKearney, J. (2007). A new marketing tool: Enhanced localization. Presented at the Game Localization Round Table, Localization World International Conference. Seattle, 16 October.

Morris, D. (2013). A new (and way better) model for licensed games, Game Developers Conference, available online at: www.gdcvault.com/play/1018054/A-New-(and-Way-Better) (Retrieved January 9, 2015).

Nashak, R. (2013). BBC, cross-media and video games. Localization Summit, GDC, available online at: http://www.gdcvault.com/play/1018047/BBC-Cross-Media-and-Video (Retrieved January 26, 2015).

Newzoo. (2014). 2014 global games market report, available online at: www.newzoo.com/product/2014-global-games-market-report (Retrieved February 26, 2015).

Newzoo. (2015). The global growth of esports, available online at: www.gamesindustry.biz/articles/2015-02-17-report-esports-revenues-to-hit-usd465m-in-2017 (Retrieved May 17, 2015).

Nichols, R. (2013). Who Plays, Who Pays? Mapping Video Game Production and Consumption Globally. In N.B. Huntemann and B. Aslinger (Eds.), *Gaming Globally. Production, Play and Place* (pp. 19–40). New York: Palgrave Macmillan.

Nichols, R. (2014). *The video game business*. London: Palgrave Macmillan.

Pilcher, T., & Brooks, B. (2005). *The Essential Guide to World Comics*. London: Collins and Brown.

Pfenning, R. (2012). Michael Anobile on the history and development of the localization industry, available online at: http://blog.csoftintl.com/michael-anobile-on-the-history-nd-development-of-the-localization-industry (Retrieved November 11, 2014).

Portnow, J., Protasio, A. and Donaldson, K. (2013). Snapshot 1: Video Game Development in Brazil. In N.B. Huntemann and B. Aslinger (Eds.), *Gaming Globally. Production, Play and Place* (pp. 75–78). New York: Palgrave Macmillan.

Prensky, M. (2001). Digital natives, digital immigrants. *On the Horizon*, 9(5), 1–6.

Remo, C. (2009). Wolfenstein removed from sale in Germany due to Nazi symbols. Gamasutra, available online at: www.gamasutra.com/view/news/116313/Wolfenstein_Removed_From_Sale_In_Germany_Due_To_Nazi_Symbols.php (Retrieved March 30, 2015).

Salen, K. and Zimmerman, E. (2003). *Rules of Play: Game Design Fundamentals*. Massachusetts: MIT Press.

Sargent, B. B. (2011). European online language preferences revealed in flash Eurobarometer report, common sense advisory, available online at: www.commonsenseadvisory.com/default.aspx?Contenttype=ArticleDetAD&tabID=63&Aid=1447&moduleId=390 (Retrieved November 9, 2014).

Saussy, H. (2006). *Comparative literature in an age of globalization*. Baltimore: Johns Hopkins University Press.

Shaw, A. (2013). How Do You Say Gamer in Hindi?: Exploratory Research on the Indian Digital Game Industry and Culture. In N.B. Huntemann and B. Aslinger (Eds.), *Gaming Globally. Production, Play and Place* (pp. 183–202). New York: Palgrave Macmillan.

Šisler, V. (2013). Video Game Development in the Middle East: Iran, the Arab World, and Beyond. In N.B. Huntemann and B. Aslinger (Eds.), *Gaming Globally. Production, Play and Place* (pp. 251–270). New York: Palgrave Macmillan.

Slattery, T. (2014). 7 languages, 7 platforms: Delivering bungie's destiny to the world. Presented at the Game Localization Round Table, October 29, 2014, Vancouver.

Valve. (2014). Steam hardware & software survey, available online at: http://store.steampowered.com/hwsurvey (Retrieved November 9, 2014).

Wheeler, P. (2013). China in your hands. Presented at Casual Connect International Conference. October 23, 2013.

Zanettin, F. (2008). *Comics in translation*. Manchester/New York: St. Jerome Publishing.

Zynga. (2014). Annual report 2013, available online at: http://investor.zynga.com/annual-proxy.cfm (Retrieved November 11, 2014).

Gameography

Angry Birds, mobile game. (Rovio, 2009–present).
Destiny, MMO game series. (Activision Bungie, 2014).

Monopoly, table game. (Monitor Media, 2002–2006).
Mother 3, roleplaying game. (Brownie Brown/ HAL Laboratory: Nintendo, 2006).
Ski Safari (China), mobile game. (Defiant Development, Yodo1, 2012).
Ski Safari, mobile game. (Defiant Development, 2012).
StarCraft, MMO game series. (Activision Blizzard, 1998–present).
The Witcher (CD Projekt, 2007: Atari).
The Witcher: Enhanced Edition (CD Projekt, 2008: Atari).
The Witcher 2 (CD Projekt Red, 2011: CD Projekt Red/ Namco Bandai).
The Witcher 3 (CD Projekt Red, 2015: CD Projekt Red/ Namco Bandai).
Travian (Travian Games GmbH, 2004–Present).
World of Warcraft, MMO game series. (Activision Blizzard 2004–present).

Glossary

Adaptation   Term used to refer to a creation (or source text) that changes artistic medium, such as a novel becoming a film, or a video game becoming a comic book. It can also refer to the remaking of a film or TV series, generally for another geographical market or to exploit an already proven text at a later point in time. In Translation Studies it is usually applied to forms of translation that display a considerable distance in formal and lexical aspects between source and target text.

Anime   A term used within Japan to refer to all types of animation regardless of national origin, yet outside of Japan used specifically to refer to Japanese animation.

Attention economy   A concept that highlights that in today's age of information overload and choice, the (rare) good sought by producers is attention. Consumer attention is the prerequisite for sales and in order to stand out and receive attention, products require heavy marketing.

Audiovisual translation   Practice of translating texts contained in audiovisual products. Also used to refer to the part of Translation Studies that focuses on the various modes of translation of audiovisual media.

Authentic speech   Speech as spoken spontaneously by speakers in everyday situations.

BADaptation   Term introduced by Hunter and Verevis (2011) to challenge those views of adaptation and remaking that routinely employ a rhetoric of betrayal and degradation, that criticize an adapted text for being 'unfaithful' to its idealized source.

Banal cosmopolitanism   Academic concept coined by sociologist Ulrich Beck (2006) to describe an allegedly quiet revolution in everyday life through the creeping emergence of the mixing of national cultures, multiple loyalties, and the transnationalization of law and politics. Instead of remaining firmly determined by national policies and identities, in a globalizing world people's lives are increasingly cosmopolitanized, Beck argues, in banal and hence unnoticed ways. This happens as a consequence of both coerced choices (e.g., migration) and unconscious decisions (e.g., through consuming foreign products and developing a taste for them).

'Canned' content   Synonym for 'finished content', i.e., those TV programs that receive no or only minor adaptation (subtitling, voice over, or dubbing) when imported. The term is used to differentiate this form of tradable audiovisual product from so-called 'TV Formats', like *Big Brother* or *Who Wants to be a Millionaire?*, which are sold internationally for a complete (or nearly complete) local remake.

Co-creation   In video games, the process of generating content, which is specific for different locales, in harmony with the lead creators.

Cosmopolitan(ism)   The notion of the cosmopolitan citizen, concerned with the wellbeing of the world rather than that of a delineated locality, has been fashionable at various times in history. Ongoing globalization processes have renewed interest in the twenty-first century and led to important revisions. According to one of the concept's most prominent proponents, Ulrich Beck (2006), the human condition has become cosmopolitan due to global risks (e.g., financial crises, environmental destruction, and the threat of terror), global trade and migration, and advanced communication technologies. With this focus on the transforming reality, Beck rejects common criticisms that cosmopolitanism is a conscious and voluntary choice, mostly of the elite. Everyday life experiences, he argues, result in the formation of transnational connections, create a global 'we-feeling' and effect that cultural ties, loyalties, and identities expand beyond national borders.

Cosmopolitanization   Concept coined by Ulrich Beck and described as "the sum total of a series of coerced choices or unintended side effects" (2006: 19), which result in the cosmopolitan condition.

Cultural discount   Concept introduced by management scholars Hoskins and Mirus in 1988 to theorize that a television program developed in a specific context has its value diminished when introduced into a new market. This is, the authors presumed, because people in foreign markets lack the cultural capital to properly understand and relate to the imported program. Related concepts, are 'cultural proximity' and 'preference for the local' (De Sola Pool, 1977; Straubhaar, 1991, 2007).

Cultural essentialism   Refers to the idea that cultures have an essence, i.e., are things in themselves. Opponents of cultural essentialist thinking argue that cultures are constructed through discursive practice. In other words, they do not exist in their own right but only in the realm of discourse.

Cultural imperialism   Term that describes the ways in which the cultural output of a powerful country has influence over another, less powerful country, often with the culture of developed countries seen to be dominant over developing countries.

Cultural odor   Academic concept introduced by globalization theorist Koichi Iwabuchi in 2002 to describe the ways in which the cultural features of a country of origin are associated with a particular product in the consumption process.

Cultural proximity   Academic concept coined by media scholar Joseph Straubhaar in 1991. At the most basic level cultural proximity describes the "seemingly common attraction audiences feel for cultural products, such as television or music, that are close in cultural content and style to the audience's own culture(s)" (2007: 26). In its original conception cultural proximity was linked to national cultures, in later revisions the concept was expanded and refined to include local and regional cultures, transnational cultural ties resulting from, for example, colonialism, and other transnational proximities based on shared values, themes, and genre. The concept builds on the work by De Sola Pool in the 1970s.

Cultural reductionism Used to describe the tendency to explain observed phenomena with culture/cultural difference alone. For example, the failure of TV Formats to gain popularity in some markets is commonly explained with cultural differences. Other important factors, such as scheduling, marketing, time of release, and production quality, are ignored.

Domestic market A term used to describe the trading of products and services within their country of origin.

Domestication Translation strategy, which aims to transform the source text in such a way that it suits the characteristics and cultural standards of the destination locale. The target text becomes more authentic, may even be seen as original, while the source text becomes invisible. The term is associated with Lawrence Venuti (1995) and is used in opposition to 'foreignization'.

Downloadable content (DLC) Refers to material that is distributed online to supplement and expand upon a released video game.

Dubbing Commonly describes the process of replacing actors' voices with those of different performers speaking the language of the importing market. In the film industry, this practice is also called 're-voicing' to distinguish it from the post-production processes, in which additional or supplementary recordings are mixed with the original production sound to create the finished soundtrack.

Essentialism A view of science, grounded in logical empiricism, that pursues knowledge about the essence of things, i.e., what things are in themselves. This tradition is hotly contested by proponents of constructivism, who argue that things have no meaning in themselves but are given (multiple) meaning(s) by those observing them.

Fansphere A different part of reality where individuals with a passion about particular creations interact virtually.

Fidelity A term often used to describe how 'faithful' an adaptation or translation is to the source text, although this notion is roundly critiqued within contemporary adaptation studies.

Flying producer A senior producer, who is familiar with the original production of an internationally franchised/formatted TV program. (S)he advises the local production team in person and over the phone and often oversees local productions in their early stages, to pass on production knowledge and to ensure a certain quality standard is met and the brand takes no harm.

Foreignization   Translation strategy that aims at keeping the 'foreign taste', the 'otherness' in the translated text. The term is associated with Lawrence Venuti (1995) and is used in contrast to 'domestication'.

Format bible   A term associated with the trade in TV Formats. A format/production bible is a compilation of instructions and information, including technical requirements, lessons learned, shooting schedules, crew lists, a budget sample, and anything else that could be of value to the production team. Furthermore, the bible includes information about the original pitch, audience ratings, and sometimes market research findings, and marketing tips. Tangible items can complement the bible; the most common are videos from the original production and/or other local adaptations, software for the graphics (logos, labels, text, etc.), sound, insertable footage, and scripts in the case of scripted formats.

Franchise   The right or license granted by a company or an individual to another company or individual to market its products or services in a specific territory. In the case of TV formats, the license allows the licensee to remake the format for the territory the license was acquired for, usually a country, a region, or a multi-territory deal based on language.

Free to play (F2P)   Refers to video games that do not require an up-front payment; is often contrasted with 'pay to play' games that do require payment.

Global-Local Nexus   An academic term coined by Morley and Robins in 1995 to describe the new and intricate relations between global space and local space. They use the concept to draw attention to the complex interrelationship in which globalization is itself associated with processes of re-localization.

Glocal   In industry terminology, a glocal approach to product distribution means acknowledging and implementing local preferences globally without losing brand identity. As an academic concept, the term was introduced into Anglo-Saxon sociological discourse in the early 1990s by Roland Robertson. He uses the concept to express the interdependence of the local and the global and to argue that the two concepts should not be seen as binary opposites but two sides of the same coin.

Glocalization   Business strategy that integrates the local within the global in all aspects, incorporating the creative input of partners in each locale while maintaining a cohesive IP/brand across territories. Sociologist Roland Robertson uses the term to highlight both the limitations of globalization processes and the duality of glocality, meaning standardization and differentiation are not binary opposites, and hence exclusionary, but occur simultaneously.

Intellectual Property (IP)   Refers to creative work that is the product of human intellect and that is protected by law from unauthorized use.

International market   Term commonly used as an antonym to domestic market to describe the trading of goods and services beyond the country of origin.

Internationalization   At the most general level, the term refers to companies' moves and strategies for growth outside the domestic market. It also describes the practice of designing and producing products that allow for the integration of minor locale variations.

Intertextuality   A link between different texts, operating in the perception and experience of audiences. Intertextuality has always existed but is growing in importance in today's 'attention economy', where texts needs to be instantly recognizable to stand out amongst the enormous choice we all face on a daily basis.

Japanese, French, Italian, German, Spanish (JFIGS)   A term used in video game and localization studies to refer to the major non-English markets that games are localized for.

Localization   The multifaceted process of adapting a product to the requirements and preferences of a different market and target audience. Localization can refer to many different product levels and aspects and varies in degree.

MAB   The Media Across Borders project and network that was launched in 2012 with the support of the AHRC network grant.

Machine Translation (MT)   The use of computer software to translate text from one language to another.

Massively Multiplayer Online Game (MMO)   Refers to a video game that is able to support very large numbers of players playing together over a network.

Meme   An academic term introduced by Richard Dawkins in 1976 to describe cultural ideas and practices that spread from person to person through processes of imitation. He introduced the term as a cultural equivalent to genes in order to help explain the dispersal of ideas and cultural phenomena. The term has come to be particularly associated with the ways in which content is spread online.

Millennial   Person born during the first decade of the twenty-first century.

Mukokuseki   A Japanese term often used within discussions of anime to describe a lack of national characteristics and racial/ethnic signifiers in a text.

Multimedia Interactive Entertainment Software (MIES)   A term that is used to describe video games in a way that emphasizes their differences from other media such as film and television. Related to **TMIES**, that refers to the translation of the above.

Orality markers   In audiovisual translation, expressions and mannerisms that occur in natural speech; more present in original productions than in dubbed ones.

Place   A fundamental geographical concept, which has been subject to long-standing academic controversy and variable use. It is theorized particularly in relation to the geographical concept of space. In the simplest sense, space is general, place is specific. The value of the concept of place for media and communication scholars lies in its theorization as a 'sense of place', as providing a feeling of belonging and identification.

Paratexts Any kind of official or unofficial creation linked to a main cultural product, such as film trailers, websites, magazines based on a TV program, or merchandising. Due to the need for extensive marketing in today's 'attention economy' and with ongoing transmedialization and multi-platform distribution, paratexts have grown substantially in both quantity and significance. Paratexts can have a greater financial value than the original text, and identifying the main text can become increasingly difficult.

Playability In game localization, an essential feature of translated texts that enhances the usability and immersion of players.

Polysemiotic (also **multisemiotic**) In the field of linguistics, it refers to items or creations that may convey meaning through various channels (visual, acoustic ...) requiring the engagement of receivers with different senses, composing a much richer and complex experience.

Preference for the local Widely accepted and perpetuated thesis, both in academia and TV industry circles, stating that audiences prefer domestic to imported programs, especially when of roughly similar quality. In television scholarship, the thesis is particularly linked to Joseph Straubhaar (1991, 2007). Like the cultural discount thesis it was developed to explain flows (or the lack thereof) in the international trade of television programs.

Quantum nation A spontaneous association of individuals within the fansphere that share a particular (media) interest and that supersede geopolitical and geocultural space-time. Term coined by Bernal-Merino in the present volume when talking about video game fans but applicable to other products and their fan communities.

Remake A cultural production that is based on an earlier production, usually within the same medium. For example, a new version of an old film (e.g., *Carrie*) or a TV series that originated in one market and is remade for another (e.g., the Danish crime series *Forbrydelsen* remade in the US/*The Killing* and Turkey/*Cinayet*; or the Israeli TV drama series *BeTipul* (In Therapy)/*In Treatment* remade in over a dozen countries). The term is sometimes used analogously with 'adaptation', although that term is more commonly used to refer to works that move across different media (novel to film, for example).

Return on Investment (ROI) The amount of profit or cost saving that is realized as a result of an investment.

Re-versioning To make a new, different version of something. The term is commonly used for internationally broadcast documentaries, where the original presenter is edited out and replaced with a 'local' presenter, the original soundtrack is replaced with different music, or some audio-visual material is added or taken out. This is done, for instance, to give the program a local feel, to make it the right length for the targeted scheduling slot, or to adhere to regulatory requirements.

Re-voicing   The act of recording new speech-based audio files to replace previous ones.

Shared-authorship   In localization studies, the practice of integrating creators in other countries to better achieve the successful adaptation of a non-domestic product.

Semiotics/Semiology   The study of signs (linguistic, visual, acoustic, tactile, etc.) within systems of signification.

Sim-Ship   Simultaneous shipment distribution model mostly used in the video game industry.

Skippers   The demographic segment that has been raised in the mobile Internet era and who skip any content not directly related to their immediate interest.

Source text (ST)   The 'original' text that is the object of translation or adaptation.

Subtitling   Practice of translating the dialogue of a cultural product produced in a foreign-language (e.g., film, TV program, or opera). In film and television, subtitles are usually displayed at the bottom of the screen.

Target text (TT)   The adapted/translated version of the source text.

Text   A signifying structure composed of signs and codes, which is essential for communication. It can take the form of speech, writing, a painting, a film or anything else that can be read as signifying something.

Transcreation   Translating content freely to maximize the characteristics of the target language and culture.

Transcultural   Academic concept used to describe cultural phenomena that exist beyond or across cultures. It can refer to hybrid cultures, which result from cultural forms moving across geographical boundaries and/ or periods of time and consequently causing cross-cultural interaction. Or it can refer to the fact that in today's globalizing world, cultures as ways of life are increasingly generated and communicated across numerous territories with perceived different cultures.

Transcultural adaptation studies   Acknowledges that borders are porous and perpetually subject to (re-)negotiation and reappraisal, and that the relationship between the local and the global, between the particular and the general, is symbiotic and interdependent. The latter claim echoes that expressed in the concept of glocalization.

Translation   The act of expressing linguistic content in a different language.

Transnational   An academic concept promoted by scholars calling for a rethinking of widely held assumptions about (national) identity, sovereignty, and citizenship. The notion of the transnational is based on the assumption that social experiences are complex and dynamic products of multiple regional, ethnic, and institutional identities. Far from being static or bounded by national borders, it is argued, in a globalizing world social, political, and economic forces operate on supra-national, trans-regional, and trans-local scales and scopes.

TV Format   In the narrow sense, used throughout in this book, a TV Format is defined as a package of production rules and instructions, which is sold in the form of a 'format bible' and licensed for reproduction in another market. In the broader sense, it can be used to refer to the formulaic regularity that is common to much of television programming.

User Interface (UI)   Refers to the interface that allows humans to interact with electronic devices such as computers.

Yeşilçam   A Turkish term for the local cinema industry named after *Yeşilçam* ('Green Pine') Street in Istanbul where many of the studios and production facilities were based from the 1950s until the industry collapse in the 1980s. The term functions as a metonym for the Turkish film industry, similar to the use of Hollywood to refer to the cinema of the US, and is often used to specifically refer to the popular film industry rather than to the art cinema productions in the country.

List of Contributors

Irene Artegiani holds a degree in Translation and Interpreting from the University of Forlì and an MA in Audiovisual Translation from the University of Roehampton. She is currently working as a specialized translator and subtitler into Italian and carries out independent research around quality issues in subtitled production. Her specific interests include the translation of dialect and humor.

Rocío Baños is Senior Lecturer in Translation at the Centre for Translation Studies (CenTraS) at University College London, UK. She holds a Ph.D. in audiovisual translation from the University of Granada. Her main research interests lie in the fields of translation technology, translation training, and audiovisual translation, especially in dubbing. She has published various articles on audiovisual translation, edited a dossier on dubbing in *Trans: Revista de Traductología* (2013), and co-edited a special issue of the journal *Perspectives: Studies in Translatology* entitled "Corpus Linguistics and Audiovisual Translation: in search of an integrated approach" (2013).

Miguel Á. Bernal-Merino, Ph.D. in the localization of multimedia interactive entertainment software at Imperial College, is a researcher in game localization and media translation. He lectures at the University of Roehampton and collaborates with universities across Europe. Miguel is the co-founder and elected chair of the 'IGDA Localization SIG'. He has co-managed the 'Game Localization Round Table' (for Localization World), the 'Localization Summit' (for the Game Developers Conference) from its conception, as well as the AHRC-funded '*Media Across Borders*' network. He is also part of the advisory board of the Brand2Global conference series and the author of several publications on media translation. His latest monograph is *Translation and Localisation in Video Games. Making Entertainment Software Global* (2014).

Aaron Calbreath-Frasieur received his Ph.D. from the University of Nottingham's Department of Culture, Film, and Media. His research examines media franchises in relation to industrial practices, using the Muppets franchise as the primary case study. Areas explored within the study of franchises include: media brands, transnational co-production, and transmedia storytelling. He served as articles editor for *Scope: an Online Journal of Film and Television Studies* in 2010/11. His publications include work on world building in franchises and transmedia storytelling.

Frederic Chaume is Professor of Audiovisual Translation at the Universitat Jaume I (Castelló, Spain), where he teaches audiovisual translation theory, dubbing, and subtitling, and Honorary Professor at Imperial College London. He has taught regularly at the universities of Roehampton, Las Palmas, Malaga, Granada, Valencia, and Seville. He is author of *Doblatge i subtitulació per a la TV* (Eumo, 2003), *Cine y Traducción* (Cátedra, 2004), *Audiovisual Translation: Dubbing* (St. Jerome, 2012), and co-author of *Teories Contemporànies de la Traducció* (Bromera, 2010). He has given over 40 invited lectures on translation for dubbing across Europe and at international translation studies conferences. For the past 24 years, he has been working as a professional translator for TV stations, dubbing and subtitling companies, film distributors, and producers. He is the director of the research group TRAMA and has been awarded the *Berlanga Award* for his support to dubbing and training in the field.

Rayna Denison is Senior Lecturer at the University of East Anglia. Rayna is a specialist in Asian film and television, but particularly Japanese media culture, and has recently led an AHRC-funded project called *Manga Movies* that examined the connections between manga and its many forms of adaptation in Japanese media. She has recently published articles in *Velvet Light Trap* and *Cinema Journal*, has co-edited a book collection titled *Superheroes on World Screens,* and has published a book in the Bloomington Film Genres series titled *Anime.*

Andrea Esser is Principal Lecturer in Media and Communications at the University of Roehampton, London, and Director of the AHRC-funded *Media Across Borders* (MAB) network. Her research interests revolve around media internationalization and transnationalization, media management, and the globalization of culture. Recent work considers transnational television audiences; transnational TV production networks; and the TV format phenomenon—the growth of the format market, patterns of flow, formats' role in production and scheduling, and the complexities of local adaptations. Before joining Roehampton University, she worked in media consulting and publishing and lectured at Goldsmiths and other London universities. In 2014/15 she spent six months as a guest researcher at Aarhus University, Denmark.

Alberto Fernández Costales is Lecturer and Researcher at the University of Oviedo (Spain), where he teaches applied linguistics, foreign language teaching, and methodology. He has been a visiting scholar at Imperial College (London), the Catholic University of Leuven (Belgium), and the University of Regensburg (Germany). His research interests lie in applied linguistics, Translation Studies, video games localization, bilingualism and multilingualism, foreign language teaching, sociolinguistics, and the relationship between language and technology. He has been engaged in more than 15 international research projects and has published widely in the fields of applied linguistics, education, and Translation Studies.

Dionysios Kapsaskis is Senior Lecturer in Translation at the University of Roehampton, London. His research extends across the fields of Translation Studies (especially the relation between translation and film) and Comparative Literature (especially the relation between French literature and continental philosophy). His publications include articles on challenges to the subtitling profession in a changing translation marketplace and on translation as a form of original writing in the work of Marguerite Yourcenar. He also guest-edited a volume entitled *Translation and authenticity in a global setting* (*Synthesis* 4, 2012). For the past 20 years, Dionysios has been working professionally as a specialized translator and subtitler into Greek.

Martin Nkosi Ndlela is Associate Professor in Media and Communication at Hedmark University College in Norway. His research interests include issues of adaptation and localization of popular television formats such as *Big Brother*, *Idols*, and *MasterChef* in Africa. His recent publications include "Television across boundaries. Localization of Big Brother Africa", in *Critical Studies in Television 8(2)* and "Global Television Formats in Africa. Localizing Idols", in Oren, T. & Shahaf, S. (2012) *Global Television Formats. Understanding Television across Borders*. He sits on the editorial board of the Journal of African Media Studies.

Laurence Raw is Professor in the Department of English, Baskent University, Ankara, Turkey. He is widely published and a frequent guest speaker at conferences. His recent publications include *Character Actors in Hollywood Horror and Science Fiction Films 1930–1960, Merchant Ivory Interviews* and *Adaptation, Translation and Transformation*. He regularly blogs on issues of translation, adaptation, and media at laurenceraw.blogspot.com.

Iain Robert Smith is Senior Lecturer in Film at the University of Roehampton, London. His research interests include popular world cinema, cross-cultural adaptation and the transnational dimensions of cult film and television. His published works include articles on a Turkish remake of *Star Trek*, a Bollywood reworking of *Oldboy*, and a Filipino spoof of James Bond. He is the author of *The Hollywood Meme: Transnational Adaptations of American Film and Television* (2016) and co-editor of *Transnational Film Remakes* (2016) alongside Con Verevis. He is co-chair of the SCMS Transnational Cinemas Scholarly Interest Group and co-director of the AHRC-funded research network *Media Across Borders*.

Jeanette Steemers is Professor of Media and Communications and Co-Research Director of the School of Media, Arts and Design at the University of Westminster. Her books include *European Media in Crisis* (2015 with J. Trappel and B. Thomass), *The Media and the State* (2015 with T. Flew and P. Iosifidis), *Regaining the Initiative for Public Service Media* (ed., 2012 with G. Lowe); *Creating Preschool Television: A Story of Commerce, Creativity and Curriculum* (2010), *Selling Television: British Television in the Global Marketplace* (2004), *European Television Industries* (2005, with P. Iosifidis and M. Wheeler), and *Changing Channels: The Prospect for Television in a Digital Age* (ed., 1998). She has an industry background having worked as an analyst for CIT Research and research manager at children¹s producer, HIT Entertainment.

Sylwia Szostak gained her Ph.D. in the University of Nottingham's Department of Culture, Film and Media. It examines the impact of international media flows on Polish television in the post-Soviet era, with particular attention to the influence of American fiction television. Sylwia has published essays in the *Journal of European Television History and Culture* and in the edited anthology *Popular Television in Eastern Europe During and Since Socialism* (eds., Timothy Havens, Anikó Imre, and Katalin Lustyik). Upon completion of her Ph.D. she worked as a research associate at Loughborough University's Department of Social Sciences. She currently works in the TV industry in Poland.

Index

accent 25, 56, 90–1, 96, 184
acoustic 2, 6, 77, 79, 80–1, 226–27
adaptation: BADaptation 141, 221; cross-cultural 38–9, 42, 50; degree of 106, 109; studies 7–8, 141, 152, 223, 227; transcultural 11, 141–9, 227
additions 74, 130–1
advertisement 78–9, 115, 194
Africa 10, 23–4, 26–7, 30, 78, 99, 102–3, 108–9, 113–23
Americanization 100, 104–5
anime 2, 9, 36–47, 49, 51, 73, 75, 77, 152, 155, 156, 159–160, 163–4, 221
appeal 9, 11, 19, 20, 28–31, 36–7, 43, 49, 50, 55, 63, 70, 88, 102, 117, 121, 141
Arab countries 9, 53–67
artificial 127, 137, 208
Asia 4, 12, 30, 36, 47, 151–166, 205
Assassins' Creed 184, 194
attention economy 14, 221
audience: configurations 31, 113, 119; international 36, 42–3, 85, 119; local 20, 57, 72, 105, 113, 142–3, 147, 149; national 8, 19–20, 23, 26, 28, 30–1, 44, 103, 113; regional 63; target 1, 24–5, 73–4, 79, 82, 93, 128, 134–5, 183–4, 186–7, 197, 225; transnational 24, 121
audience ratings 25, 126, 128 171, 224
audience research 11, 19–20, 26, 29, 58, 62, 183–201
authenticity 86, 96, 97, 221
authentic speech 11, 221

Barátok közt 12, 167, 171
belonging 21, 30–2, 55, 63, 89, 226
Betty, La Fea 3, 12, 25, 167, 175–6
Big Brother 3, 10, 19, 24, 26, 113–15, 117–121, 222
boundaries 21, 23, 118; cultural 55; disciplinary 5; geocultural 212;

geographical 119, 212, 227; national 62, 113, 118–19
brand 3, 12, 36, 54, 57, 63, 79, 101, 106, 120, 172; consumption 55; identity 207, 224; permanence 13, 203, 211, 216
branding 68, 101; emotional 79

canned content 116, 169, 222
captioning 68, 70
cartoon 2, 4, 43, 54, 58, 70–9
children's television 9, 37, 53–67, 73–7, 99–112
class 28–30, 88, 119–20, 157
co-creation 5, 13, 202, 208, 215–16, 222
code 73, 75, 77, 80–1, 207–8, 214, 227; filmic 79–80, 82; linguistic 77, 80–1, 90; musical 77; paralinguistic 77, 80–1; sound 81; visual 80, 82
codes and conventions 56, 63
code switching 91, 185, 197, 198
comedy 49, 81, 91, 125
commercials 78–9, 100, 193
community 31–2, 55, 58–9, 64, 68, 89, 102, 105, 107, 142–3, 146–7, 149, 205, 211, 213
competition 1, 25, 55, 61, 101, 119
complexity 5–6, 14, 20, 22–4, 30–2, 50, 89, 95–96, 117, 163, 205
consumer 1–2, 5, 9, 13–14, 22, 43, 54, 64, 114, 119, 126, 183–4, 195, 202, 204–7, 210–12, 221; behavior 68, 79, 120; culture 55, 65; participation 68–69; requirements 120; sameness 205, 211
context 6–7, 9, 11, 14, 18, 31, 38, 40, 42, 45, 49, 53, 86–7, 91, 95–6, 99, 104, 106, 117, 126, 132, 137, 141, 143–4, 148, 159–60, 168, 190, 192, 198; local 38, 100, 106, 142, 170, 174; national 41, 102, 105,

173; production 42, 49, 159, 162, 171; socio-cultural 7, 11, 14, 124, 126, 137
conventions: global popular 56, 63; translation 97, 125–6, 128, 134, 137, 186; genre 127, 135; community 146; Yeşilçam 144, 148
co-productions 37, 40–3, 49, 56, 59, 61–4, 101–5, 107–8, 110–11, 114, 151
cosmopolitan(ism): banal 26, 27, 221; cosmopolitanization 26, 222; lifestyle 196; pop 49; definition 222
creativity 72–3, 77, 81–2, 180
cross-cultural: adaptation 9, 38–9, 42, 46, 50, 148; exchange 42, 49–50; fandom 49; processes 40
cultural affiliations (multiple) 10, 24, 31
cultural borders 12, 38
cultural considerations 113, 115, 118, 121
cultural essentialism 20–1, 22, 31, 222
cultural difference 9, 12, 19, 22, 25, 37, 50, 109, 120, 148, 174, 223
cultural discount 8, 20, 28, 30, 43, 47, 50, 57, 117, 222 *see also* preference for the local
cultural distance 121–2
cultural diversity 32, 142, 195
cultural domination 55
cultural hybridity 24
cultural imperialism 44–5, 47, 104–5, 109, 113, 115, 122, 222 *see also* Americanization
cultural odor 43–4, 47, 49–50, 222
cultural proximity 28, 102, 115, 118, 186, 222
cultural references 27, 86, 134, 184–5, 191–92, 196
cultural reductionism 8, 31, 223
cultural sensibilities 24
cultural standardization 114
culturally specific 56, 82, 107, 157; non- 44
culture-bound 135

developing markets 167, 170
dialect 10, 27, 85–97, 117
dialogue 11, 70, 77, 80–1, 89, 90, 92–3, 97, 124, 125, 127–33, 135, 137–38, 145, 169, 176, 184, 227; dubbed 124–8, 131–2, 135, 137; translated 124–6
digitalization 1–2, 9, 13, 69, 72, 81
documentary 75

Dogtanian and the Three Muskehounds 37, 42, 48
domestic: market 54, 160, 223; production 12, 29, 59, 129, 130–2, 137, 167–70, 180
domestication 27, 73–4, 81, 88, 184–5, 187, 196–7, 223
Dora the Explorer 78, 110
Doraemon 2, 5, 75, 77–8
drama: action 156, 160; melo- 142–3, 145, 158; television 3, 14, 23, 36, 57, 61, 71, 124, 132, 138, 152, 155–56, 158–60, 162, 169–173, 180
dubbed 2–3, 6, 8–9, 11, 24, 36, 44–5, 50, 57, 62, 68–72, 79, 81, 85, 101–2, 124–9, 131–8, 187, 191–2, 196, 207, 223
dubbing 2, 6, 8–9, 11, 24, 50, 62, 68–71, 79, 81, 83, 86, 124–40, 187, 192, 196, 207, 209, 222, 223
Dünyayı Kutaran Adam 141–2, 144–9

educational television 104, 111
efficiency 7, 11
elites 30, 120
emotion 87, 89–90, 93, 96, 148; *see also* emotional branding
English as lingua franca 24, 26, 118, 186; international/global language 185, 192, 195, 198
Europe 3, 5, 9, 23, 26, 29, 30, 37, 42, 48–9, 53–67, 70–1, 73, 106, 118, 154, 157, 167–9, 189, 194–5
Exorcist, The 141–3
extratextual: constraints 11; factors 11, 88; sources 126, 129

factual entertainment 3, 57
fandubs 68, 72
fansphere 13, 212, 223
fansubs 68, 72
fidelity 51, 177, 223
film studies 7–8, 19–20, 27, 72 *see also* adaptation; *see also* remakes
foreignization 27, 88, 184–5, 187–8, 193–7, 224
format adaptation 7–8, 20, 23, 30, 99–112, 113–23, 167–182; scripted 167–182
franchise 3, 5, 7, 10, 12, 20, 26, 43, 56, 99–101, 104, 107–111, 120, 151–164, 224
franchising 10, 12, 101, 154, 163, 109–11, 123, 151–66
Friends 127, 129, 132–6, 138

game experience 187–8, 190–3, 195–7, 207
game localization 5–7, 13, 79, 183–4, 187, 196–9, 206, 208, 226
gender 28–9, 32, 54, 60, 108, 110, 116, 188, 190
geocultural 7, 55, 212, 226
geolinguistic 55
globalization 8, 19, 21, 27, 37–8, 54, 72, 115–16, 120, 158–9, 214
global-local nexus 9, 36, 38, 224
glocalization 1, 5, 13, 55, 115–16, 202–9, 212–13, 215–16, 224

Hana Yori Dango 12, 151–164
Heidi 4, 42
heterogenization 55, 122
homogenization 37, 55, 109, 122; cultural 22, 109–10, 115–16
hybridized: language 87; media forms 110; *see also* cultural hybridity

iconicity 75
Idols 10, 24, 29–30, 113, 117–122
Il Commisario Montalbano 10, 85–97
indigenization 101, 105
infrastructure 54, 205
intellectual property 68, 101, 111, 203, 224
interactivity 2, 202, 208
intermediality 97
international markets 1–5, 8, 10, 12–13, 20, 22–3, 28, 36, 41, 43–44, 53–58, 61, 64, 100–101, 119, 122, 152, 170, 180, 202–11, 214, 224
internationalization 1, 5, 11, 13, 38, 43–4, 58, 85, 108, 192, 202–3, 205, 207–9, 216, 225
intertextuality 10, 86, 97, 151, 153, 162, 225
intonation 77, 89, 90, 93, 96
Italian 9–10, 27, 36–38, 40–3, 47–9, 85, 87–94, 97, 134, 173, 184, 186, 202, 204, 211, 214–15, 225
Italy 5, 24–5, 27, 42, 57–8, 85–7, 134, 171, 173, 204

Japan 4–5, 12, 37–43, 47, 50, 73, 77–8, 152, 154, 156–61, 163, 186, 203–4, 221
Japanese 2–3, 9, 12, 23, 37–45, 47–51, 56, 62, 73–5, 77–8, 151–3, 155–164, 194, 204, 210, 212–5, 221, 225; Japaneseness 38, 41–5, 48–50

Killing, The 71, 226
knowledge transfer 172

language: attitudes 183–4, 194–7; colonial 117–18; preferences 190–1, 193, 195, 197, 210; registers 89–90; source 70, 86, 187, 194
linguistic: codes 73, 75, 77, 80–2, 90; patterning 124, 127, 135; registers 89–90; supervisor 129, 132
localization: considerations 7–9, 25, 113; definition 225; needs 10, 202; practices 1, 5, 8–9, 14, 53, 100–2, 214; quality 210; strategies 21, 32, 57–58
local market 55–6, 63, 168–9, 173, 180
local producers 10, 56, 102, 168
look and feel 29, 185, 188, 193, 197

manga 12, 36–7, 39–42, 51, 74, 151, 155–8, 160–1, 163
manipulation 74, 80–2
Mario Bros 43, 185, 207
marker(s): orality 11, 125, 129–36, 138, 225; phonetic 90; societal 90
marketing 13, 22–3, 32, 54, 79, 101, 120, 161, 204–5, 212, 221, 223–224, 226
meme 40, 225
merchandizing 110, 226
Middle East 54, 59–60, 63
millennial 207, 225
minority languages 117, 193–4
mother tongue 193–5, 197, 216
mukokuseki 44, 47, 48, 50, 225
multicultural 59, 117, 205
multimedia: products 13, 185–6, 195, 197; software 6, 184, 202–3, 208, 225; translation 68

Na Wspólnej 171–2, 174–5, 178
Nanny, The 27, 179
narrative 11–12, 45–6, 80, 85–7, 89, 94–7, 100, 102, 142–3, 145–6, 149, 151, 155, 157–8, 162, 172, 184, 207–8
national: cultures 19, 22–3, 27, 30, 46, 114, 116–17, 119, 148, 151, 221, 223; identities 19, 22, 215; imaginary 20, 31; markets 53, 118, 122 *see also* local markets
nation-centric fallacy 20
naturalness 135, 137
negotiate/-ion 12, 41, 53, 104, 105, 107, 120, 122, 151
Next Top Model 3, 25–6, 28–9

omission 89, 136, 138
original: game 188, 193; language 71, 192; flavor 194; proficiency 195; text 39, 88, 132, 192

paralinguistic: code 77, 80–1; features 129, 131
parameters 96
paratexts 12–14, 50, 85–6, 185, 195, 197, 226
participation 9, 45, 58, 64, 68, 115
particularity 31, 87, 117
place 20–1, 27–8, 30, 32, 54, 60, 62–3, 101, 116, 225–6
playability 6, 203, 207–9, 214, 216, 226
player satisfaction 13, 207
Poland 5, 12, 99, 105, 167–175, 178–180, 211
policy 9, 23, 53–5, 58, 62–3, 115, 144
polysemiotic 6, 187, 226
Powerpuff Girls 2, 78
preference for the local 8, 13, 20, 28, 226 *see also* cultural discount
professional: aspects 126–8; context 94; factors 133, 137; practices 6; lives 171; market 70; translators 184

quality: control 128, 132–3; of dubbing 62, 132–3, 137, 192, 196; poor 145, 196; standards 128, 132–133, 137

reception 9, 19–20, 22, 25, 27, 31–2, 36, 38, 41, 48–50, 107, 126, 129, 151, 153–5, 158, 160, 183, 195, 198, 202
recontextualize 77
references: cultural 27, 86, 134, 184–5, 191–2, 196
regionalism 95
regulation 9, 55, 60–1, 63–4, 156, 169, 215
remakes 2–3, 7, 12, 29, 151–3, 155–6, 162–4, 226
reproduction 41, 105, 110–11, 136, 151–2, 228
research and development 12, 167–8, 174, 179
revoicing 68, 70
reworking 2–3, 38–9, 42, 97
risk 27, 41, 96, 168, 170, 172–3, 175–6, 178, 180, 222
routine 57, 114, 197

scripted formats 12, 167, 169, 178, 180, 224
scriptwriting 12, 125, 129, 135–6, 172

semantic: structure 75; potential 80; redundancies 133
semiotic: adaptation 75; context 91; levels 2; model 80, 126; transfers 68, 85
Sesame Street 10, 56–7, 60, 78, 99–111
sexual content 73
Şeytan 141–9
shared-authorship 6, 216, 227
Sherlock 36, 50
Sherlock Hound 9, 36–51
Siete Vidas 127, 129–33, 135
Simpsons, The 24, 27
sitcom 11, 70, 105, 125, 127, 130, 133, 135, 168, 177, 179
soundtrack 57, 70, 202, 223, 226
source text 11–12, 51, 91, 133, 138, 184–5, 192, 196–7, 221, 223, 227
Spain 2, 5, 13, 28, 41, 79, 81, 125, 127, 129, 185, 188, 194–5, 204, 211
Spanish 11, 13, 23, 36–7, 71, 78, 81, 124–5, 127, 129, 131–8, 184–6, 191–7, 202, 204, 210–11, 215, 225
Speed 2, 5, 11, 81
Spider-Man 2, 77–8
Spontaneity 124–5, 129, 136, 137
spontaneous conversation 126–7, 129, 131–3, 135–7
standardization 95, 110, 114, 116, 127, 131–2, 224
Star Wars 141, 144
strategy/ies: broadcast 128; business 175, 203, 224; critical 7; distribution; industrial 177; marketing 79; subtitling 91
subtitles 10, 71–2, 85–7, 91–7, 185, 187, 192, 195, 206, 208–209, 227
subtitling 2, 6, 8–9, 68–71, 79, 81–2, 85, 91, 185, 187, 192, 227
symbol 81–2, 120

talent competition 27, 29–30, 121
target: language 6, 71, 80, 88, 124, 133, 187–8, 192–3, 227; text 12, 70, 88, 135, 184, 193, 221, 223, 227
technology 1, 13, 21, 69–70, 81, 101, 104, 121, 173, 187, 195, 197, 208, 212
telenovela 25, 30, 168, 175–7
Teletubbies 56, 111
television: audiences 8–11, 19–20, 22–4, 26, 28, 30–1, 36, 55–7, 63, 110, 113, 115, 118–22; 137, 156, 158, 162–3, 169; formats 3, 6–8, 10, 12, 19–20, 23–7, 30, 50, 56–7, 62, 99–102, 109–10, 113–14, 116–22, 152, 159, 163, 167–80, 224, 228

tendency 9, 13, 22, 38, 43, 45, 88, 92, 95, 195, 223
tension 37, 41, 50, 88, 161, 163–4, 183–4, 186
territory 5, 8, 20, 57, 62, 114, 224
training 12, 147, 174, 177
transadaptation 68
transcreation 2, 5–6, 9, 69, 72–3, 77–82, 187, 227
transcultural 11, 24, 49, 142, 148, 227
translatability 86, 88
transition 68, 88, 179
translation: audiovisual 6, 8–9, 24, 68–73, 75, 77, 80–82, 124, 126, 135, 183, 187, 221, 225; community 68; constrained 68; cultural 46, 99, 180; definition 227; goblin 69–70; interlinguistic 75; intersemiotic 75, 82, 85; loyal 132; mode 68, 126; multimedia 68; no- 187, 192, 194; non-professional 68; screen 68–9; strategies 88, 90, 134, 184, 187, 192, 198; studies 5, 6, 72–3, 82, 124–5, 183–4, 186–7, 190, 193, 196, 198, 221, 230–1; target-oriented 81
transmedia 152, 155, 163, 226
transnational: borrowing 12, 163; collaboration 59; definition 227;

franchise 111, 151–2, 154, 156–9, 163; intertextual network 151; negotiation 151; reception 151
Turkey 5, 141, 143, 145, 211, 226

Ulysses 31 37, 43
universal 43, 46, 48, 53, 55, 72, 108, 145, 213
unnatural 125, 137

variations: linguistic 87, 90, 93; local 171, 173, 213, 225; national 110
video games: company 4, 204–6, 212–3, 215–6; localization 5, 13, 183, 185–7, 190–1, 196–8, 208, 225–6; translation 70, 183–187, 190–2, 194–8
violence 55, 60, 73, 143
voiceover 2, 6, 9, 68–70, 208, 210, 213, 214, 222

Who Wants to be a Millionaire? 3, 19, 205, 222
World of Warcraft 2, 208

X Factor, The 29–30

Yeşilçam 12, 142–5, 147–9, 228